The Future
of Management

The Future of Management

Industry 4.0 and Digitalization

Scientific editors
Piotr Buła · Bogdan Nogalski

Jagiellonian University Press

Scientific editors
Prof. Piotr Buła, Ph.D.
Department of International Management, Cracow University of Economics
Department of Business Management, University of Johannesburg

Prof. Bogdan Nogalski, Ph.D.
WSB University in Gdańsk
Committee on Organizational and Management Sciences of the Polish Academy of Sciences

Scientific reviewer
Prof. Szymon Cyfert, Ph.D.
Department of Organization and Management Theory, Poznań University of Economics and Business

Publication coordination
Piotr Sedlak, Ph.D.
Department of International Management, Cracow University of Economics

Cover design
Sebastian Wojnowski

Publication financed by Cracow University of Economics

ISBN 978-83-233-4859-7
ISBN 978-83-233-7123-6 (e-book)

www.wuj.pl

Jagiellonian University Press
Editorial Offices: Michałowskiego 9/2, 31-126 Kraków
Phone: +48 12 663 23 80, Fax: +48 12 663 23 83
Distribution: Phone: +48 12 631 01 97, Fax: +48 12 631 01 98
Cell Phone: +48 506 006 674, e-mail: sprzedaz@wuj.pl
Bank: PEKAO SA, IBAN PL 80 1240 4722 1111 0000 4856 3325

Contents

Preface

The world is standing on the very edge of the fastest industrial revolution ever. A revolution which will rapidly increase the efficiency of many production processes. Automation (both mechanical and the one happening with computer processes) will reduce the demand for human work and release a huge amount of time we can use for further development. Industry 4.0 has been a buzz word recently. It is about interconnecting devices and giving them the possibility of making autonomous decisions. It is certainly a way of increasing efficiency of production, but it will also have impact on the facilitation of other processes within the organization.

At the same time, it is said that we are on the verge of an ecological catastrophe and that we have merely a few years before irreversible climate changes may endanger the future of our species.[1] Some say, that the development of AI will solve most of our problems. We believe that the need for the activity of human beings will be even bigger.

Piotr Buła
Bogdan Nogalski

---

[1]   World Scientists' Warning of a Climate Emergency, https://academic.oup.com/bioscience/advance-article/doi/10.1093/biosci/biz088/5610806 (access: 2 November 2019).

Industry 4.0: Social Impacts and Operations Management Challenges

Prof. Grażyna Leśniak-Łebkowska, Ph.D.   https://orcid.org/0000-0003-3035-6676
Warsaw School of Economics

Abstract

The new Industry 4.0 is designed to respond to major global challenges, such as global warming, ageing population, globalisation, deregulation, depletion of raw materials, growth of the young (born digital) generation with rising demands and expectations, political frictions, economic growth uncertainties, social unrest, mass migrations, etc. On the reverse side—the Industry 4.0, which is to meet new expectations also has its dark side if not managed wisely with a human-centred focus. It is the set of social costs of transition. In such settings corporate leaders attempt to rethink not only the winning logic of competitiveness but also with whom and how they have to cooperate "in the crafting of a new societal deal that helps individuals cope with disruptive technological change."[1]

Facing up to the Fourth Revolution is the major challenge for managers in their professional career in the industry. They have to find their way of managing transition from the past routines and present problems to brand new reality to be invented and constructed, based on the innovations offered by technology revolution with its overwhelming disruptive power and competition based on the Amazon Effect.
In this article focus will be put on the transition process to be navigated by three types of companies: old fashioned and lagging behind the new stream of inventions, adopting new technology in a human-friendly way, and new-born entrepreneurial digital platform companies. For all of them, the key success factor is accelerated and focused education.

Keywords: industry revolution, innovations, cyber security, retail, digitalisation

---

[1]   E. Greenberg, M. Hirt, S. Smit, *The Global Forces Inspiring a New Narrative of Progress*, "McKinsey Quarterly" 2017, p. 1.

Table 1. Revolutions (not only) in industry

Industrial Revolutions	Major drivers of change
1st Industrial Revolution 1765 until the mid-1800s	**The water and steam engine** enabled the growth of manufacturing productivity, transportation and other areas where hard human work could be replaced by steam power. It did not reduce employment, quite the contrary—it fostered the industrial activity of mass production due to mechanisation, moving workforce from agriculture to factories, thus initiating the emergence of management science.
2nd Industrial Revolution 1870 until 1914 At present its significance continues to grow	**Electricity, gas and oil** enabled further facilitation of work, replaced horsepower, illuminated life space in households and cities, thus making it possible to work and be active longer than the daylight. It caused a high growth of productivity, economy and quality of life. Major inventions included the combustion engine, the steel industry, chemical synthesis. New communication modes (telephone and telegraph). Automobile and plane. Model of large factory. Electrification is still in progress, as 1.3 billion people do not have access to electricity yet, mainly in Africa and India. Electricity became a public good. New industries emerged active in energy generation, transmission, distribution and use. Electricity changed the work of all other industries. It has been called "the greatest engineering achievement of the 20th century." New sources of energy aimed at decarbonisation of the economy are forced at present to enable further growth without sacrificing climate safety.
3rd Industrial Revolution From 1950s	**Computers, IT systems and programmable logic controllers (PLCs)** The era of information organised for diverse needs of users, scalability. Nuclear energy. Rise of electronics (transistors, microprocessors). Miniaturised materials to develop biotechnology and space research. Rise of high-level automation and robotics in manufacturing. The emergence of the Internet (the end of the second millennium).
4th Industrial Revolution Underway	The first industrial revolution not rooted in a new source of energy but rather constituting a new technological phenomenon in itself: **digitalisation** enabling the construction of a virtual world from which we steer the physical world.[2] It builds upon the 3rd revolution inventions. The key issue is connectivity and interaction of all production means in real time. Enabling solutions for Factories 4.0 to connect different objects in a production line and different players (Cloud Computing, Big Data Analytics, Industrial Internet of Things (and Services), Machine Learning, Virtual and Augmented Reality, 3D Printing and Artificial Intelligence). The use of technology blurring the border between physical, digital and biological spheres to completely uproot industries all over the world. Transformations of entire production, management and governance systems. Energy still becomes an issue. Diversified alternative sources of renewable energy to be adopted (geothermal, wind, solar, water) to reduce the adverse impact of carbonisation on climate, health and reduce costs.

Source: prepared by the author.

---

[2] Although the digital transformation already has a 10-year history with the launch of the first smartphone, cloud computing and social media, all of them increasing the scale and ease of communication, the pace of its spread in the business applications has not reached the stage of maturity yet.

1. Industrial revolutions: Change of technologies, products and mindset

From a historical perspective, Revolution 4.0 is the natural step ahead on the road of achievements and shortages of previous revolutions to meet the evolving needs of the growing global population.

The already existing applications for the industrial sectors of the economy represent a broad range of new possibilities, such as "predictive maintenance, improved decision-making in real time, anticipating inventory based on production, improved coordination among jobs, etc. Day after day, all these improvements are gradually optimizing production tools and revealing endless possibilities for the future of Industry 4.0."[3]

Adaptability and agility become the distinctive features of Industry 4.0 in view of dramatically changing conditions. From a psychological point of view it creates a permanent strain on people on how to survive, how to innovate and become the winner in the competitive gain. It is difficult to manage people oscillating between hope and fear, opportunity and threat. They expect job safety and such management that will secure it. Thus, the focus changes from the strategy of competing for the future with a strategic intent, core competences and industry foresights,[4] to a disciplined execution of operations. It is, in a sense, a comeback to the era of quality movement with its concepts of J. Juran and E. Deming[5] on converting tools and methods into capability.

Embedded capability as the master use of a resource became the vehicle of change towards inventing a new future. It was rooted in the early 1990s, when the digital era followed by world-class companies from Internet start-ups to biggest multinationals changing the approach to competition. Instead of reacting to competitive moves they started leading the revolution with passion to make radical innovations fuelled by strategic imagination.[6] So, this new mindset and strong capability fostered a radical change in manufacturing instead of small incremental improvements with limited potential.

2. Organisational contingencies of innovations

In order to create adequate conditions for innovations, a company needs to combine two components: creativity and execution, with creativity needing freedom and execution needing resources and discipline. In reality, a number of ingredients of the management

---

[3]   www. sentryo.net (access: 5 June 2019).
[4]   G. Hamel, C. K. Prahalad, *Competing for the Future*, Harvard Business School Press, Cambridge (Mass.) 1993.
[5]   Both of them are the pioneers of the quality movement. See: R. T. Westcott, *The Certified Manager of Quality/Organization Excellence Handbook*, 4th ed., ACQ Quality Management Division, Chicago 2013.
[6]   G. Hamel, *Leading the Revolution*, Harvard Business School Press, Cambridge (Mass.) 2000.

system should be logically integrated with soft factors playing an important role in this process. The major ones are embraced in the vision framework (Figure 1).

Aligning the culture with formal systems and management structure leads to a platform for sustainable growth.

Every admired company has its value-based purpose and distinctive culture. The executive group plays the key role in elaborating the inspiring and agreed vision taking into account different perspectives, promoting it across the organisation, managing conflicts, guiding execution through development of the action plans in all related areas of competence and not foresaking teamwork and responsibility for integrated implementation. It is a continuous process of setting and sharing values that lead execution.

The organisational structure determines the way of dividing jobs to be done, information flows and decision-making patterns. The more formalised and centralised the structure, the less flexibility and initiative is left to employees. That is why Industry 4.0 promotes more organic structures to encourage creativity, impact and responsibility.

People-related issues are no longer the unique domain of the HR department responsible for major processes of recruitment, development and retainment of the best

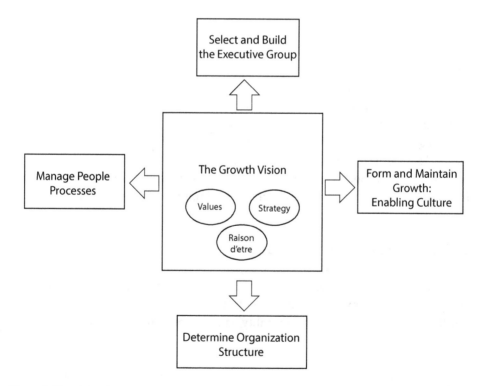

Figure 1. The vision framework

Source: based on M. Lipton, *Guiding Growth. How Vision Keeps Companies on Course*, Harvard Business School Press, Boston, Massachusets 2003, p. 28.

possible employees to meet organisational needs. Human factors become strategic in view of their potential contribution to company survival and growth. Although new technologies tend to reduce employment in all areas that could be automated, the turbulent environment requires intelligent responses of well-educated cadres on all organisational positions. Some human values cannot be substituted, especially in critical situations. Lagging behind new demands may pose new risks on operations.

Growth should be guided by a vision of the future. Entrepreneurial trend-setting companies need visionaries with capabilities to guide growth and its new pathways. Technology is the key enabling factor, while human needs are the initial and final reference factors for the evaluation of ideas and achievements.

Innovation, being the cornerstone of Industry 4.0, wherever it is being elaborated, requires a full readiness of people engaged to:
- Think big, be ambitious.
- Be enterprising and investigative.
- Be nonconformist and flexible.
- Be open-minded to irrational and outside the box ideas.
- Be ready for failures and being wrong, it is a good lesson learned.
- Stop pretending to know everything and being a perfectionist.
- Stand up for crazy ideas.

Without such an attitude creativity becomes compressed to filtered, old ideas.[7]

3. To be or not to be hyper-connected: The cyber security challenge

The big promise is that "communication between tools and controls will be instantaneous and all intra, inter and exterior networks will be interacting with each other. These connection nodes will facilitate the adjustment of production rates in real time. Tomorrow plants will be intelligent, will function on their own, and remote control will be the norm."[8] They will be automatically adapting to inputs they receive thanks to nine types of sensors of lighting, acceleration, magnetism, coprocessor of movement, sounds, orientation, distance, temperature and humidity, and atmospheric pressure.[9] For example, quality failures will immediately trigger an automatic analysis thanks to communication sensors, determine the cause of the problem and initiate automatic

---

[7]   Ibidem, p. 159.
[8]   *Industrial Cyber-security: Monitoring and Anomaly Detection*, Report produced by Sentryo in collaboration with Schneider Electric, Siemens, and CEA, www.sentryo.net (access: 5 June 2019). This report illustrates informal exchanges, joint projects, solution tests and field experience of the authors. The goals are to share a realistic and pragmatic vision of industrial monitoring and detection systems and to enhance the knowledge on industrial systems and the implementation of monitoring and anomaly detection solutions.
[9]   It is worth noting that the price of sensors goes down with the connectivity of objects growth.

corrective action. A smart plant will also adjust its production output to demand fluctuations being evidenced in the company dynamic sales database. It will allow for greater flexibility and will support competitiveness, while keeping costs under control.

Industrial devices are designed according to strict physical security and safety standards in order to work in unfriendly to humans, rough conditions with extreme temperature ranges, vibrations, and electromagnetic noise. The ubiquity and flexibility demanded by Industry 4.0 trend pose specific contradictory demands on industrial devices. They should be flexible, easy to deploy, and not necessarily require any special security or IT skills. These opposing design requirements make producers very prone to introducing software bugs. Vendors have not yet successfully solved this problem.

A smart plant will unfortunately be broadly exposed to security risk of operations. New services have emerged to protect manufacturing plants against cyberattacks of hackers. They integrate the operation system with the IT system, which becomes critical for maintaining continuous screening of all systems.

Security Operating Centres are likely to become units responsible for performing these controls, which offers new career opportunities for humans.

Politecnico di Milano (POLIMI) and the Trend Micro Forward-Looking Threat Research (FTR) Team conducted a joint research on robotics-related risks.[10] They analysed the impact of system-specific attacks and demonstrated attack scenarios on actual standard industrial robots in a controlled environment.

In their security analysis, they found that the software running on these devices was outdated; based on vulnerable OSs and libraries, sometimes relying on obsolete or cryptographic libraries. They had weak authentication systems with default, unchangeable credentials. Additionally, the Trend Micro FTR Team found tens of thousands of industrial devices residing on public IP addresses, which could expose industrial robots to further increasing the risk of hacking. In conclusion, the authors of the report alerted the industrial control sector to undertake more intensive efforts in this area. Moreover, using a standard robot installed in their laboratory, the researchers showed how remote attackers could violate fundamental laws referring to robots setup to the point where they can alter or introduce minor defects in the manufactured product, physically damage the robot, steal industry secrets, or injure humans. They also designed threat scenarios on how attackers capitalised on these attacks.

Nevertheless, robotics and automation represent major trends in Industry 4.0 smart factories. The International Federation of Robotics forecasted the need for employing 1.3 million industrial robot units in factories globally, mainly in such operations as welding, packaging, food processing or die casting, what makes the market value for

---

[10]   Research Report: *Rogue Robots: Testing the Limits of an Industrial Robot's Security*, ed. by F. Maggi (Trend Micro Forward-Looking Threat Research), D. Quarta, M. Pogliani, M. Polino, A. M. Zanchettin, S. Zanero (Politecnico di Milano), https://documents.trendmicro.com/assets/wp/wp-in... (access: 10 June 2019).

robotic systems reach a level of about US $32 billion.[11] The customers are from large- and medium-sized enterprises, mainly from industries critical for every nation, such as: automotive, aerospace, alternative energy, defence, plastics, electrical and electronics, glassmaking, welding, food and beverages, metal fabrication, wood industries, paper and printing, pharmaceutical, packaging and palletising, distribution centres, die casting, off-road vehicle manufacturing, railway, foundry and forging.[12]

4. "The Amazon Effect" challenge

The Internet has enabled the initiation, and nowadays the boom, of online retailers and e-commerce at the cost of heavy equity brands in old distribution models. Consumers are able to access virtually any product or service using their mobile devices. The agency FutureCast[13] specialising in helping brands and agencies adapt in the ever-evolving marketing systems, described the new situation as "the Amazon Effect," which is the impact that the digital marketplace has on traditional business in view of changing customer preferences and a new competitive landscape. Today, consumers, with special regard to millennials, expect their buying experience to be immediate and friction-less. Thus, the role of brands has outperformed any other advantages of competitive offerings. Amazon, through creating the platform, offers not only convenience but also influences value characteristic and extensive networks. Those, in turn, further influence consumer expectations. The research of FutureCast proves that the largest generation, i.e. the millennials, are two times more likely to be adopters of new technology and digital trends, and they have very specific behaviours and attitudes in the market. In regards to brands, they attribute high value to six areas related to brand performance regardless of the industry sector or product:

- Social Circle (a part of the consumer's close social circle).
- Self-Does (emotional connection to the brand).
- Innovative (brand in a constant state of beta).
- Trusted (consumer needs put first).
- Purposeful (doing good for the larger community).
- Accessible (simplifying the lives of consumers).

Next Gen X puts almost equal value on mindsets. The FutureCast study also allows to draw conclusions from benchmarking modern brands and mass appeal brands,

---

[11]   International Federation of Robotics, *Highlights*, http://www.ifr.org/index. php?id=59&df=2016FEB_ Press_Release_IFR_Robot_density_by_region_EN_QS.pdf (access: 5 April 2017).
[12]   Research Report: *Rogue Robots…*
[13]   See: www. thefuturecast.com. Its motto is: "The FutureCast. Established tomorrow." Below their research results are reported.

such as Amazon, Apple, Netflix, Tom's Shoes and Uber. It turned out that Amazon outperformed all other brands when scored against the mindsets of millennials, with Apple as a follower, also across generations.

The main reason was the consistent ability to reduce friction in the consumer journey and stay at the forefront of market innovation. This is the lesson that should be learned by other brands to stay relevant and develop relationships.

Amazon became the most successful disruptor of retail trade achieving the leading position in e-commerce (both on-line and through physical outlets). Its early entry and deliberate strategy of platform development secured it an unquestionable dominance. By mid-2018 Amazon was already responsible for approximately 50% of the US e-commerce sales and 5% of all combined offline-online sales.

Two new inventions may further strengthen its leadership in setting new trends on the retail market: Fulfilment by Amazon and Merch by Amazon. These two programmes offer new services to potential partners from SMEs, which are not able to navigate the growth path fast enough and to build scale to stay competitive. Through the Fulfilment project, Amazon offers them its business infrastructure, such as warehouses, shipping, administrative paperwork, etc., for a fee. Merch by Amazon may strongly appeal to designers of T-shirts who have artwork concepts ready to be leveraged worldwide with no upfront costs, with Amazon taking care of everything else needed in retail distribution through the largest e-commerce platform. Amazon takes royalties only for the sale of T-shirts, while the rest is free of charge.[14]

Taking into account the impact of the Amazon Effect, retailers and manufacturers have a difficult task to compete on the base of costs and product differentiation.

The bargaining power of manufacturers who want to sell through such platforms is also limited, so the cost, quality and customisation has become critical to meet customer expectations.

However, there are attempts to battle the Amazon Effect. One of them is by Kroger and Ocado who announced their first robotic warehouse in the US to take on Amazon in the competitive online grocery market, which in the US is still relatively untapped, not exceeding 2% of sales as compared to 6% in the UK. It could be explained by the perishable nature of grocery food items and a relatively low profit margin. From the entry strategy point of view it is logical to choose the weakest defended segment of the market and next to strengthen the position. According to Reuters, Ocado is known for the innovative robotics used in their warehouses to process and pack food orders.

> The company newest machines can pull together a 50-item grocery order in as little as five
> minutes—potentially slashing Kroger's labor costs at a time when US grocers are looking

---

[14] It is roughly estimated that for a T-shirt sold for USD 20 the designer may receive USD 7. All parties involved navigate the offerings and positioning through Amazon's SEO.

for ways to profitably deliver milk, eggs and other necessities to customer doorsteps. This is the first of 20 high-tech warehouses (or "sheds") planned for the US in a bid to edge out Amazon and Walmart and become America's top online grocery delivery service.[15]

5. Transition paths to the new market reality in Poland

Since 2016, Dell Technologies together with Intel have been conducting a survey on a group of large- and medium-sized companies in Poland on their road to the adoption of new models of digitalisation maturity.[16]

In their 2018 conclusions they pointed out that 73% of interviewed managers plan to adopt broader new digital business models, but only 5% are real transformation leaders, 24% implementing, while the dominant group represented a reserved attitude with 34% of them with the lowest level of digitalisation. The main barriers, in the opinion of 91% of managers, were related to:

- Changes in legislation.
- Shortage of financial and other resources.
- Excess of information.
- Lack of support from the company leadership.
- Lack of consistent strategy and vision of digital transformation.

The McKinsey team of researchers elaborated a very inspiring report on the potential impact of digitisation on Poland's improvement of productivity and contribution to economic growth within the next decade.[17] It should be based on online communication between different parts of the production process, the use of advanced data analytics, which will favour low operating costs of intelligent production systems as well as an easy adaptation to market needs. Optimistic projections of the possible increase in economic value by 27–47% in the EU-15 leading countries within the decade, are based on such advantages of Poland as a high number of science graduates, high quality and affordability of talents, broad Internet access of households and intensity of its use.

The authors distinguished four ways for digital transformation: digitally enabled process optimisation, access to broader market space, more innovative products and increase in labour participation. Each of them consists of specific steps (Table 2).

---

[15]   www.2.novacura.com (access: 5 June 2019).
[16]   Dell Technologies Digital Transformation Index. Source: aleBank.pl (access: 11 September 2018).
[17]   McKinsey Global Institute Report, *Digital Poland*, by D. Boniecki, W. Krok, W. Namysł, M. Borowik, J. Iszkowska, M. Rabij, 2016.

Table 2. Digital transformation

Digitally enabled process optimisation	Access to broader market space	More innovative products	Increase in labour participation
Digitally supported value—chain management Process automation Optimisation of resource utilisation through advanced analytics	Access to niche clients Global reach without a physical footprint Data based analysis of client needs	More effective R&D processes New business models New ways of communicating with clients	The possibility of remote work Greater specialisation within advanced technological processes

Source: based on McKinsey Global Institute Report, *Digital Poland*, 2016, pp. 1–25. Based on the research on Hidden Champions in Poland conducted in 2018, we can identify three types of enterprises, which require different ways to reach their target markets with a view to using the potential of Industry 4.0.[18]

The first and largest group consisted of mature companies of all sizes with an established market position in the respective supply network and strong brand recognition. In view of market changes they frequently had to change ownership, (including the privatisation of state-owned companies and foreign direct investments) and deeply reengineer their companies to meet the high industry standards to gain international recognition. In case of producers of tangible products, large scale, capital and competences became a must to survive. Examples of such fast growing Polish private companies are TZMO (Toruńskie Zakłady Materiałów Opatrunkowych), Fakro (global producer of roof windows), Drutex (one of the top leaders in window manufacturing in the EU) and Wiśniowski (international seller of garage and property gates). Other companies selling to foreign investors are, e.g. Solaris (busses) Morpol (global leader of salmon processing) and Korona Candles.

Their major focus was on sustaining strong relationships and adopting evolutionary methods for large scale innovations as part of Revolution 4.0 (products, technologies, sales, services), at the same time educating their employees, building partnerships and a client base, educating them about their efforts to innovate and stay close to their needs. The organisational inertia and worsening financial performance may slow down the transition, eventually leading to the failure of some. However, their potential attracts new investors ready for takeover. A special category in this group is constituted by a debt recovery company Kruk, which disrupted the service model of this type of business.

The second group is created by young entrepreneurial start-ups, hungry for success. They usually have well-educated leaders or creative inventors, but scarce financial resources (in relation to their ambitions) and management competences, a weak market

---

[18]   The examples are extracted from the research report on Hidden Champions in Poland (co-author) conducted in 2018 in the CEE region for EBRD, coordinated by the Bled School of Management (IEDC).

position and limited trust of the community. Support for their business depends on the business idea and scalability, with reliable managerial competences. Start-ups not necessarily build upon Revolution 4.0 ideas, but at least they start business from scratch and do not have a heavy past behind them. Young start-upers are usually digital savvies and have an ease in using digital communication and work tools. The success ratio in this group is rather low, only a few are able to build their strong position in a niche due to a unique product, service or solution, frequently based on a distinctive technology and know-how. Many companies of this type stay hidden in the public sphere and try to overcome the existing market and financial barriers in a step-by-step approach to build a broader presence. There are numerous examples of such companies identified in the research on hidden champions initiated by Herman Simon, who defined this special category of companies as attaining leadership positions in their respective markets and industry sectors and enjoying decent financial performance to foster further growth.[19] An example of international success is HTL Strefa going global with their innovative safety lancets, CD Project and City Interactive (computer games), WATT (solar collectors), Carlex Design (automobile, maritime and aviation designs).

The third group brings together companies named "born global" by nature, which are ICT platform-based companies with intangible products created with full development of Revolution 4.0 innovations. Their leadership is based on global data profiling with the use of innovative technologies. Usually they operate in networks and adopt a coopetition strategy to cooperate and compete with their partners. Examples of such companies in Poland are: Cloud Technologies with automated data profiling and selling, Growbots with an automated B2B sales platform, Codiwise (applications for mobile phones), RTB (state-of-the-art retargeting technology for top brands worldwide. Its proprietary ad buying engine is the first and only in the world to be powered entirely by deep learning algorithms, enabling advertisers to generate outstanding results and reach their short-, mid- and long-term goals).

Conclusions

The key observations made in major areas of the contemporary strategies and methods of operational management allow to conclude that increased growth will be more and more closely related to the accelerating technological disruption and rising societal tensions. Industry leaders will have to reshape their strategies, operations and workforce to stay ahead of competition.

Industry 4.0 does not appear in a vacuum. It has already started to deeply change the rules of the market game, disrupting business models and undermining the

---

[19]   Simon, Kutcher & Partners, *Hidden Champions. Lessons Learned from 500 of the World's Best Unknown Companies*, Springer, Berlin 1999.

value of companies which are not resilient to market turbulences and lacking strong leadership and survival capabilities. It is worth pointing out the unquestionable role of financial institutions' engagement to enable this transition as well as supportive policies of the state.

The winning companies, regardless of their lifespan on the market and traditions, are determined innovators capable of mastering their uniqueness in their industry sectors or narrow niches, consistently following a fast growth trajectory, frequently on an international and global scale. Some adopt a diversification strategy to better manage the demand risks, which requires flexibility of manufacturing systems and agility in management to keep a high pace of growth.

The soft factors behind business success refer to culture, and especially to team spirit, passion, determination of dedicated staff, fast learning, knowledge and creativity, even more than financial factors. More than ever, the following set of competences becomes highly valued: quality focus, operations excellence, service support, top designs, competitive pricing, omni-channel marketing, and customer-friendly financing. The key issue is the mindset of being open to new ideas and conditions, going beyond traditional business, engaging in CSR activities, understanding and undertaking new opportunities.

The departure point for further growth is not as important as the drive ahead with the use of Industry 4.0 vehicles and understanding threats. Such transition requires a strong transformational type of leadership, effective management and disciplined execution of strategic changes.

Defensive reactions against the new reality, ignoring education adjusted to new contingencies and sticking to obsolete knowledge lead to failure. One could not expect lifelong employment with outdated skills and mindset. It is evident that many traditional jobs will disappear but, on the other hand, a broad range of new professions and jobs are to be created. The transition has just started with digitisation and Big Data profiling allowing for the optimisation of business ventures and processes. Robotics and automation followed by cybersecurity solutions are already changing manufacturing operations. Distributed financial systems, like blockchain, are globally tested as innovative forms of support for innovations.

As it was pointed out at the World Economic Forum in Davos in 2017, creating a shared future in a fractured world makes a point for international collaboration as a means of solving critical global challenges. The existing modern ICT platforms help to communicate, but real capability to communicate, cooperate and successfully coordinate complex ventures on the global scale are strongly dependent on trust and credibility in human relations.

Bibliography

Constable G., Somerville B., *A Country of Innovation: Twenty Engineering Achievements that Transformed Our Lives*, Joseph Henry Press, Washington D.C. 2003.

Crandall N. F., Wallace M. J., *Work & Rewards in the Virtual Workplace*, AMACOM, New York 1998.

Davis S., Meyer Ch., *BLUR. The Speed and Change in the Connected Economy*, Addison-Wesley, Reading, Massachussets 1998.

Evans Ph., Wurster Th., *Blown to Bits. How the New Economics of Information Transforms Strategy*, Harvard Business School Press, Boston, Massachussets 2000.

Greenberg E., Hirt M., Smit S., *The Global Forces Inspiring a New Narrative of Progress*, "McKinsey Quarterly" 2017.

Hamel G., *Leading the Revolution*, Harvard Business School Press, Cambridge (Mass.) 2000.

Hamel G., Prahalad C. K., *Competing for the Future*, Harvard Business School Press, Cambridge (Mass.) 1993.

Industrial Cyber-security: Monitoring and Anomaly Detection, Report produced by Sentryo in collaboration with Schneider Electric, Siemens, and CEA, www.sentryo.net (access: 5 June 2019).

International Federation of Robotics, *Highlights*, http://www.ifr.org/index. php?id=59&df=2016FEB_Press_Release_IFR_Robot_density_by_region_EN_QS.pdf (access: 5 April 2017).

Lipton M., *Guiding Growth. How Vision Keeps Companies on Course*, Harvard Business School Press, Boston, Massachusets 2003.

McKinsey Global Institute Report, *Digital Poland*, by D. Boniecki, W. Krok, W. Namysł, M. Borowik, J. Iszkowska, M. Rabij, 2016.

Research Report: *Rogue Robots: Testing the Limits of an Industrial Robot's Security*, by F. Maggi (Trend Micro Forward-Looking Threat Research), D. Quarta, M. Pogliani, M. Polino, A. M. Zanchettin, S. Zanero (Politecnico di Milano), https://documents.trendmicro.com/assets/wp/wp--in… (access: 10 June 2019).

Simon, Kutcher & Partners, *Hidden Champions. Lessons Learned from 500 of the World's Best Unknown Companies*, Springer, Berlin 1999.

Simon, Kutcher & Partners, *Hidden Champions of the 21st Century. The Success Strategies of Unknown World Market Leaders*, Springer, Berlin 2010.

Tarlow M., Tarlow Ph., *Digital Aboriginal*, Warner Books, New York 2002.

Westcott R. T., *The Certified Manager of Quality/Organization Excellence Handbook*, 4th ed., ASQ Quality Management Division, Chicago 2013.

Business Model Changes in the Presence of Challenges Brought by Industry 4.0

Prof. Jan Brzóska, Ph.D. Eng.   https://orcid.org/0000-0002-0753-6444

Prof. Lilla Knop, Ph.D. Eng.   https://orcid.org/0000-0001-6796-7695
Silesian University of Technology

Abstract

The business model is a new research area, becoming more and more clear on the research map of strategic management sciences. Global competition, the requirements of sustainable development, the construction of an innovative economy and Industry 4.0 induce the need for creating new or changing current business models. The business models of companies applying various types of innovations constituted the main focus of the research. These companies used digitisation for creating value for clients as well as maintaining (capturing) it, and gaining competitive edge. The purpose of the paper is the presentation of modern business models using features and elements of Industry 4.0. The work underlines their attributes as well as directions of changes of current business models adapting to effective functioning under the conditions of the fourth industrial revolution. It identifies the antecedents of creating and changing business models in the aspect of implementing Industry 4.0. The paper presents the role of innovation and digital technologies as elements in creating value through business models. It also presents case studies, i.e. undertakings using the elements of Industry 4.0 to create their own business models based on renewable energy.

Keywords: Industry 4.0, digital economy, business models, photovoltaics, passive buildings

Introduction

The dynamics of the surroundings, especially the increasing competition and the progressing globalisation, pose new challenges before organisations within their strategic and operational management. This leads to the search for the creation and application of even more complex systems, methods and management instruments. At the moment, business models deciding about competitiveness potential and effectiveness of a given organisation are one of the major management instruments, representing a generator of value for a client and growth of goodwill. Business models capture the concepts of creating value based on various sources; this may be resources, processes or competences, and now numerous innovations play a significant role in creating value and achieving competitive edge. The creation of new business models or a change of the existing ones is affected both by the internal conditions of a given organisation and external factors resulting from the surrounding dynamics. One of such substantial external factors affecting the concept of new business models or adaptive changes in the functioning business models, is the fourth industrial revolution, or the so-called Industry 4.0. This term is defined differently and even understood in varying ways. In the case of this study, one may assume that Industry 4.0 is a definition of innovative solutions and technical processes as well as concepts concerning the organisation (management) of the value chain.[1] Within the scope of these processes

> within modularly structured smart factories, the cybernetic and physical systems moni-
> tor real (physical) processes, create virtual copies of the real (physical) world and take de-
> centralized decisions. Through the Internet of things, the cybernetic and physical systems
> communicate with each other and cooperate with each other and the people acting in real
> time. Through the Internet of services, the internal as well as inter-organizational services
> are offered and used by the users of the value chain.[2]

The main component (foundation) and condition for practical functioning is thorough utilisation of digital economy (widely comprehended digitization). The purpose of the paper is to present modern business models using features and elements of Industry 4.0. It shows the attributes as well as directions of changes in current business models adapting themselves to efficient functioning under the conditions of the fourth industrial revolution. It also presents case studies, i.e. undertakings using elements of Industry 4.0 to create own business models based on renewable energy. Business models of companies applying various types of innovations were the object of the research. Those companies used digitisation for creating value for the client and maintaining (capturing) it as well as gaining competitive edge. The studies in question and the implementation of the paper objectives concerned the following research questions:

- What are the specific antecedents for creating and changing business models in the aspect of implementing Industry 4.0?
- What is the meaning of innovation and digital technology in creating value through business models?

---

[1]   J. Barata, P. Rupino Da Cunha, J. Stal, *Mobile Supply Chain Management in the Industry 4.0 Era: An Annotated Bibliography and Guide for Future Research*, "Journal of Enterprise Information Management" 2018, 31 (1), pp. 173–192.

[2]   M. Herman, T. Pentek, B. Otto, *Design Principles for Industry 4.0 Scenarios: A Literature Review*, Working Paper No. 1, Dortmund 2015, p. 11.

The presented paper is mostly the result of the authors' research performed for many years within the scope of the research projects related to innovation management and business models in companies and regions.[3] The developed methodology of business models research in the aspect of creating value through innovations consists of three steps. The first step is analytical and consists in studying works devoted to the conditions and concepts of digital economy and Industry 4.0. The second step is related to the conditions and theories of business models, in particular to their structure and creating value through innovations and instruments of digital economy. One presented concept of digital economy models regards Industry 4.0. The third step concerns empirical studies presenting the structure of two business models using the concept of the New Era of Innovation model.

1. Digital economy, creating a communication network: The foundation of Industry 4.0

The concept of the fourth industrial revolution, also called Industry 4.0, is a result and consequence of the development of humanity, including technical progress. We have seen three significant points of development across the history of the world, which have given rise to new technologies and organisations:

- The first industrial revolution (Industry 1.0) meant the mechanisation of work. The discovery and application of the steam engine introduced production companies into the industrialization era. Workshops and manufactories were forced out by factories employing often a few hundred employees.
- The second industrial revolution (Industry 2.0) based on the generation of electrical energy allowed for replacing steam engines with electrical drives. Electrification enabled the organisation of mass, bulk production based on production lines. Factories and concerns were established, and they employed thousands of employees.
- The third industrial revolutions (Industry 3.0). Computerisation (including digitisation), automation, the application of highly efficient computers as well as data and information processing systems, allowed for the application of ICT for controlling machines and devices. The efficiency, quality and flexibility of production increased incrementally. Production management systems were introduced that optimised the utilisation of resources and responded to client needs. The meaning of competences and skills of human capital increased.

---

[3] Currently, two projects are carried out in this area at the Faculty of Organization and Management of the Silesian University of Technology: *Methods and Management Instruments Influencing the Growth of the Organization's Innovativeness* (internal project: 2018/2019) and the *Network of Regional Special Observatories in the Entrepreneurial Discovery Process* (EDP)—Project Leader—Marshal's Office of the Silesia Voivodeship (2017/2019).

At the moment, we stand on the threshold of the fourth industrial revolution, also called Industry 4.0, meaning the integration of systems and creation of networks that integrate employees as well as digitally controlled machines and devices using ICT programmes and the Internet. Materials and components manufactured or used for production can be digitally traced, they are able to communicate independently with each other. The vertical flow of information concerning individual components is directed to the control centre (platform) of a given organisation and back from the centre to components and subunits. Another orientation of the information flow is executed in horizontal direction: between machines engaged in the production process and the company production control system. Within the said new depiction of the industry's functioning concept, it is necessary to apply the instruments of technology and digital economy to a very broad extent. There are many definitions of digital economy, but all of them underline a common consecutive element of this concept—i.e. the role and meaning of ICT technology within all domains of life, particularly within contemporary economy.[4] Of course, there are many factors and movers for the development of digitisation (digital economy), the most important of which include dynamically developing knowledge and innovations that enable not only the exponential growth of ICT techniques and technologies, but also innovations within many fields, such as nanotechnology, medicine, bioengineering, material engineering or distributed power engineering. Within this context, it is necessary to answer the question of: What is digital economy based on, and what creates digital economy? At this point, it is necessary to mention:

- the development and utilisation of the Internet of Things, i.e. a system wherein objects, equipped with special sensors, communicate and exchange data with computers and other devices. The process takes place using various network solutions, in particular wireless ones;[5]
- artificial intelligence—systems, machines, devices, products mirroring human intelligence while executing tasks that are able to interactively correct them based on gathered information. They increase the abilities and productivity of human capital;
- cloud computing. Computing clouds are also used to store data and represent data repositories made available through networks of very large capacities as well as equipped with fast access mechanisms. The following clouds are used: Private Cloud managed by a company using it and Public Cloud;

---

4   J. Lee, B. Bagheri, H. Kao, *A Cyber-Physical Systems Architecture for Industry 4.0-based Manufacturing Systems*, "Manufacturing Letters" 2015, 3, pp. 18–23; M. Goliński, *Gospodarka cyfrowa, gospodarka informacyjna, gospodarka oparta na wiedzy – różne określenia tych samych zjawisk czy podobne pojęcia określające różne zjawiska?*, Szkoła Główna Handlowa, Warszawa 2013, pp. 180–184.

5   N. G. Nayak, F. Dürr, K. Rothermel, *Software-defined Environment for Reconfigurable Manufacturing Systems*, 5th International Conference on the Internet of Things (IOT), Seoul 2015, pp. 122–129; R. Mącik, *Internet rzeczy – postrzegane przez młodych konsumentów korzyści i zagrożenia – wyniki badań wstępnych*, "Przedsiębiorczość i Zarządzanie" 2016, 17 (4), pp. 11–27.

- the dissemination and commercial utilisation of social media;
- the application, as a standard, of multimodular (including CRM and e-commerce), integrated information systems for Enterprise Resource Management (ERP) using mass data analyses gathered automatically (Big Data). Such systems enable delivering management information using a hierarchical system for each level of management within economic entities (Business Intelligence);
- the development and popularisation of mobile technologies. Mobile technologies do not only include GSM cellular network technologies. Mobility can be characterised first and foremost by wireless communication (radio communication, connectivity using infrared waves, Bluetooth technology) between devices, not necessarily of the same kind or serving the same purpose. New forms of mobile technologies include augmented reality, i.e. systems connecting the real world with computer-generated content.[6] Other forms of mobile technologies, so called beacons, i.e. small radio transmitters using the technology of Bluetooth Low Energy that communicate with mobile devices, transfer valuable information to users in the surrounding world, i.e. offers of shops in the vicinity. In turn, Near Field Communication (NFC) is a radio communication standard that allows for the exchange of data within 20 cm. Cellular phones equipped with NFC transmitters enable mobile payments;
- 3D printing, i.e. manufacturing three-dimensional physical objects based on a computer model. They are more and more often applied in building prototypes and ready-made objects;
- blockchain, i.e. a decentralised and distributed database within an open-source model in the Internet. It is used to register transactions, settle payments and for traceability of products. It is a public and open register of transactions, processes and products;
- smart grids allowing for communication between all participants of the energy market in order to deliver power services ensuring the reduction of costs and increase of efficiency as well as the integration of distributed energy sources and smart metering covering electronic meters of electrical energy that enable two-way communication between the meter and energy provider, also remote reading of consumed energy.

The mentioned elements of digital economy permit the creation of networks covering integrated digital, physical and human systems. These created **"social networks"** often provide hyperconnectivity, meaning billions of connections between people, organisations, devices, data and processes resulting in the growing interdependence and cooperation of these elements. It is expected that the networks of Industry 4.0

---

[6]   P. Kwiatkowski, *Technologie mobilne – rosnący potencjał*, "Harvard Business Review Polska" 2016, 164.

would allow better flexibility of economic entities and other organisations. They will provide better business interactions, more benefits for clients, employees and partners compared to traditional economy. They are the antecedents of creating and changing business models within many sectors of economy, including the renewable energy sector.

2. Innovative business models: A strategic component of Industry 4.0

The business model is a new research area, becoming more and more clear on the research map of strategic management sciences. There are many premises justifying the exploration of business model issues both for practitioners and theoreticians of management. Of course, global competition, the requirements of sustainable development or the construction of an innovative economy (including Industry 4.0) induce the need for creating and applying even more complex company management systems and searching for effective management methods and instruments.[7] Within this aspect, changes of the existing business models as well as the implementation of their new concepts represent one of the most important systems and instruments of contemporary management. Their meaning results from the following reasons:

- contemporary business models allow for creating value based on various types of innovations, including digital technologies;
- the application of a business model as a transparent concept of capturing and creating value. This applies both to value for the client and for company owners. The created value is based on innovations;
- the ability to create unique combinations of resources as well as cybernetic-physical-human networks capable of generating value;
- treating the business model as a system of mutually dependent activities and processes strongly focused on creating value;
- the ability to search for instruments and methods creating competitive edge through the implementation of innovations;
- treating the business model as an architecture of business operations, which could make the organisation more effective by generating profit;
- business models may be used as instruments for managing the existing companies, furthermore, they represent the basis for planning start-ups, while creating substantial organisational innovations at the same time.

---

[7] A. Janik, A. Ryszko, *Mapping the Field of Industry 4.0 Based on Bibliometric Analysis* [in:] *Vision 2020: Sustainable Economic Development and Application of Innovation Management from Regional Expansion to Global Growth*, Proceedings of the 32nd International Business Information Management Association Conference (IBIMA), 15–16 November 2018, Seville, Spain, ed. by Kh. S. Soliman, International Business Information Management Association, 2018, pp. 6316–6330.

The observed dynamics of strategies and business models of organisations cover all sectors of the economy and apply both to large, as well as medium and small organisations. Changes of business models are the manifestation of a pursuit of these organisations to achieve competitive edge and effectiveness of operations, as well as limit risk. These changes and the creation of new business models are affected both by internal and external conditions. Of course, among the latter, an important role is played by globalisation, increasing competition as well as pro-innovative and environmentally friendly politics. At the moment, the application of various kinds of innovations (including ICT technology) plays a major role in creating value. The concepts and implemented business models show methods and processes related to creating value both for the client and the stakeholders. The first one concerns the satisfaction of client's needs, solving his/her problems; this means specifically the formation of value exchange with the client. The changing role of the client from a passive buyer to a prosumer significantly affecting the activation of user-driven innovations is a material challenge for the development of business models possible because of the digital economy instruments. The same applies to treating business models as a carrier of many types of innovation that allow for achieving competitive edge through their implementation. In turn, the developed and implemented business model may represent a valid and effective organisational innovation, as manifested by the business models of transport or hotel service providers. Only these synthetically presented attributes, expectations and challenges standing before business models point to the complexity, interdisciplinarity and multidimensionality of the business modelling issue. Within this context, the issue of business models has been very interesting within the recent period for both theoreticians and practitioners of management. This interest is accompanied by very differentiated approaches and understandings of business modelling (a multitude of definitions and concepts), thus the stipulations concerning the necessity to create a common scientific platform for a better and more effective study of the business model.[8] Cognitive difficulties (definitions, structure) result from the multidimensional and interdisciplinary nature of the business model, determining the research approach.[9]

As mentioned, the development of studies over business models has resulted in many definitions and concepts.[10] In the context of the subject in question, the ones related

---

[8]   C. Zott, R. Amit, L. Massa, *The Business Model: Recent Developments and Future Research*, "Journal of Management" 2011, 37 (4), pp. 1019–1042.

[9]   M. Kalinowski, L. Vives, *Multi-perspective View on Business Models. Review and Research Agenda*, "Academy of Management Proceedings" 2013, 1, pp. 1–6.

[10] See also: H. W. Chesbrough, *Business Model Innovation: Opportunities and Barriers*, "Long Range Planning" 2010, 43 (2–3), pp. 354–363; N. M. Dahan, J. P. Doh, J. Oetzel, M. Yaziji, *Corporate-NGO Collaboration: Co-creating New Business Models for Developing Markets*, "Long Range Planning" 2010, 43 (2–3), pp. 326–342; D. J. Teece, *Business Models, Business Strategy and Innovation*, "Long Range Planning" 2010, 43 (2–3), pp. 172–194; C. Zott, R. Amit, L. Massa, *The Business Model....*;

to creating the value and meaning of innovation within business modelling are valid. In this case, business models can be treated as a system of resource configuration and mutually dependent activities focused on creating value. In many discussions, the fact of close relationships between the business model and creation of value for clients and company is underlined, and the role of configuration of tangible and intangible factors is emphasised together with the option to capture a part of income from the value.[11] In concepts of the business model, two main dimensions are underlined. The first one is the way in which the value for a client is created, particularly which elements of the business models play a key role and how the value will be rendered.[12] The second dimension of the business model is capturing value for a company that provides profit for it. Its size depends to a high extent on the architecture and character of resources as well as tasks included within the business model.[13] One must also underline their mutual harmonisation and level of innovation. A higher level of harmonisation between elements of the activities system affects the growth of the created value, and thus the ability of its greater appropriation. The dependency between value for a client and capturing values is related to networks of value and strategic selections being components of the business model. Within the theory of business models, addressees of the created value are perceived differently. Treating the business model as a specific combination of resources, generates value through transactions both for clients and organisations.[14] Stakeholders are also depicted as addressees of the value, implementing the term of creating and capturing value within the value network.[15] In turn, creating a unique value and competitive edge is

S. Svejenova, M. Planellas, L. Vives, *An Individual Business Model in the Making: A Chef's Quest for Creative Freedom*, "Long Range Planning" 2010, 43 (2–3), pp. 408–430; C. Zott, R. Amit, *Business Model Design: An Activity System Perspective*, "Long Range Planning" 2010, 43 (2–3), pp. 216–226; R. Boulton, B. Libert, S. Samek, *Cracking the Value Code*, Arthur Andersen, HarperCollins, New York 2000, pp. 244–258.

[11] F. Newth, *Business Models and Strategic Management. A New Integration*, Business Expert, New York 2012, p. 8; M. Jabłoński, *Kształtowanie modeli biznesu w procesie kreacji wartości przedsiębiorstw*, Difin, Warszawa 2013, pp. 31–38.

[12] A. Osterwalder, Y. Pigneur, *Business Model Generation: A Handbook of Visionaries, Game Changers and Challengers*, Strategyzer Series, Wiley, Amsterdam 2010, pp. 26–29; T. Gołębiowski, T. M. Dudzik, M. Lewandowska, M. Witek-Hajduk, *Modele biznesu polskich przedsiębiorstw*, Szkoła Główna Handlowa, Warszawa 2008, pp. 56–68; H. Chesbrough, R. S. Rosenbloom, *The Role of the Business Model in Capturing Value from Innovation: Evidence from Xerox Corporation's Technology Spin-Off Companies*, "Industrial Corporate Change" 2002, 11 (3), pp. 529–555.

[13] C. Zott, R. Amit, L. Massa, *Business Model…*; R. Casades-Masanell, J. E. Ricart, *From Strategy to Business Model and onto Tactics*, "Long Range Planning" 2010, 43 (2–3), pp. 195–215; B. Nogalski, A. A. Szpitter, J. Brzóska, *Modele i strategie biznesu w obszarze dystrybucji energii elektrycznej w Polsce*, Wydawnictwo Uniwersytetu Gdańskiego, Gdańsk 2017, pp. 17–27.

[14] H. Chesbrough, R. S. Rosenbloom, *The Role…*, pp. 530–555; A. Osterwalder, Y. Pigneur, *Business…*, pp. 26–29.

[15] S. M. Shafer, H. J. Smith, J. C. Linder, *The Power of Business Models*, Indiana University, Business Horizons, Bloomington 2005, 48, pp. 199–207; L. Knop, *The Process of Cluster Management* [in:] *Management*

related to innovations (innovation level), for which the business model is a carrier.[16] Innovations allow for creating value for the client (new products, new methods of client service) as well as for stakeholders (environmental protection, new technologies, new value chains, growth of effectiveness).[17] The implementation of innovation is to prevent imitation threats.[18] The business models themselves may represent organisational innovation important for competitiveness.[19] An example may be the business model of hidden revenues and digitisation. This means that we offer our products and services in digital form, therefore easier and faster distribution is possible. The model of hidden revenues means that the products and services are available free of charge and users are not the main sources of revenue. Revenues are generated by other entities, e.g. advertisers.[20] This model was used by the start-up Qpony.pl Sp. z o.o. utilising mobile technologies, especially mobile applications. Features of the business models of digital economy relevant for Industry 4.0 are presented in Table 1. It is worth pointing to the multidimensionality of the value proposal and differentiation of revenue types.

The dynamic growth of innovativeness and development of digital technologies created a potential enabling the construction and application of innovative business models significantly varying from current business modelling concepts. Table 2 presents ten most "revolutionary" business models.

---

of *Network Organization. Theoretical Problems and Dilemmas in Practice*, ed. by W. Sroka, Š. Hittmár, Springer, Heidelberg 2015, pp. 105–120; N. M. Dahan, J. P. Doh, J. Oetzel, M. Yaziji, *Corporate...*, pp. 328–332.

[16] G. Hamel, *Leading the Revolution*, Harvard Business School Press, Boston 2002, pp. 59–68; C. K. Prahalad, M. S. Krishnan, *New Age of Innovation*, McGraw-Hill, New York 2008, pp. 15–29; J. Brzóska, *Innovations as a Factor of Business Models Dynamics in Metallurgical Companies*, Proceedings of 23rd International Conference on Metallurgy and Materials, Brno, Czech Republic, May 2014, pp. 1842–1849.

[17] K. Dohn, A. Gumiński, W. Zoleński, *Early Warning Concept in Identifying Risks in Business Activity* [in:] *Risk Management in Public Administration*, ed. by K. Raczkowski, Springer, Cham 2017, pp. 149–187; A. Szmal, M. Jodkowski, *Technical-Economic Perspective of Using Composite Alternative Fuels in Metallurgical Production*, 24th International Conference on Metallurgy and Materials, Brno, Czech Republic, June 2015, pp. 2–4; J. Baran, A. Janik, A. Ryszko, M. Szafraniec, *Making Eco-Innovation Measurable—Are We Moving towards Diversity or Uniformity of Methods and Indicators?*, SGEM Conference Proceedings 2015, 2, 2, pp. 787–798; M. Kramarz, *Flexibility Strategy in Delayed Differentiation Model of Steel Products* [in:] *Intelligent Systems in Production Engineering and Maintenance, ISPEM, 17–18 September, Wroclaw 2018*, ed. by A. Burduk, E. Chlebus, T. Nowakowski, A. Tubis, Springer, Cham 2019, pp. 731–741.

[18] K. Obłój, *Tworzywo skutecznych strategii*, PWE, Warszawa 2002, pp. 97–99.

[19] G. Hamel, *Leading...*, pp. 69–72.

[20] M. Kardas, *Pojęcia i typy modeli biznesu* [in:] *Zarządzanie, organizacje i organizowanie. Przegląd perspektyw teoretycznych*, ed. by K. Klincewicz, Wydawnictwo Naukowe Wydziału Zarządzania Uniwersytetu Warszawskiego, Warszawa 2017, pp. 298–318.

Table 1. Features of the digital economy business model relevant for Industry 4.0

Dimension	Business model attributes	Specification				
Value creation dimension	Platform type	Web-based platform	Mobile app			
	Key activity	Data services	Community building	Content creation		
	Price discovery	Fixed prices	Set by sellers	Set by buyers	Auction	Negotiation
	Review system	User reviews	Review by marketplace	None		
	Key value proposition	Price/cost/efficiency	Emotional value	Social value		
	Transaction content	Product		Service		
	Transaction type	Digital		Offline		
	Industry scope	Vertical		Horizontal		
Value delivery dimension	Marketplace participants	C2C	B2C	B2B		
	Geographic scope	Global	Regional	Local		
Value capture dimension	Key revenue stream	Commissions	Subscriptions	Advertising	Service sales	
	Pricing mechanism	Fixed pricing	Market pricing	Differentiated pricing		
	Price discrimination	Feature based	Location based	Quantity based	None/other	
	Revenue source	Seller	Buyer	Third party	None/other	

Source: K. Tauscher, S. M. Laudien, *Understanding Platform Business Models: A Mixed Methods Study of Marketplaces*, "Journal on Management" 2018, 36 (3). pp. 319–329.

Table 2. Ten most "revolutionary" business models

Business model	Enterprise example—disruptor	Business model description
Subscription Model	Netflix, HelloFresh, Dollar Shave Club, Kindle, One	The user pays a fixed fee for access to the offered product /service.
Freemium Model (free and premium connection)	Spotify, Dropbox, LinkedIn, Skype, The New York Times, Farmville	The product or service (mostly software, computer game, Internet service) is available for free, however using advanced functions or gaining some virtual goods requires purchasing the premium version.
Free Model	Google, Facebook, Snapchat	The final user has free access to a product service, however the operator acting as a service provider earns on advertisements and the sale of information on consumer preferences, who are users of the free service.
Market Place	eBay, Alibaba, Friendsurance, priceline.com, Upwork	The company makes the platform available for transactions made by third parties.
Access over Ownership	Zipcar, ParkCirca, Peerby, Car2Share	Users may use the services without the need to purchase the product which is used while using the service.
Hyper Market	Amazon, Zalando, Coolblue	Companies engaged in e-commerce offer a very wide assortment of goods and services, often making the products or services available based on exclusivity principle.
Experience	Apple, Tesla, Disney World, Tomorrowland	Companies use the propensity of users to pay more based on previous experiences resulting from using the products or contacts with the company.
The Pyramid	Amazon, and other e-shops	Companies generate a large part of their revenues using the cooperating entities and sellers of other goods.
On Demand	Uber, Operator, Tsk-Rabbit	Companies offer products/services "immediately" available for users at the moment of the demand's emergence.
Ecosystem	Apple, Google	Companies create a closed ecosystem of products and services that makes the users buy other products of the same company.

Source: J. Gajewski, W. Paprocki, J. Pieriegud, *Cyfryzacja gospodarki i społeczeństwa. Szanse i wyzwania dla sektorów infrastrukturalnych*, Instytut Badań nad Gospodarką Rynkową, Gdańska Akademia Bankowa, Gdańsk 2016, p. 19.

In turn, when studying the trends and concepts related to the development of digital economy business models, A. Jabłoński and M. Jabłoński[21] distinguish the following:

- business models in the sharing economy representing a very wide scope of business and social activity, covering unconventional forms of consumption activities, such as exchange, barter trade, rental, sharing and replacement;
- business models using Big Data. Running a business and social activities is based on the application of Big Data's usefulness. The key attributes include variety, pace, size, reliability and ability to create value using Big Data;
- circulating economy business models oriented at the development of a regenerative economic system. These are business models related to the recovery of materials and energy, using resources within the recycling processes, extensions of product life as well as components through activities such as: repair, modernisation or resale or offering services instead of sale;
- sustainable business models of digital economy. Business models consider the balance of ecological, social and economic factors. The proposal of value must ensure both ecological, social and economic value through offering products and services. These models are to include the achievement of fair success for employees;
- social business models within the digital economy. This is a business model of operating companies, the development stimulation factors of which are social aspects expressed by the sustainability of economic, ecological and social issues with the engagement of the society and their dynamic communication focused on selected business model attributes, based on digital platforms stimulating growth and fostering the achievement of success. Economic revenue may also be the manifestation of such success.[22]

Start-ups are other important entities of Industry 4.0. From this perspective, they may be perceived as an "undertaking that satisfies at least one of two conditions: belongs to the digital economy sector . . . or creates new technological solutions within IT/ITC."[23] However, S. Blank and B. Dorf define the start-up as "temporary organization engaged in the search for scalable, repeatable and profitable business model."[24] These are the features of such companies: relatively low expenditures and costs of initiation of economic activities, increased risk comparing to standard undertakings, better return on investment comparing to standard undertakings, basing the business model on knowledge and innovativeness, using different forms of support often related to cooperation.

---

[21] *Perspektywy rozwoju modeli biznesu przedsiębiorstw – uwarunkowania strategiczne*, ed. by A. Jabłoński, M. Jabłoński, CeDeWu, Warszawa 2019, p. 48.

[22] Ibidem, p. 80.

[23] *Polskie startupy*, Raport Fundacji Startup Poland, 2017, p. 16.

[24] S. Blank, B. Dorf, *Podręcznik startupu. Budowa wielkiej firmy krok po kroku*, transl. B. Sałbut, Helion, Gliwice 2013, p. 19.

The presented synthetic review of innovative business models shows a significant meaning of various types of innovations in creating value. The fundamental meaning of creating value for the growth of competitiveness and development of companies means that digital technologies and instruments related to the contemporary industry have even more impact on new business models.

3. Innovative business models—case study

3.1. Methodology of the study

The concept of the New Era of Innovation is a very interesting approach that allows for analysing and creating innovative business models (including innovation, Industry 4.0), as created by C. K. Prahalad, M. S. Krishnan.[25] The operational business model according to the New Era of Innovation principles is presented in Figure 1. The business models create three basic components: the first two are social architecture and technical architecture, representing specified resources, while the third one is business processes.

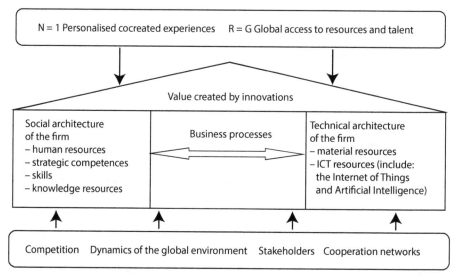

Figure 1. Operational business model according to principles of the New Era of Innovation

Source: prepared by the authors based on C. K. Prahalad, M. S. Krishnan, *New Age of Innovation*, McGraw-
-Hill, 2008, p. 6.

---

[25]   C. K. Prahalad, M. S. Krishnan, *New Age...*, pp. 13–47.

Based on the performed studies of the business modelling theory and own research, we may define the business model as a configuration of business processes combining and developing resources, shaped in the form of social and technical architecture, creating a value. The paper uses the analysis of two cases, whose business processes and resources are focused on renewable sources of energy and digital technology that allow for balancing energy. It also assumes the creation of value for the client as well as the option of its creation by the client. In case of the methodology developed and applied in the studies, elements of the business model based on the New Era of Innovation principles were used, i.e. an undertaking was briefly presented followed by a discussion of the business model elements:

- social architecture including first and foremost: human resources and strategic competences, skills and knowledge resources;
- technical architecture including: material resources (size and structure of property, potential characteristics, sources of supplies, organisation, global resources) and ICT resources (systems);
- business processes including: processes map and business processes;
- created value, including: sources of achievable value and its innovation effects.

3.2. Business model: Photovoltaic farm within a developer's undertaking

The business model of such a company consists in using the technology of processing solar light into electrical energy, i.e. generating electrical current from solar radiation using the photovoltaic effect. Based on using smart networks and the application of smart metering software, it is possible to transfer the surplus of energy to the network. The undertaking is an element of a developer's investment within a residential building estate "Słoneczne wzgórze" (transl. Sunny Hill) consisting in the first stage of 24 buildings with four apartments each. The installation will be operated by tenants of the estate and the farm maintenance personnel. The installed power of each building is 11 kW. The elements and features of the business model are presented in Table 3. Total financial expenditures amounted PLN 1,056,000 and the return on investment period, considering additional funds, is around four years.

Table 3. Elements and features of the business model: A photovoltaic farm within a developer's undertaking

Operational time — Elements of the model	20 years (starting on 1 March 2019)
Social architecture	
Human resources (including prosumers) Strategic competences, skills and knowledge resources	Installation maintenance personnel (services contract), tenants (owners of apartments within the estate). Maintenance of the farm by natural persons and a periodical services contract with the maintenance personnel. Strategic competences include the knowledge of law concerning RES and duties of the DSO within the scope of connecting and cooperating with prosumers. The ability to obtain financial assistance by the developer. Experience in settling net energy principles by balancing electrical energy.
Technical architecture	
Material resources (size and structure of property, characteristics of potential, sources of supplies, organisation, global resources) ICT resources (systems)	Having one's own apartment. RES installation, 960 pieces of panels Sharp Solar 275 Wp. Efficiency ca. 98%. Connection as well as metering and settlement system. The application of smart grids and proper software, including a two-way meter. Using the Internet and smartphones for net metering by apartment owners.
Business processes	
Processes map Business processes	The basic process consists in the production of electrical energy based on solar energy. The remaining processes: optimisation of own energy consumption, settlement of and balancing of energy, net metering and settlement of net energy. This consists in deduction by the DSO from the bill of the generated surplus that has been sent to the grid, imposing only the fee for transfer of energy received from the DSO. Possible process control using the Internet and smartphone. Maintenance and repair process (after the guarantee period).
Created value	
Sources of attained value	The basic source of value is the application of RES. Value for the prosumer is the generated electrical energy used for own needs and the surplus is sent to a power company for balancing purposes. Provision of energy independence (within the scope of electrical energy).
Effects	• Production of energy 230,400 kW/h; • Savings in virtue of own production of energy PLN 149,760; • Fixed fees for distribution of energy PLN 18,432; • Savings in total resulting from the fees for electrical energy—per annum: PLN 131,760

Source: prepared by the authors.

3.3. Business model: Low-energy (passive) office building in the Scientific and Technological Park "Euro-Centrum" in Katowice[26]

The presented undertaking is an example of using many types of innovations and information technologies. This is a low-energy (passive) office building in the Scientific and Technological Park "Euro-Centrum" in Katowice. The elements and features of the business model are presented in Table 4.

Table 4. Elements and features of the business model concerning a passive building

Elements of the model ⟍ Time	Min. 30 years (commissioning in February 2014)
Social architecture	
Human resources Strategic competences, skills and knowledge resources	Employment of specialists within the scope of energy and environmental protection. Skills within maintenance of the applied technical and digital systems and installation. Large object management skills. Property market marketing skills.
Technical architecture	
Material resources (size and structure of property, characteristics of potential, sources of supplies, organisation, global resources) ICT resources (systems)	Within the scope of structural and construction solutions, the following was applied: column and slab construction system, walls insulated with Styrofoam with a thickness of 30 cm; glazed centre of the building providing the maximum possible amount of daylight; automatic facade shutters stopping excessive transfer of sun radiation and protecting the rooms against heating; triple glazed windows of high insulation power, achieving a transfer coefficient of 0.7. The building installation includes, among other things: • geothermal probes located within vertical bore holes at a depth of ca. 50 m (total length of bore holes is 4 km) that represent the bottom source of heat for the heat pumps; • 6 heat pumps, heating the building by raising the water temperature in the installation and transferring it to the system of heating and cooling ceilings BKT. Heating power of the pumps is 256.8 kW. Cooling power is 186.9 kW; • integrated smart metering system and utilisation of smart grids; • 10 solar collectors (vacuum) located on the building roof, using solar radiation energy to warm up water in the accumulation tanks; • 3 sets of photovoltaic panels: roof panels; • 231 modules, installed within the system; • double-axis photovoltaic tracker system, i.e. 3 tracking systems with 36 installed modules, tracking the apparent movement of the Sun;

---

[26] Based on information included on the website of the Scientific and Technological Park "Euro-Centrum" in Katowice.

Time Elements of the model	Min. 30 years (commissioning in February 2014)
	• heat recovery system within the air handling unit (recuperator) in order to recover 80% of thermal energy from the expelled air; • process cold installation adapting the internal temperature to the laboratory and implementation rooms requirements. The passive building at the Scientific and Technological Park "Euro-Centrum" in Katowice also has a modern Data Centre.
Business processes	
Processes map Business processes	The basic process consists in the management of the building (BMS) that allows for integrating and managing the systems from one place and controlling operational parameters of individual devices. An Internet-guided monitoring process of the installations, including power systems. The remaining processes: building administration; rental and cooperation with tenants; maintenance and repair process; office building maintenance; human resources management.
Created value	
Sources of attained value	The basic source of value is the application of the RES solutions and obtaining energy savings.
Effects	The value for tenants is a modern and safe interior and a good location. The power of total photovoltaic installation is 107 kWp, which is enough to cover the annual demand for energy of the technological systems of the building, i.e. heating, ventilation and air-conditioning. Promoting the Scientific and Technological Park "Euro-Centrum" in Katowice and building its image as a centre of renewable energy and effectiveness.

Source: prepared by the authors.

In case of the second undertaking, it is worth mentioning the significant number of applied innovations and information technologies, relevant for Industry 4.0. The passive building "Euro-Centrum" satisfies the EU requirements concerning this type of constructions from both the technical and economic point of view. As assumed, the building uses only 12.5% of energy that would have otherwise been used by an analogical traditional building. In 2012, the construction has been honoured during the contest "Innowator Śląska" (transl. "The Innovator of Silesia"), and in 2013 has been awarded with the European Green Building Award. Implementation of the project was possible because of the additional funds from the European Regional Development Fund.

The presented cases assumed that the basic source of value is the application of renewable sources of energy. The applied technical resources correspond with the digital economy assumptions wherein the omnipresence of digital technologies answers the needs (even these subconscious) of clients. Technical resources are followed by social ones, not only in the context of possessed skills and competences of employees, but also a broad prosumer approach. Changes in business processes result both from the created value and the resources necessary for its creation. This means, among other things, net metering or the Internet of things.

Summary

The results of theoretical and empirical studies show the multidimensional character of circumstances that create the new and modify the existing business models. Dynamically developing knowledge and innovations allow not only the incremental increase of ICT techniques and the level of technologies, but also innovations within all sectors of life, mostly in economy, having its impact on the management of business and non-business organisations. Proper business models will be decisive for the implementation and development of the modern industry. Specific antecedents for creating new and changing the existing business models are instruments of digital economy, used skilfully to create social networks including both digital, physical (infrastructural) and human systems. The success of Industry 4.0 companies will be affected by both digital and production technologies as well as modern infrastructure and properly competent human capital.

Moreover, a review of theory and case studies shows that value based on innovations represents a central dimension of the contemporary business model. This is created by the application of innovations which are frequently related to the newest ICT technologies. The presented business models constitute examples of undertakings that use many innovations, especially technological (process), organisational and marketing (prosumer relationships). This was possible due to the application of modern information technologies attributable to Industry 4.0.

Bibliography

Baran J., Janik A., Ryszko A., Szafraniec M., *Making Eco-Innovation Measurable—Are We Moving towards Diversity or Uniformity of Methods and Indicators?*, SGEM Conference Proceedings 2015, 2, 2.

Barata J., Rupino Da Cunha P., Stal J., *Mobile Supply Chain Management in the Industry 4.0 Era: An Annotated Bibliography and Guide for Future Research*, "Journal of Enterprise Information Management" 2018, 31 (1).

Blank S., Dorf B., *Podręcznik startupu. Budowa wielkiej firmy krok po kroku*, transl. B. Sałbut, Helion, Gliwice 2013.

Boulton R., Libert B., Samek S., *Cracking the Value Code*, Arthur Andersen, HarperCollins, New York 2000.

Brzóska J., *Innovations as a Factor of Business Models Dynamics in Metallurgical Companies*, Proceedings of 23rd International Conference on Metallurgy and Materials, Brno, Czech Republic, May 2014.

Casades-Masanell R., Ricart J. E., *From Strategy to Business Model and onto Tactics*, "Long Range Planning" 2010, 43 (2–3).

Chesbrough H., Rosenbloom R. S., *The Role of the Business Model in Capturing Value from Innovation: Evidence from Xerox Corporation's Technology Spin-Off Companies*, "Industrial Corporate Change" 2002, 11 (3).

Chesbrough H. W., *Business Model Innovation: Opportunities and Barriers*, "Long Range Planning" 2010, 43 (2–3).

Dahan N. M., Doh J. P., Oetzel J., Yaziji M., *Corporate-NGO Collaboration: Co-creating New Business Models for Developing Markets*, "Long Range Planning" 2010, 43 (2–3).

Dohn K., Gumiński A., Zoleński W., *Early Warning Concept in Identifying Risks in Business Activity* [in:] *Risk Management in Public Administration*, ed. by K. Raczkowski, Springer, Cham 2017.

Gajewski J., Paprocki W., Pieriegud J., *Cyfryzacja gospodarki i społeczeństwa. Szanse i wyzwania dla sektorów infrastrukturalnych*, Instytut Badań nad Gospodarką Rynkową, Gdańska Akademia Bankowa, Gdańsk 2016.

Gołębiowski T., Dudzik T. M., Lewandowska M., Witek-Hajduk M., *Modele biznesu polskich przedsiębiorstw*, Szkoła Główna Handlowa, Warszawa 2008.

Goliński M., *Gospodarka cyfrowa, gospodarka informacyjna, gospodarka oparta na wiedzy – różne określenia tych samych zjawisk czy podobne pojęcia określające różne zjawiska?*, Szkoła Główna Handlowa, Warszawa 2013.

Hamel G., *Leading the Revolution*, Harvard Business School Press, Boston 2002.

Herman M., Pentek T., Otto B., *Design Principles for Industry 4.0 Scenarios: A Literature Review*, Working Paper No. 1, Dortmund 2015.

Jabłoński M., *Kształtowanie modeli biznesu w procesie kreacji wartości przedsiębiorstw*, Difin, Warszawa 2013.

Janik A., Ryszko A., *Mapping the Field of Industry 4.0 Based on Bibliometric Analysis* [in:] *Vision 2020: Sustainable Economic Development and Application of Innovation Management from Regional Expansion to Global Growth*, Proceedings of the 32nd International Business Information Management Association Conference (IBIMA), 15–16 November 2018, Seville, Spain, ed. by Kh. S. Soliman, International Business Information Management Association, 2018.

Kalinowski M., Vives L., *Multi-perspective View on Business Models. Review and Research Agenda*, "Academy of Management Proceedings" 2013, 1.

Kardas M., *Pojęcia i typy modeli biznesu* [in:] *Zarządzanie, organizacje i organizowanie. Przegląd perspektyw teoretycznych*, ed. by K. Klincewicz, Wydawnictwo Naukowe Wydziału Zarządzania Uniwersytetu Warszawskiego, Warszawa 2017.

Knop L., *The Process of Cluster Management* [in:] *Management of Network Organization. Theoretical Problems and Dilemmas in Practice*, ed. by W. Sroka, Š. Hittmár, Springer, Heidelberg 2015.

Kramarz M., *Flexibility Strategy in Delayed Differentiation Model of Steel Products* [in:] *Intelligent Systems in Production Engineering and Maintenance, ISPEM, 17–18 September, Wroclaw 2018*, ed. by A. Burduk, E. Chlebus, T. Nowakowski, A. Tubis, Springer, Cham 2019.

Kwiatkowski P., *Technologie mobilne – rosnący potencjał*, "Harvard Business Review Polska" 2016, 164.

Lee J., Bagheri B., Kao H., *A Cyber-Physical Systems Architecture for Industry 4.0 Based Manufacturing Systems*, "Manufacturing Letters" 2015, 3.

Mącik R., *Internet rzeczy – postrzegane przez młodych konsumentów korzyści i zagrożenia – wyniki badań wstępnych*, "Przedsiębiorczość i Zarządzanie" 2016, 17 (4).

Nayak N. G., Dürr F., Rothermel K., *Software-Defined Environment for Reconfigurable Manufacturing Systems*, 5th International Conference on the Internet of Things (IOT), Seoul 2015.

Newth F., *Business Models and Strategic Management. A New Integration*, Business Expert, New York 2012.

Nogalski B., Szpitter A. A., Brzóska J., *Modele i strategie biznesu w obszarze dystrybucji energii elektrycznej w Polsce*, Wydawnictwo Uniwersytetu Gdańskiego, Gdańsk 2017.

Obłój K., *Tworzywo skutecznych strategii*, PWE, Warszawa 2002.

Osterwalder A., Pigneur Y., *Business Model Generation: A Handbook of Visionaries, Game Changers and Challengers*, Strategyzer Series, Wiley, Amsterdam 2010.

Perspektywy rozwoju modeli biznesu przedsiębiorstw – uwarunkowania strategiczne, ed. by A. Jabłoński, M. Jabłoński, CeDeWu, Warszawa 2019.

Prahalad C. K., Krishnan M. S., *New Age of Innovation*, McGraw-Hill, New York 2008.

Shafer S. M., Smith H. J., Linder J. C., *The Power of Business Models*, Vol. 48, Indiana University, Business Horizons, Bloomington 2005.

Polskie startupy, Raport Fundacji Startup Poland, 2017.

Svejenova S., Planellas M., Vives L., *An Individual Business Model in the Making: A Chef's Quest for Creative Freedom*, "Long Range Planning" 2010, 43 (2–3).

Szmal A., Jodkowski M., *Technical-Economic Perspective of Using Composite Alternative Fuels in Metallurgical Production*, 24th International Conference on Metallurgy and Materials, Brno, Czech Republic, June 2015.

Tauscher K., Laudien S. M., *Understanding Platform Business Models: A Mixed Methods Study of Marketplaces*, "Journal of Management" 2018, 36 (3).

Teece D. J., *Business Models, Business Strategy and Innovation*, "Long Range Planning" 2010, 43 (2–3).

Zott C., Amit R., *Business Model Design: An Activity System Perspective*, "Long Range Planning" 2010, 43 (2–3).

Zott C., Amit R., Massa L., *The Business Model: Recent Developments and Future Research*, "Journal of Management" 2011, 37 (4).

Communication in Traditional and Network Organisation: Transformation

Prof. Jerzy Kisielnicki, Ph.D.   https://orcid.org/0000-0002-2451-7202
Warsaw University

Abstract

I wish to compare the communication systems of network and traditional (hierarchical) organisations. The communication system as a tool supporting the management system may be, depending on the situation, a component delaying or supporting the implementation of the Industry 4.0 concept. The author also examines the factors that impact the smooth functioning of modern communication systems, focusing in particular on the role of ICT as a determinant of the operation of such systems. Communication systems of organisations depend on many factors, of which the main ones include: 1) the purposes that these systems are to serve and 2) the resources allocated to them. Communication systems are analysed in numerous works of literature on organisation and management sciences. In order to present communication in organisation management, the author applied a model approach simplifying managerial communication. The selection of analysed sources is anchored in the study of literature and research reports as well as in his own experience as a designer and researcher.

Keywords: communication systems, network organizations, models of communication

Introduction

We wish to compare the communication systems of network and traditional (hierarchical) organisations. The communication system as a tool supporting the management system may be, depending on the situation, a component delaying or supporting the implementation of the Industry 4.0 concept. The implementation of this concept requires a shift from hierarchical communication systems to the use of network solutions. We will also examine the factors that affect the smooth functioning of modern communication systems. We are particularly interested in the role of ICT as a determinant of the operation of such systems. Communication systems of organisations depend on many factors. The crucial ones include the purposes that these systems are to serve and the resources allocated to them. Communication systems are analysed in numerous works of literature on organisation and management sciences. In order to present communication in organisation management, we will employ a model approach that outlines managerial communication in a simplified way. The selection of analysed sources is anchored in the study of literature and research reports as well as in our own experience as designers and researchers.

Models of communication systems and their elements

The cybernetic model of contemporary communication was first presented in the literature by Shannon and Weaver. The Shannon–Weaver model of communication has been called the "mother of all models."[1] It is considered when many senders and receivers exist and when information channels are broadened and extended. Thereby, we can prove that when analysing the extended model presented in the figure, the risk of losses and changes in sent information increases. This model justifies the assertion that IT systems allow the information transmission process to be organised in such a way that we reduce the possibility of noise as an element of information loss.

The notion of communication model is applied in various contexts, and research into communication is multidisciplinary. Such research is associated with theories and research in the fields of psychology, economics, sociology, political science, and sciences. In our discussion, we focus on management and organisations. We analyse the processes pertaining to two key management issues, namely efficient transmission of reliable and up-to-date information and knowledge to all authorised members of the organisation. Today's communication system fulfils the following two tasks:

- Transfer of information.
- Transfer of knowledge, including the transformation of information into knowledge by means of BI information systems.

The primary objective of communication projects is to design such a process of information and knowledge transfer within an organisation that will satisfy user needs. At the same time, the implementation process should be effective, smooth and efficient. In the related literature, similar aspects of communication processes were addressed by many researchers.

Analysis of the communication system concerns both intra-organisational processes and those between the organisation and its environment. The communication model in an organisation is shaped by the following groups of factors:

---

[1] D. Woods, E. Hollnagel, *Joint Cognitive Systems: Foundations of Cognitive Systems Engineering*, Taylor & Francis, Boca Raton 2005.

1. The management process structure as the backbone of the communication model;

2. Semantics, meaning the content being sent;

3. The communication system infrastructure (hardware and software), meaning hardware and software tools used in the communication system.

A specific communication system is chosen depending on the situation of the examined organisation, including its needs as well as both tangible and financial resources available. This choice is also influenced by the progress in hardware and software solutions.

The management process structure and its role in the communication system

Management is an element of the communication model that directly affects the structure of the communication process. This structure is represented graphically or descriptively as an organisational chart. The organisational management chart may be analysed from the perspective of models of individual (among various actors in the organisation) and global communication (among some or all actors in the organisations and between the organisation and its environment). The communication structure is a derivative of the management style of a particular organisation. Elements of the communication model include: individual organisational posts, their agglomerates (units, departments, divisions), and existing relationships (ties). The communication model structure both connects and divides in this respect. The basic relationships that are reflected in the communication system are: linear (hierarchical, formal), expressing superior-subordinate relations, and functional, including matrix relationships.

Communication structures can be analysed and assessed against a variety of criteria. The central criterion is the number of intermediate levels. The number of levels (intermediate tiers) determines both the degree of organisational complexity and the way in which knowledge and information are transmitted and absorbed. There is a tendency to reduce the number of intermediate levels and transmit information and knowledge directly. In many organisations, however, a system of traditional hierarchical communication is applied.

The effectiveness and efficiency of the information system depends on the functioning of its individual tiers as well as on the operation of the so-called feedbacks. Tiers providing appropriate "portions" of information and knowledge should get signals of receipt and understanding in relation to the transmitted content and if the message was an order, of the stage of task completion.

Contemporary communication systems are becoming increasingly network-based and relational. The network communication system bears the following essential characteristics:

- Flexible actions undertaken in order to continuously improve the effectiveness and efficiency of the organisation as a whole;

- A constant flow of information and knowledge among all those involved: employees, investors, suppliers, customers, which is connected with cooperation in different cultures and time zones within a uniform global network;
- Building teams that can quickly deliver high-quality solutions based on the knowledge gained from work in network teams.

The model of network links comprises direct links, yet they exist among all employees of the organisation whether they cooperate with one another or not. The relational system can be accused of being more "lavish" to a certain extent. However, it is more secure than a network system. Among all employees of the organisation, there are direct links that can be activated at any time. Each row of the matrix contains communication links between individual employees in the organisation. In practice, a hybrid model is used. It can be referred to as a network-relational or object-relational model where links between objects are network-based and links inside objects are relational. In each analysed communication system, the role of people responsible for the design of the information and knowledge transmission system also involves building a system of mutual trust between individual members of the organisation.

As an example we could use the implementation of MRP systems and the design and implementation of BI systems in large organisations such as banks, trading and manufacturing companies.[2] The network communication system was well received by the project workers. It turned out to be both efficient and effective. The use of this type of communication made it possible to achieve obvious results such as increased speed of information transfer and a reduced scale of disinformation. What is the added value? This communication model enabled the application of agile methodologies during a research project.[3]

Semantics as a description of the transmitted content

A semantic description is a part of a comprehensive communication model that addresses the content and meaning of transmitted data, information, knowledge, and their aggregates. For example, it takes the form of words, phrases, ideas, sentences, and texts. Communication requires more and more information and knowledge that is transmitted in units or as specific aggregates. Global networks such as the Internet make contents

---

[2]   F. Baumann, R. Hussein, D. Roller, *State of the Art of BPM—Approach to Business Process Models and Its Perspective*, "International Journal of Electronics Communication and Computer Engineering" 2015, 6 (6), pp. 649–657.

[3]   J. Kisielnicki, *Intellectual Capital in the Knowledge Management Process—Relations-Factors* [in:] *Business Environment in Poland*, ed. by A. Z. Nowak, B. Glinka, P. Hensel, Wydawnictwo Wydziału Zarządzania Uniwersytetu Warszawskiego, Warszawa 2008; idem, *Zarządzanie projektami badawczo-rozwojowymi*, Wydawnictwo Nieoczywiste, Warszawa 2017; idem, *Zarządzanie i informatyka*, Placet, Warszawa 2017.

accumulate very fast. The development of IT tools today allows large data sets, or Big Data, to be used. According to some authors[4] Big Data is a term referring to large, variable and diverse data sets that are difficult to process and analyse; yet, such an analysis is valuable as it can lead to gaining new knowledge. In a report by L. Douglas[5] Big Data is referred to as a 3V model: a large volume of data; high data velocity; a wide variety of data. It is now assumed that Big Data consists of the following four dimensions called the "4Vs": volume—the amount of data counted in tera- or petabytes; variety—the diversity of data that come from different, often incoherent, sources; velocity—the speed of new data inflow and data analysis, in nearly real time; value—the value of data, the most important data are distinguished from among the mass of insignificant information. Big Data also refers to sets of information that require new forms of processing in order to: support decision-making, discover new phenomena, and optimise processes. Managing large sets is a challenge faced by contemporary communication processes.

Apart from sets of information and knowledge, communication systems also comprise networks of relations between individual elements and their aggregates. Sets of notions as aggregates are often termed concepts. Their presentation creates conceptual schemas that, as a description of a certain domain of knowledge, can serve simultaneously as a basis for inference. Such a set of information and relations is defined as ontology. Ontology is a formal representation of a user-defined knowledge domain. It is the records of sets of concepts and relations between them. Creating ontology fulfils the tasks of the users of the communication process in a formalised way.[6] Thanks to the communication system, users will obtain the needed data, information, knowledge, ideas, and strategies. Thereby, their information needs are satisfied. The analysed part of the communication system also includes a set of concepts, techniques and notations aimed at projecting the semantics of data, or their meaning in the outside world. The literature uses different types of notations to present information, knowledge and their aggregates in accordance with the facts.[7]

How transmitted information and knowledge are recorded can be defined as a semantic model representing a particular ontology. An example of a simple semantic model is the entity-relationship model. The term "semantic model" or "conceptual model" is sometimes also used to refer to a specific diagram (or another linguistic-graphic form)

---

[4]   T. Erl, W. Khattak, P. Buhler, *Big Data Fundamentals: Concepts. Drivers & Techniques*, Prentice Hall, Upper Saddle River 2016.

[5]   *Gartner Business Activity Monitoring (BAM)*, 2013, http://www.gartner.com/it-glossary/bam-business-activity-monitoring (access: 2 January 2018).

[6]   D. Fensel, H. Lausen, *Enabling Semantic Web Services: Web Service Modeling Ontology*, Springer, Heidelberg 2006.

[7]   A. Tatnall, *Web Technologies: Concepts, Methodologies, Tools and Applications*, Information Science Reference, Hershey, New York 2010; M. Dumas, M. La Rosa, J. Mendling, H. A. Reijers, *Fundamentals of Business Process Management*, Springer, Heidelberg 2013; *Domain-Specific Conceptual Modeling*, ed. by D. Karagiannis, H. C. Mayer, J. Mylopoulos, Springer, Heidelberg 2016.

that reflects the reality described by data. The semantic model consists of a network of concepts and relationships between these concepts. Concepts are ideas, objects or topics of interest to the user.

Effective communication requires a number of factors to be taken into account, regardless of the communication model applied. As was written,[8] it is important to convey relatively full information and knowledge in this process. Nonetheless, the difficulty of conveying information and knowledge in a multicultural and global world must be realised. Our core task is a knowledge transfer system. It is this system that influences communication models in organisations. M. Polanyi[9] noticed that there is knowledge that man is not aware of. In his work, he distinguished two types of knowledge:

- Tacit knowledge existing only in the mind of the person who possesses it, produced by experience and not fully realised ("I know that I can do it"), manifested only through skilful action.
- Explicit knowledge (formal knowledge) expressed as signs and recorded on knowledge carriers.

In the communication system, we should pay particular attention to cultural problems that can be categorised as tacit knowledge. The weight of this issue is noted by many researchers. The works by A. Trompenaars and Ch. Hampden-Turner[10] report interesting findings in this respect. Inter-cultural communication is a meaningful part of communication processes that affect communication models in organisations. According to F. Trompenaars and Ch. Hampden-Turner, the condition of the economy is not determined solely by economic laws. Also communication systems influence the economic situation of organisations and countries. Their research covered a group of fifteen thousand senior managers from 43 different countries who were responsible for international projects. The results showed that even people who performed international tasks and were in constant contact with representatives of other nationalities used national stereotypes in communication systems. Moreover, what could be noticed was that those stereotypes were reinforced in their case. Those works resulted in the so-called "Trompenaars model." It is a framework for semantic analysis of inter-cultural communication and serves to understand communication systems and activities of international corporations. It can be employed to design communication systems and to understand transmitted content. There are seven components of the model:

---

[8]   Among others L. Beamer, I. Varne, *Intercultural Communication in the Global Workplace*, McGraw-Hill/Irwin, Boston–New York 2011.

[9]   M. Polanyi, *Personal Knowledge: Towards a Post-Critical Philosophy*, University of Chicago Press, Chicago 1974.

[10]   B. F. Trompenaars, Ch. Hampden-Turner, *Siedem wymiarów kultury. Znaczenie różnic kulturowych w działalności gospodarczej*, transl. B. Nawrot, Oficyna Ekonomiczna, Kraków 2002; idem, *Business Across Cultures*, Capstone Publishing, Oxford 2003; idem, *Culture for Business*, 2017, http://www2.thtconsulting.com (access: 4 May 2019).

- Universalism vs particularism (What is more important, rules or relationships?).
- Individualism vs collectivism (Can we function in a group or individually?).
- Neutral vs emotional (Do we display our emotions?).
- Specific vs diffuse (How to separate our private and working lives?).
- Achievement vs ascription (Do we have to prove ourselves to achieve status or is it given to us?).
- Sequential vs synchronic (Do we do one thing at a time or several things simultaneously?).
- Internal vs external control (Are we able to control our environment or are we controlled by it?).

Understanding these factors can help us control our behaviour and know and understand the behaviour of people who grew up in other cultures.

The analysis of research results is based on the view that the communication system, including the knowledge transfer system, should comprise, among other things, solutions that take into account factors such as values, habits, and applied cultural models. How participants of the communication process perceive time, family, history, ethics in progressing the career ladder and how they see the hierarchy of needs—all this, even subconsciously, influences decision-making processes. The diversity of the world we live in should be taken into account. We should remember that there are differences in adopted management styles and conflict-resolution and negotiation tactics in other countries. If we not only remember but also know them, we can effectively communicate in a multicultural world. It should always be borne in mind that a prominent element of information is the context of what we communicate. It is not always possible to send context directly.

Communication system infrastructure

The use of data, knowledge and information resources and their transmission requires infrastructure appropriate to the management system and to the semantic content of information and knowledge. Infrastructure consists of hardware and software tools as well as networks connecting them. At this point, we wish to focus on some elements that are essential to the communication process. The changes in the infrastructure supporting communication systems are directed towards building faster and faster computers with increased capacities. It should be taken into account that new possibilities in the communication system will occur when quantum computers become widespread. The reason will be that the quantum bit (qubit) does not have a fixed value of 1 or 0, like a standard computer, but may remain in an intermediate state. The application of this notation will have a significant impact on the efficiency of computers as tools supporting complex decision-making based on multiple criteria and will help solve multidimensional decision problems.

The establishment of network organisations is aided by the emergence and development of mobile technologies. It is their development that contributes to the enhanced computing power of mobile devices, increased data throughput, and users gaining access to databases and knowledge whenever and wherever they need them. Mobile technologies contribute substantially to the changes in both business and society. They have led to the formulation of new rules and patterns of communication behaviour. In their works, researchers clearly pointed to the immense potential of wireless solutions for the development of communication systems.[11] Even the most complex management structures can work in this way. The intensive advancement of mobile technologies in recent years has enabled the improvement of communication processes. This has been achieved through the deployment of mobile infrastructure, smartphones, and accelerated data transmission processes. With the rapid development of mobile technologies, it will soon be possible to talk about organisations whose employees have access to the data they need, regardless of place and time. As a result, mobile technologies allow for the minimisation of constraints ensuing from the distance between the sender and the receiver.

These changes are aimed at supporting the management of network organisations. The contemporary communication model within a computer network provides all hosts with the same authorisations. This is interchangeability which depends on specific client-server architecture.

As argued by M. Castells,[12] mobile solutions result in the emergence of a new power theory based on the management of communications networks in the information era. Hence, we can recognise that hierarchical structures typical of traditional organisations are gradually making room for network structures. Network organisations use BI systems, in particular Business Activity Monitoring (BAM) solutions, to a greater extent than traditional ones. Their application allows the operation of the entire organisation to be analysed comprehensively in real time.

When comparing communication infrastructures of network and traditional organisations, we can assume that any hardware and software solution can support the management system of a hierarchical organisation. This is not the opposite relationship. A network organisation, even with a decentralised management system, needs modern infrastructure with high network capacity, as well as Big Data technology supported by Business Intelligence systems together with tools such as Business Activity Monitoring. As claimed by E. B. Kerr and S. R. Hiltz,[13] international network organisations with inter-cultural management are much more demanding than national network organisations.

---

[11]   J. Wan, L. Zhuohua, Z. Keliang, L. Rongshuang, *Mobile Cloud Computing: Application Scenarios and Service Models*, 9th International Wireless Communications and Mobile Computing Conference (IWCMC), Sardinia 2013, pp. 644–648.

[12]   M. Castells, *Communication Power*, Oxford University Press, Oxford 2013.

[13]   E. B. Kerr, S. R. Hiltz, *Computer-Mediated Communication Systems: Status and Evaluation*, Academic Press, Cambridge 2013.

Determinants of communication in network organisations

The effectiveness of communication systems in network organisations depends on a wide range of factors. The impact of determinants on improvement projects is not identical. We can divide them into:

1. Absolute—we cannot spend more on the improvement of the organisation's communication system than a certain amount, we cannot install only a piece of software or hardware we need.
2. Relative—which can be overcome with a particular effort. For example, installing the software that we consider necessary requires the involvement or training of staff or the installation of new types of computers, or we may call for some adaptation of the premises.
3. Apparent—which appear to be significant, but on closer examination, it turns out that removing them requires little effort. For example, we want to introduce a new type of software, and it seems that we will have difficulty training staff, yet—upon a careful analysis of IT staff skills—it turns out that it is the software that employees know but have never had the opportunity to use it.

The determinants can be grouped into the following categories:

1. Technical, related to technical and technological progress in the area of IT infrastructure, i.e. hardware, both core and application software, and the communications system (attention should be paid to access to global networks such as the Internet and the speed of information transfer).
2. Economic, referring to both the amount of financial resources and formulas of profitability for innovative activities measured by various evaluation indicators of output, financial incentives.
3. Organisational, depending on the applied management formula (centralisation-decentralisation), organisational structure, application of outsourcing solutions.
4. Sociological and psychological, i.e. preferences, management styles, negotiation and conflict-resolution methods, organisational culture, non-financial incentive systems, ethical issues.
5. Legal, existing legal regulations, i.e. certificates, quality management system, safety standards.

Among economic determinants, financial factors play a special role. The organisation allocates certain resources for the modernisation of its communication system. They can be used both for hardware and software purchases and for the improvement of qualifications of system users. Practically, the money for modernisation is a specific amount limited by two thresholds. The "upper" threshold means that we cannot spend more money than we have. The "bottom" threshold means that no solutions to improve the communication system may be introduced until a certain minimum amount of funding needed to carry out an innovative project is allocated. The "upper" one implies that we cannot spend more funds than we have because such overspending would have a negative impact on the functioning of the organisation.

The strength of each determinant is different. The simulation calculus is helpful in analysing the influence of individual factors, as it answers the question: What do we gain if the constraint is overcome? The simulation approach requires action and reflection on whether the money spent will be used optimally. As demonstrated by the performed analyses, it is the technical barrier that affects users most. Modernisation of the communication system necessitates the use of appropriate IT equipment. What can determine communication system modernisation is the computer itself, mobile devices or peripherals such as optical readers for large data volumes, scanners, printers, and data transmission devices. A technical determinant is also the lack of access to necessary computer systems, especially those connected with knowledge acquisition and management systems.

Economic determinants pertain to situations where we cannot implement the most needed information system due to a lack of sufficient financial resources. Modernisation of the communication system is influenced by prices and taxes. An organisation that does not have adequate resources to buy hardware chooses to lease it or uses cloud computing, as highlighted by Qi, Cheng and Boutaba.[14] However, organisations sometimes opt for the cloud technology not because of expenditure but because this solution is more convenient, safer, etc., for them at the moment. Thus, the user can upgrade the communication infrastructure with less resources than when buying necessary hardware.

Organisational determinants are equally common in business practice. There are objections against many communication systems because of the problems with coherence of diverse infrastructure. Integrators and inter-operable platforms do not always work properly. The location of the team of system administrator(s) managing the entire communication is a particularly sensitive issue. How the administrator is linked with all organisational units is not always clear. Not fully defined competences and responsibility are still another element classified among organisational determinants.

The socio-psychological barrier is a natural reaction to changes in the organisation. It can be termed immunological barrier or negative coopetition, as indicated by P. Parigi, J. J. Santana and K. S. Cook.[15] Members of the organisation where changes are forthcoming try to discredit the changes and it is where they focus their activities. In extreme cases, manipulation of the transmitted information may undermine confidence in the communication system. A mechanism may also be triggered whereby information unfavourable to the sender is not conveyed.

---

[14] Z. Qi, L. Cheng, R. Boutaba, *Cloud Computing: State-Of-The-Art and Research Challenges*, "Journal of Internet Services and Applications" 2010, 1 (1).

[15] P. Parigi, J. J. Santana, K. S. Cook, *Online Field Experiments. Studying Social Interactions. Context*, "Social Psychology Quarterly" 2017, 80.

The opinion survey of designers in MBA studies, which the author has conducted in 2014–2016, on the applicative efficiency of IT systems allowed the specification of elements negatively influencing communication systems in organisations. The students most often referred to the following as communication barriers within and between organisations:

- Poor quality of the source data, including their incomparability resulting from different rules for their acquisition.
- Inadequate hardware and software, including financial problems, meaning a lack of funds for appropriate equipment, and a lack of user qualifications for using the systems.
- Unspecified requirements both for the speed of the system operation and for the scope of needed information.
- Unclear definition of economic and legal rules for the communication system operation, including unspecified roles and authorisations of individual participants in communication processes.
- Routine and resistance to new solutions as well as reluctance to transmit information and knowledge that senders deem unfavourable to themselves.
- Long-standing or imaginary dislike for the receiver—here, the reasons may be very different, often cultural and frequently irrational.

The studies by T. Ariyachandra and H. Watson[16] focused on three groups of determinants:
- Organisational factors: Are planned changes in the communication system supported by the management board and the sponsor, and are the objectives and vision of the solution clear?
- Factors related to the efficiency of the communication process: Is it oriented towards business needs and interactive change implementation and management?
- Factors related to infrastructure capacity (in terms of technology): Are factors such as the system design focused on business and the user, system scalability, data quality and integration appropriate?

W. Delone and E. McLean[17] identified the following determinants of today's communication systems: quality of information, quality of the system (including its functionality and ease of use), quality of the system maintenance. These factors directly translate into the requirements for the use of communication systems and the satisfaction of system users. Identifying, and then overcoming, the determinants affects the operational efficiency of any communication system.

---

[16] T. Ariyachandra, H. Watson, *Which Data Warehouse Architecture Is Most Successful?*, "Business Intelligence Journal" 2006, 11 (1).

[17] W. Delone, E. McLean, *The DeLone and McLean Model of Information Systems Success: A Ten-Year Update*, "Journal of Management Information Systems" 2003, 19 (4).

Communication in network and hierarchical organisations and its impact on IT project success—research results

The analysis of the research evaluating successes and failures of IT projects was performed on the basis of the ISBSG database.[18] The database contains historical data on completed IT initiatives from a number of public and private institutions operating in various industries and administrations. These initiatives concerned both the development of new and the modification of existing software. The analysis shows that most IT projects exceed the pre-defined cost and time. Many publications offer a more detailed examination indicating the reasons for failures of IT projects. L. Mieritz[19] and S. J. Spalek[20] list the following reasons for failures: lack of communication within the team and with stakeholders, unrealistic budget and schedule, complexity and a prototypic nature of IT systems, lack of sufficient resources or team qualifications.

We have conducted comparative analyses of the quality of communication systems within R&D project teams for many years.[21] Here, we wish to present their synthetic results. The reference list contains monographs that outline the analyses of individual projects. Due to a relatively long time span of the research, detailed comparisons could not be made between individual projects. The factors distorting such examination included: sizes of projects and their different scopes, differences in the used infrastructure, differences in costs and times of implementation. However, expert opinions on the quality of communication systems in project management, that is on successful implementation, may provide quite precise assessments. It is assumed that project success is decisively influenced by the management system that, in turn, depends on the quality of the communication system as a system for transmitting information and knowledge.

The research focused on comparing two most popular communication systems used in project teams: traditional (hierarchical) and network. The research on communication systems in project teams was conducted for projects carried out in different years (1996–2015). The investigation covered 28 management systems for R&D projects concerning the design or implementation of IT systems. I participated personally in 18 projects as a performer of tasks or a project manager. The data for research on other projects were obtained from documentation and interviews with project participants. My involvement in those projects concerned supervision over their implementation.

---

[18] https://www.isbsg.org/2015/08/03/research-papers-that-have-used-or-refer-to-the-isbsg-repositories/ (access: 5 May 2019).

[19] L. Mieritz, *Survey Shows Why Projects Fail*, Gartner Research Report 2012.

[20] S. J. Spalek, *Critical Success Factors in Project Management: To Fail or Not To Fail, That is the Question!*, PMI Global Congress Proceedings, McGraw-Hill, London 2005.

[21] J. Kisielnicki, *Intellectual Capital…*; idem, *Zarządzanie projektami…*; idem, *Zarządzanie i informatyka…*; J. Kisielnicki, O. Sobolewska, *Knowledge Management and Innovation in Network Organisations*, IGI Global, Hershey, New York 2019.

Difficulties in conducting the research were caused by the practical impossibility to compare the effects produced by two teams using different communication systems, due to the unique nature of the analysed situations (which is a rule in research projects). Such an experiment would require identically qualified teams carrying out the same project, hence the quantitative results are based only on expert estimates.

Most studied projects involved improvement of the existing business management system. Substantial materials were collected during the implementation of projects covering, among others: IT application in accounting for big textile mills, improvement of the IT-supported benefit calculation system in the Polish Social Insurance Institution, implementation of the MRP II/ERP system in a pharmaceutical company, IT applications to support the management system for a regional capital city, development of an IT application strategy for the National Bank of Poland (NBP), IT application to improve the management system for prisons and the police, participation in the SYNAT project (development of a national scientific research information system), design of a BI system supporting organisational creativity.

This set of projects provides a picture of a very broad research spectrum. The investigation covered both business (20 projects) and administrative (8 projects) organisations. Although most projects (19) were successful, they encountered many threats in the course of implementation. Success was assumed to be a situation where the planned project scope, implementation time and costs would not increase by more than 10% in the last two years.

Teams of 20–60 people took part in the implementation of each project. These were both designers and cooperating specialists in various industries. Such a minimal size of the implementing team was chosen because I was interested in teams where implementation required the cooperation of various teams. The research questions that I tried to answer were:

- What is the effectiveness of basic communication systems in project teams (do the team members feel that they have received full information and knowledge about the performed tasks from other team members)?
- What rules should be applied to manage a project team so as to ensure the best flow of information and knowledge in achieving the set objectives?
- What communication system can be recommended for the implementation of R&D projects?

The effectiveness of a communication system is understood as the degree to which the project objectives have been attained, i.e. success as specified above. The analysis covered: documents (conceptual design and documentation of project implementation including: costs, times, scopes), special questionnaires filled in by both selected managers and designers, reports on the implementing team's discussions (in which I participated) about the causes of failures or difficulties in project implementation.

Discussions were the primary research method, supplemented by the analysis of documents and questionnaires. Documents and questionnaires showed that there were problems to be solved. Discussions about changes in the management system provided recommendations on what should be done to address these issues. Experts were very often involved in the discussion on the causes of threats. They were outsiders including specialists from cooperating teams as well as users. Any major deviation from the assumed standard (plan, schedule) was debated and considered. The analysis of documents and questionnaires verified the answer to the question of whether the taken decisions had been effective. One of the basic questions asked after project completion was: Would you like to work on the next project in the same team?

In order to enhance the analysis of the communication system, the examination occasionally covered the time within which the information given to a particular person would reach all team members. In that case, the information was transmitted as an e-mail, and the time when the message would be read was analysed. The frequency of using a database or the frequency of sending and receiving e-mails was also investigated. The ancillary question concerned the degree of understanding and the usefulness of information to the recipient. The combination of the speed of information transmission, information comprehension, usefulness and appropriate use has a decisive influence on project success understood as its implementation within the planned time span, scope and costs.

The factors that disturb communication processes in project implementation can be divided into the following groups:

- Caused by external factors: delay in the delivery of technical and financial resources, inadequate documentation provided by the user, change of legislation, change in the management system of the organisation for which the project is carried out, random factor, and a team member's incapacity for work (illness).
- Resulting from internal factors such as: poor communication, lack of knowledge and experience in project implementation, conflicts between team members, errors in project management.

All the factors listed as internal are very strongly linked with the communication system. The research results formed the basis for improving the existing information transmission system. Communication systems were also analysed against the following criteria:

- Deviations from planned costs, time, adopted parameters.
- Failure to spot threats in time.
- Conflicts during task performance.
- Lack of cooperation and failure to share knowledge with partners.
- Willingness to work on the next project in the same team.

The examination of those communication systems revealed that:

- Out of 18 network communication systems, 15 projects were successful (i.e. over 80%) according to the previously adopted criterion.
- Out of 10 traditional communication systems, 5 projects were successful (i.e. 50%).

Certainly, not only communication systems are responsible for success. However, the answer to the previously mentioned question: "Would you like to work again in the same team?" was symptomatic. The following responses were given in this respect:

- Traditional, hierarchical communication system: positive responses: 60–70% of managers and about 30% of designers.
- Network communication system: positive responses: 70–80% of those surveyed (it was impossible to make a precise differentiation between managers and designers for this system).

The number and gravity of conflicts were much lower in teams working in network communication systems than in hierarchical systems. The analysis of results showed that the data transmission time was about 30% shorter in network systems than in hierarchical ones.

The research on the functioning and effectiveness of communication systems makes it possible to argue that the network system has an advantage over the traditional (hierarchical) one, notably as regards the following elements:

- Monitoring of implementation. Risks to implementation and deviations from planned costs, time, adopted parameters of IT systems, were spotted earlier than in hierarchical systems, hence intervention decisions could be made in good time. Also, almost all staff working in network systems felt responsible for the project.
- Cooperation and knowledge transfer in task performance. There was good cooperation between co-workers in task performance and transfer of information and knowledge to their partners. No artificial barriers existed such as a division into leaders and employees. Generally, each worker is a leader and a performer of tasks, depending on the situation.
- Problem solving. Conflicts in task implementation were much less severe than in hierarchical systems, and if they arose, they were quickly resolved within the team.

The communication system used in a network team requires a number of conditions to be met. The level of qualifications of individual employees and their willingness to work together are most important. Such a system is difficult for individualists and people wishing to make an administrative career. In the recommended system, the career path is directly associated with professional development. Nonetheless, it should be emphasised that this is a system where projects are difficult to manage. The leader of the entire project bears a great responsibility, being in charge of team selection and organisation, as well as the creation of an appropriate atmosphere. Compared to the hierarchical system, the project leader should give up many managerial powers and delegate them to the implementing teams. Yet, the leader's responsibility for project implementation does not change. Therefore, many project managers, even those aware of their limitations, prefer the hierarchical system as allowing for easier control of the work done by their subordinates and strengthening their formal authority.

It is quite difficult to provide unequivocal answers to the questions:
1. Which of the analysed communication systems is more effective under all circumstances of research project implementation?
2. What is the economic efficiency of replacing a hierarchical communication system with a network one?

I would like to conclude by noting that it is not only the communication system that determines the working efficiency of the project team. It is also very important to select project team members and decide on the incentive system for those implementing the project. The former problem has already been flagged up, but the general principle should be to support communication systems through appropriate incentives. Developing an incentive system is a separate issue strongly dependent on the organisational culture and conditions prevailing on the labour market. The system will be different in India, Great Britain, Poland and the United States. Nonetheless, the communication system is the element that influences the efficiency of the project team regardless of the project scope and type, the method of employee selection or offered incentives.

Conclusion

The effectiveness and efficiency of a communication system depends on manifold factors. It is not always possible to identify them. Therefore, I wish to point out that not only communication models determine the efficiency of information and knowledge transmission systems. Some factors influencing this process are highlighted at the end of this chapter. Work on this issue should be continued. However, as described in the article, the operation of communication systems is highly dependent on the employed communication models. In most situations, the network model has an advantage over the hierarchical one. This is evidenced by our research and the related literature alike.

Glossary

Communication is a process of continuous, multi-level action undertaken to make decisions effectively and to increase our knowledge of the surrounding reality. The contemporary communication system fulfils the following core tasks: transfer of information, transfer of knowledge, transformation of information into knowledge.

Hierarchical communication model represents information and knowledge transfers with linear and hierarchical relationships within the communication system. Its task is to convey information and knowledge clearly and accurately.

Network communication model represents information and knowledge transfers that are characterised by direct information channels independent of the physical distance between the sender and the receiver. Users use information and knowledge sources directly.

Bibliography

Ariyachandra T., Watson H., *Which Data Warehouse Architecture Is Most Successful?*, "Business Intelligence Journal" 2006, 11 (1).

Baumann F., El Hussein R., Roller D., *State of the Art of BPM—Approach to Business Process Models and its Perspective*, "International Journal of Electronics Communication and Computer Engineering" 2015, 6 (6).

Beamer L., Varne I., *Intercultural Communication in the Global Workplace*, McGraw-Hill/Irwin, Boston–New York 2011.

Berg Insight, *The Global M2M/IoT Communiactions Market—Report*, https://www.marketresearch.com/Berg-Insight-v2702 (access: 2 January 2018).

Castells M., *Communication Power*, Oxford University Press, Oxford 2013.

Delone W., McLean E., *The DeLone and McLean Model of Information Systems Success: A Ten-Year Update*, "Journal of Management Information Systems" 2003, 19 (4).

Domain-Specific Conceptual Modeling, ed. by D. Karagiannis, H. C. Mayer, J. Mylopoulos, Springer, Heidelberg 2016.

Dumas M., La Rosa M., Mendling J., Reijers H. A., *Fundamentals of Business Process Management*, Springer, Heidelberg 2013.

Eadie W. F., Goret R., *Theories and Models of Communication: Foundations and Heritage* [in:] *Theories and Models of Communication*, ed. by P. Cobley, P. J. Schulz, De Gruyter Moution, Berlin–Boston 2013.

Erl T., Khattak W., Buhler P., *Big Data Fundamentals: Concepts. Drivers & Techniques*, Prentice Hall, Upper Saddle River 2016.

Fensel D., Lausen H., *Enabling Semantic Web Services: Web Service Modeling Ontology*, Springer, Heidelberg 2006.

Gartner Business Activity Monitoring (BAM), 2013, http://www.gartner.com/it-glossary/bam-businessactivity-monitoring (access: 2 January 2018).

Kerr E. B., Hiltz S. R., *Computer-Mediated Communication Systems: Status and Evaluation*, Academic Press, Cambridge 2013.

Encyclopedia of Information Science and Technology, ed. by M. Khosrow-Pour, Hershey, New York 2017.

Kisielnicki J., *Intellectual Capital in the Knowledge Management Process—Relations-Factors* [in:] *Business Environment in Poland*, ed. by A. Z. Nowak, B. Glinka, P. Hensel, Wydawnictwo Wydziału Zarządzania Uniwersytetu Warszawskiego, Warszawa 2008.

Kisielnicki J., Sobolewska O., *Knowledge Management and Innovation in Network Organisations*, IGI Global, Hershey, New York 2019.

Kisielnicki J., *Transfer of Information and Knowledge in the Project Management* [in:] *Encyclopedia of Communities of Practice in Information and Knowledge Management*, ed. by E. Coakes, S. Clarke, IDEA Group Reference, London–Melbourne 2006.

Kisielnicki J., *Zarządzanie i informatyka*, Placet, Warszawa 2017.

Kisielnicki J., *Zarządzanie projektami badawczo-rozwojowymi*, Wydawnictwo Nieoczywiste, Warszawa 2017.

Melis K., Campo K., Breugelmans E., Lamey L., *The Impact of the Multi-Channel Retail Mix on Online Store Choice: Does Online Experience Matter?*, "Journal of Retailing" 2015, https://lirias.kuleuven.be/bitstream/123456789/472387/1/2014-12-04+-+Manuscript_.pdf (access: 8 February 2018).

Mieritz L., *Survey Shows Why Projects Fail*, Gartner Research Report 2012.

Mullins L., *Management and Organizational Behavior*, Pitman Publishing, London 1993.

Parigi P., Santana J. J., Cook K. S., *Online Field Experiments. Studying Social Interactions. Context*, "Social Psychology Quarterly" 2017, 80.

Polanyi M., *Personal Knowledge: Towards a Post-Critical Philosophy*, University of Chicago Press, Chicago 1974.

Qi Z., Cheng L., Boutaba R., *Cloud Computing: State-Of-The-Art and Research Challenges*, "Journal of Internet Services and Applications" 2010, 1 (1).

Schahaf P., *Cultural Diversity and Information and Communication Technology Impacts on Global Virtual Teams*, "An Exploratory Study, Information and Management" 2008, 45 (2).

Slater D., *Social Relationships and Identity On-line and Off-line* [in:] *Handbook of New Media: Social Shaping and Consequences of ICTs*, ed. by L. Lievrouw, S. Livingstone, Sage Publications, Thousand Oaks 2002.

Smith P. R., Zook Z., *Marketing Communications: Offline and Online Integration, Engagement and Analytics*, Kogan Page, London–Philadelphia 2017.

Spalek S. J., *Critical Success Factors in Project Management—To Fail or Not To Fail, That is the Question!*, PMI Global Congress Proceedings, McGraw-Hill, London 2005.

Tatnall A., *Web Technologies: Concepts, Methodologies, Tools and Applications*, Information Science Reference, Hershey, New York 2010.

Trompenaars B. F., Hampden-Turner Ch., *Culture for Business*, 2017, http://www2.thtconsulting.com (access: 2 May 2019).

Trompenaars B. F., Hampden-Turner Ch., *Siedem wymiarów kultury. Znaczenie różnic kulturowych w działalności gospodarczej*, transl. B. Nawrot, Oficyna Ekonomiczna, Kraków 2002.

Trompenaars B. F., Woolliams P., *Business Across Cultures*, Capstone Publishing, Oxford 2003.

Wan J., Zhuohua L., Keliang Z., Rongshuang L., *Mobile Cloud Computing: Application Scenarios and Service Models*, 9th International Wireless Communications and Mobile Computing Conference (IWCMC), Sardinia 2013.

Woods D., Hollnagel E., *Joint Cognitive Systems: Foundations of Cognitive Systems Engineering*, Taylor & Francis, Boca Raton 2005.

Xu Ch., Song L., Han Z., Zhao Q., Wang X., Cheng Z., Jiao B., *Efficiency Resource Allocation for Device-to-Device Underlay Communication Systems: A Reverse Iterative Combinatorial Auction Based Approach*, "IEEE Journal on Selected Areas in Communications" 2013, 31 (9).

Consequences of the Fourth Industrial Revolution in Social and Economic Development in the 21st Century

Prof. Kazimierz Górka, Ph.D.   https://orcid.org/0000-0002-0861-6382
Chamber of Commerce, "Bottling Industry"

Agnieszka Thier, Ph.D.   https://orcid.org/0000-0002-5915-2071
The Institute of Economics and Corporate Organisation
Cracow University of Economics

Prof. Marcin Łuszczyk, Ph.D.   https://orcid.org/0000-0001-7337-0668
Opole University of Technology

Abstract

The article is devoted to the essence, manifestations and the economic consequences of the Fourth Industrial Revolution as well as the difficulty to assess ensuing social results of the artificial intelligence. It also analyzes the practical manifestations of the foregoing in some countries, including Poland. The chapter titles of this paper are the following: The stages of Industrial Revolution, The significance of the Fourth Industrial Revolution, The implementation of the Industrial Revolution, The challenges of artificial intelligence, The economic and social effects of the Fourth Industrial Revolution.

Keywords: industrial revolution, artificial intelligence, economic effects, social effects, economic development

Introduction

Industrialisation has become a major factor for the social and economic development and the progress of civilisation, exerting an impact on the structural changes in the economy and social life. Industrialisation processes are closely intertwined with the changes in the organisation, legal status and property of various types and forms of enterprises and instruments used in the management of economy. In the 1970s, the growing importance of relationships between the enterprises and the environment and the necessity of extending the time of planning development have resulted in the emergence of *strategic planning*. The principles of *crisis management* which were formulated in the early 21st century, responded to the increasing turbulences within the environment of enterprises.

Industrialisation and the technical progress in the industry determine raising the standard of living not just through the supply of modern and relatively cheap products, but also through the growing services sector. This is because in line with the development of processing industry, the services sector has increased employment in the economy and generated a higher GDP. This, in turn, has brought a new look at the structure of the economy and the role of the industry in its development, which has resulted in the concept of a *post-industrial* society and the dawn of the post-industrial era followed by the onset of the *servitisation phase*, i.e. the superiority of services over other economic sectors.

However, it turned out that deindustrialisation cannot be carried too far as many service providers are not able to operate without being supplied with the new industrial goods. Hence, a new catchy slogan of reindustrialisation was coined. It was propagated by the EU institutions and was reflected in the economic development programmes of numerous countries, including the USA. It should be noted that the industry is not so much subject to internal development mechanisms which are stimulated by the economic policy of countries and international organisations. There are some phases discernible in its global development tendency which are revolutionary. To conclude, the world economy is currently entering the fourth stage of the industrial revolution which consists in the dissemination of IT production systems and distribution.

This paper presents the essence, manifestations and the economic consequences of the fourth industrial revolution as well as the difficult to assess ensuing social consequences and show them against the backdrop of the preceding stages of industrial development. It also aims to present the analysis of the practical manifestations of the foregoing in chosen countries, including Poland.

The stages of the Industrial Revolution

The term Industrial Revolution was coined by the British historian Arnold Toynbee in 1884, who dated the first Revolution to 1760. He referred the onset of the Revolution to the emergence of the factory industry, which was the consequence of the introduction of steam-powered engines in England and Scotland.[1] However, 1784 was to become the milestone as in that year James Watt's steam engine was installed in a loom. In turn, the second industrial revolution which took place at the turn of the 19th and 20th centuries was possible due to the emergence of electric power and a dozen industrial

---

[1]   M. Blung, *Teoria ekonomii. Ujęcie retrospektywne*, transl. I. Budzyńska, Wydawnictwo Naukowe PWN, Warszawa 2000, p. 35.

inventions such as the combustion engine, the light bulb, the telephone, the radio, or the photographic camera.[2] It also involved the introduction of serial production, and then mass production. The first example of such a system was a meat processing plant in Cincinnati, USA launched in 1870, and Henry Ford's car assembly line opened in 1913 was to become the most famous.

Moving on, the third industrial revolution (digital) was characterised by the application of computers and the Internet in the second half of the 20th century, which translated into full control over the production process and flexible production systems as well as the use of robots. The milestone year was 1969 when the programmable logical controller (PLC) Modican 084 came to the market and opened the era of industrial automation. Apart from classical production factors: land, capital, labour, the key role was attributed to knowledge (technology).

The third industrial revolution, a large step in the modernisation of the industry, was possible due to informatics and the application of industrial automation. However, it pushed the economy into the post-industrial stage, or to use an even stronger term, into de-industrialisation or a departure from the industry. In Poland and other Eastern European countries, that process became more apparent due to systemic transformation. Contrary to the name, deindustrialisation does not stand for the decline of industry, despite the fact that some depreciated or obsolete industrial plants have been shut down. What it really means is decreasing the relative role of the industry in the employment and generation of GDP.

To give a few examples, the share of the industry in GDP generation has reached 22–23% in the USA and the EU, including Poland. At the same time, the share of services reached 75–77% in the USA and the EU, and approximately 67% in Poland (merely 42% in China). Hence, the formerly described structural changes are better illustrated not by the declining role of the industry, but by highlighting the development of services, i.e. servitisation of the economy.[3] Nonetheless, the overt domination of finance over the real sphere and the services sector has led to economic disparities whose increasing criticism resulted in the implementation of re-industrialisation concepts.

In 2014, the European Union came to the forefront by launching the "Investment for Europe" programme and setting up the European Fund of Strategic Investment (the so-called Juncker's plan), and then moved into the *circular economy* viewed as the higher stage of *sustainable development*. In turn, Poland launched the "Strategy for responsible development" programme which was hailed as the programme for

---

[2]   A slightly different classification was presented by Alvin E. Toffler (1928–2016), a writer and futurologist, who distinguished agricultural, industrial and digital revolutions. He envisaged cloning and other forms of artificial intelligence applications: A. Toffler, *Future Shock*, Bantam Books, New York 1970, Polish edition: *Szok przyszłości*, transl. W. Osiatyński, E. Grabczak-Ryszka, E. Woydyłło, Zysk i S-ka, Poznań 1998; idem, *The Third Wave*, Bantam Books, William Morrow & Co., New York 1980, Polish edition: *Trzecia fala*, transl. E. Woydyłło, PIW, Warszawa 1986, 1997.

[3]   D. Kiełczewski, *Uwagi o serwicyzacji gospodarki*, "Optimum. Studia Ekonomiczne" 2012, 4 (58).

reindustrialisation.[4] It entails some ambitious objectives; however, its critics maintain that there is no funding or organisational capacity for its implementation even as late as 2030.

The above-mentioned programmes highlight the care for job creation and fighting unemployment, yet they also stress the importance of advanced products and technologies for services, in other words, striking a balance between the industrial production and the provision of services. All this heralds the emergence of a new stage of social and economic development and civilisation progress aptly termed the fourth industrial revolution (also the digital or technological revolution). Other equivalent terms are the fourth generation industry or Industry 4.0. The stages of the industrial revolution are presented in Table 1.

Table 1. Characteristics of the stages of the Industrial Revolution

Specification	Stages of the Industrial Revolution			
	I	II	III	IV
The main features of successive generations of the industry	Emergence of the factory industry	Serial and mass production	Information revolution and industrial automation	Digital evolution Cyber-physical digital systems Intelligent plants
Duration in highly-developed countries (symbolic dates)	1760–1870	1870–1960	1960–2010	since 2010
Implementation of new technologies	Introduction of the steam engine	Application of electricity and a combustion engine	Application of computers, the internet and robots	Application of fast internet, 5G and the Internet of Things Autonomous vehicles and advanced robots Mobile technologies Social media
Major economic and social consequences	Increasing human physical potential, new division of labour	Significant facilitation of physical labour and an incremental increase of work efficiency	Increasing human intellectual potential, entering the post-industrial stage and the domination of services in employment and GDP generation	Reindustrialisation programmes Personalised products and orientation on services Global reach free enterprise Diverse and controversial consequences of artificial intelligence

Source: authors' own elaboration.

---

4   *Strategia na rzecz odpowiedzialnego rozwoju*, Rada Ministrów, Warszawa 2016.

The significance of the fourth industrial revolution

The fourth industrial revolution is the result of the digitalisation of production processes and the growing role of information as well as the application of cyber and physical systems. What it boils down to is the emergence of a social network connecting people of technical infrastructure, production facilities and services present within the whole chain of creating added value, from placing orders to pick-up by the customer. In other words, industrial digitalisation stands for increasing the flow of information and boosting its transmission speed. In the new arrangement, online communication does not take place between a person and a machine, but between two machines (M2M), which helps to reduce the role of human labour.[5]

Common access, speed and the quality of information transmitted with ICT permit building intelligent plants, which are able to adapt themselves and optimise the use of resources. Another characteristic feature is the concentration on customers' individual choices and integration of the customer with the producer through the application of digital access, i.e. *product personalisation*. A smartphone and digital cyber and physical systems have become symbols of the fourth industrial revolution. The latter consist of intelligent sensors reacting to the presence of humans, then software and communication systems defined as 5C (*connection, conversion, cyber, cognition, configuration*) and also advanced robots, 3D printers, autonomous vehicles and drones. Digital technologies of the new age include a "computing cloud," Big Data applications, mobile technologies and social media.

The term "fourth industrial revolution" came into use in Germany between 2010 and 2011. At that time, a working group *Platform Industrie 4.0* was set up, serving as a centre for contacts between the industry, business and science. Hence, Industrie 4.0 has become known as the Smart Industry or the Integrated Industry to connect machines and devices, processes and products in intelligent networks.

It is considered that the third industrial revolution consisted in the automation of individual machines and production processes, and that this process has not been completed even in developed countries, including Poland. In turn, the fourth industrial revolution turned out to be a complex digital transformation of all fixed assets and their integration with the partners contributing to the chain of added value within the framework of a digital ecosystem. Such a system is efficient and relatively cheap to operate owing to, to give one example, a dramatic decrease in the cost of storing data, from USD 10,000 to USD 0.03 per annum for 1 GB. The proper training of staff and preparation of the infrastructure are prerequisite to making use of those resources, which are capital intensive.

---

[5]   M. Olender-Skorek, *Czwarta rewolucja przemysłowa a wybrane aspekty teorii ekonomii*, "Nierówności Społeczne a Wzrost Gospodarczy" (Uniwersytet Rzeszowski) 2017, 3 (51).

That brings to mind the fact that a few decades ago enterprises implemented programmes to improve the safety and hygiene of work, followed by the introduction in the 1970s of installations for environmental protection. It all started with economic outlays (in extreme cases, in the power industry, those outlays attributed to 30% or even 40% of the investment outlays). Some time later, it brought an increase in the efficiency of work, waste management, improved competitiveness on the market, etc. Initially, the changes were spontaneous, but the third industrial revolution has been offered substantial support of the state. Currently the role of the state in those issues has been growing, even though technical progress is to some degree autonomous. For these reasons the development of electronic services has accelerated as they are present in all sectors of the economy and in everyday life and contribute to building the digital society.

In summary, the constituent elements of the fourth industrial revolution may be described as follows:

- *Industrial Internet of Things* (IoT) comprising a system of collecting data via sensors of current, temperature, pressure, vibrations and noise, and storing them in the computing cloud.
- *Cyber-Physical System* (CPS) stands for a system in which the physical world communicates with the virtual world via sensors and actuators, and information on the real world is processed with the use of mathematical reflection of physical objects. The CPS system explains the environment in a better way and with the network of its sensors is used for monitoring vital functions of hospital patients or watching traffic to avoid congestion. In the industry, we can find Cyber Physical Production Systems (CPPS).
- *Cloud computing* denotes the technology used for storing data in virtual space (instead of company computers). Due to the Internet, data are accessible 24/7 from any place on the globe, just like email boxes or social portals.
- *Big data* is a field that deals with ways to analyse, systematically extract information from, or otherwise deal with datasets that are too large or complex to be dealt with by traditional data-processing application software.
- *3D printing* covers a variety of processes in which material is joined or solidified under computer control to create a three-dimensional object. Initially these were prototypes of products. The technology was patented in 1986. 3D printers came to the market in 1992, and those for household applications in 2006.

The implementation of the fourth industrial revolution

The growing number of holdings, capital groups, industrial complexes and clusters is attributable to IT and network connections. The bottom line is that under certain digitalisation conditions, the cooperation of companies is becoming more efficient and reliable, and transaction costs are substantially lower. New forms of market models emerge, e.g. sharing economy not just among households but also enterprises. Another example are strategic alliances of companies which compete on the market, yet at the same time cooperate in designing new products such as electric cars.

Owing to digitalisation, every product may be provided with digital information which in the production process are swapped, without human intervention, with other products and the environment. In this way, production facilities engage autonomously in the successive stages of the production process. Production is becoming personalised, since a client is actively engaged in the design of a product or a service by choosing any configuration from the catalogue of the available options. The intellectual process of designing and then the execution of the contract are facilitated with incremental development technologies (e.g. 3D printers).

In turn, the Industrial Internet constitutes a dynamic and global network of physical objects, systems, platforms and applications which are capable of communicating and sharing intelligence among themselves and with the external environment or people. The set of information created in this way is used for monitoring the whole production process in a plant, and the visualisation of information (the equivalent of the real world) as well as for computing and analyses necessary for making decisions and on-line control (in real time). Such monitoring capability allows avoiding flaws and technical breakdowns.

In the process of remote control, operators may connect with the "cloud" with the use of tablets and smartphones. In general terms, IoT facilitates the automation of all processes in a plant, hence it optimises control and increases energy efficiency, reliability levels and safety of work. This results in accelerating technological changes and innovation, and often brings an incremental increase in the efficiency of work and the production volume, which would not be attainable with the use of traditional methods.

New technologies, computer hardware and other devices and networks are continually emerging in this area. For example, Swiss Stock Limited headquartered in Zug came up with a novel digital solution, introducing the first stock exchange index administered by artificial intelligence. This method entails processing large sets of data taking into account numerous factors including those of social nature (e.g. ageing of the society) and is superior to DAX or Staxx Europe 600 indexes. That solution may substantially improve the forecasting of SE investment.

Motteo Andretto has announced the launch of a similar index for tracing cryptocurrencies. The new XETRA system permits computing the DAX and Europa 600 indexes applied by the German Stock Exchange in Frankfurt every second. Those indexes are based on the share prices of 30 listed companies and a large number of other parameters. Han Hai Precision Industry Co., known as Foxconn, stationed in Taiwan and running 13 large plants in China and numerous subsidiaries in other countries, employing 1 million workers and manufacturing 40% of world electronics (one of their customers is Apple), has been streamlining production by transforming their facilities into intelligent plants whose efficiency may increase many times.

Foxconn Industrial Internet is a well-known producer of industrial robots and the computing cloud. The French Group L'Oréal, which owns 25 cosmetic plants, including a subsidiary plant in Kanie near Warsaw, pioneered the concept of Industry 4.0. The group has been renowned for the standardisation and unification of the processes of production, supply and warehousing with the use of FlexNet (Apriso) with Quality Control Module. All tasks are fully automated and monitored on-line at the shop floor level.

In comparison to other European countries, Poland ranks lower in terms of the implementation of the fourth generation industrial solutions than it should, as shown by social and economic indicators. This is because the level of computerisation of Poland is a half lower than the EU average. Insufficiently trained staff and the lack of capital funding, as well as low labour costs, mean that merely 15% of larger plants are fully automated, and 75% partly automated. However, new trends are clearly visible, which is best illustrated by the growing production of 3D printers, their maintenance and provision with the necessary supplies.

Zortrax S.A. seated in Olsztyn, Poland is a well-known manufacturer of 3D printers which help to produce some household appliances, toys, and elements of houses. The company also produces new materials such as grafen. There emerge industrial plants which handle smaller orders and serve individual demand and niche customers.[6] It is worth noting the co-operation between the Digital Poland Foundation and the Data Processing Centre at the National Research Institute in programming artificial intelligence. This centre is renowned for the production of intelligent information systems supported by SI technology for the research sector, and it monitors the development of that technology both in science and business.[7]

The challenges of artificial intelligence

Artificial intelligence and its applications have been put in the forefront of the implementation of the digital revolution. In computer science, **artificial intelligence** (AI), sometimes called **machine intelligence**, is intelligence demonstrated by machines, in contrast to the **natural intelligence** displayed by humans. Colloquially, the term "artificial intelligence" is often used to describe machines (or computers) that mimic "cognitive" functions that humans associate with other human minds, such as "learning" and "problem solving."[8] In the narrow meaning, it denotes a part of computer science involved in modelling intelligent behaviour with the support of computer programmes.

---

[6]   *Raport "Internet of Things i Artificial Intelligence w Polsce,"* ed. by B. Michałowski, Instytut Sobieskiego, Warszawa 2018.

[7]   www.sztucznainteligencja.org.pl (access: 5 June 2019).

[8]   https://en.wikipedia.org/wiki/Artificial_intelligence (access: 5 June 2019).

In the broader meaning, it includes fuzzy logic, neuron networks, robotics and other areas. Such projects are meant to create computer software as well as to construct machines and devices capable of replicating some functions of the human mind, including the creation of programmes and self-learning. The key areas of artificial intelligence are as follows:

- Cognitive technologies and image processing.
- Speech processing and storing technologies.
- Automated robots and vehicles.
- Virtual assistants.
- Machine learning (self-learning of machines). Machines that are capable of drawing conclusions and making decisions.

The GPT-2 language model (a large-scale model with 1.5 billion parameters taking up 8 million of Internet pages) is a good example of an advanced programme. It drafts press releases, analyses, summaries. It also translates from other languages and answers questions pertaining to texts. Apart from that, it may impersonate celebrities and write biased commentaries. The latter capabilities raise some concern about the future of artificial intelligence, particularly referring to self-learning machines. While it is true that computers have no consciousness, and artificial intelligence is based on algorithms, the people who write algorithms may take power.

Not only does a computer win with chess masters, but also with poker champions (who cheat), which is another negative argument. Ryszard Tadeusiewicz, a biocyber-netist, maintains that computers will never seize power as they lack consciousness, and they feel no need for doing it (as they are built by humans).[9] By this token, Stephen King and Elon Musk, the most renowned opponents of the further development of artificial intelligence are wrong claiming that robots are a threat (according to Elon Musk, the manufacturer of rockets to Mars, artificial intelligence is a larger threat than nuclear power).

In the era of artificial intelligence, culture and art are continually threatened with the mass copying of works of art, including landscapes, and then disseminating them without any spatial and temporal limits. It is quite simple to record anything, then convert it to digital form, and what is the most controversial, to make modifications. In view of the foregoing, the transformation of culture with artificial intelligence technologies is becoming a more and more substantial social problem. To give an example, a text editor corrects grammatical mistakes and improves style, yet artificial intelligence applied to managing business procedures infringes the role of a human (especially in view of the fact that machines may be creative). Despite some concerns about artificial intelligence,

---

9   R. Tadeusiewicz, *Odkrywanie właściwości sieci neuronowych przy użyciu programów w języku C#*, Polska Akademia Umiejętności, Kraków 2007.

computer software has become indispensable. Consequently, the role of humans in creating culture is diminishing and it is hard to envisage the result of that process.

The economic and social effects of the fourth industrial revolution

The above-mentioned processes of digitalisation and automation have already brought effects apparent in the reduction of the time of production and an increase in sales by a few per cent a year, and even 30–60% over a few years. The economic effects are attributable to the following factors:[10]

- A new model of management based on a greater IT and analytical potential as well as a flexible organisational structure and teams (e.g. the well-known engineering / value analysis teams).
- Precision in meeting customer expectations on-line at every stage of product design and implementation.
- Design and manufacture of products so that they can be easily reused in line with the provisions of circular economy.
- Automation of analytical and computing operations (which increases their efficiency by 50%).
- Development of customised and niche products and creation of new business.
- A better use of resources and avoidance of stoppages by 30–50%, dropping the cost of resource management by 20–50%.
- Availability of cheap public services via "the cloud" and decreasing the market entry barriers.
- Designing a two-speed flexible information and analytical system "for now" and "for the future."

It is worth quoting the relatively simple examples which give an insight into the new features and functions of technology. Virtual reality brings us into a 3D world once we put on special goggles. The purchase of, e.g. furniture is facilitated as we can view any piece which we intend to purchase in 3D in our room on our smartphone. A dramatic technological leap in interior design was made possible with the advent of special 3D spectacles which allow experiencing virtual reality (VR), augmented reality (AR), or mixed reality (MR). Customers in Western Europe and the USA show an increasing preference of a cheap and readily accessible product made to customer specifications. This decreases the cost of labour and by the economies of scale lowers the unit costs of production. This process is also visible in Poland.

---

[10] K. Schab, *The Fourth Industrial Revolution*, World Economic Forum 2016, Penguin Random House, London 2017; M. Götz, J. Gracel, *Przemysł czwartej generacji*, "Kwartalnik Naukowy Uczelni Vistula" 2017, 1 (51).

In the discussion on economic benefits, the role of re-industrialisation of economy is emphasised as it helps to create new jobs. Nonetheless, this factor raises serious concern attributable to an increase in unemployment as due to automation at least 10–20% of jobs may be lost. Consequently, new social issues related to employment come to play as automation demands higher qualification, high specialisation and flexibility from workers.

New technologies are oriented towards a higher potential of workers (human centred automation) and reach further than making staff redundant. This requires a redefining of the existing work posts and the creation of entirely new jobs. At the same time, the demand for engineers and IT specialists is on the rise. However, fears of rising unemployment are becoming real and the spectres of people fighting for jobs come to play. The latter issue has already taken place during the mechanisation of manual labour. Those issues have been raised by Lewiatan, an organisation for entrepreneurs, who in their document "Manifest for the future of work" postulate new models of employment and a new order on the labour market by training professional adaptation to new conditions. The tendencies and postulates in this area may be listed as follows:

- Adapting the law, labour conditions and social security to new conditions in which enterprises are to operate.
- Implementing lifelong education (*kaizen*).
- Extending the time of professional activity and protecting the work posts by the government.
- Including in the labour market people who have not been employed as well as foreigners.
- A better work/life balance.

The Warsaw Institute for Economic Studies conducted susceptibility tests for automation covering over 900 professions in Poland. They maintain that the fourth industrial revolution may lead to the disappearance of 36% of jobs, mostly in the construction business, food processing and transportation, and merely 28% of the labour market may feel secure. The published percentage is far worse than the statistics for Benelux and Scandinavia where just 20% of work posts are at threat.

The social consequences of the fourth industrial revolution are perceived as far-reaching changes in the life of the society, even though it may be difficult to judge them unambiguously at this point We have stressed the need for changes in education, greater differentiation in the forms of employment and work time. These postulates call for adaptation and a new psychological perspective. Other issues are care for the privacy of workers and security of information as well as numerous changes in social life.

Conclusions

The fourth industrial revolution is taking place within an interesting period of social and economic development which has moved into the post-industrial stage, with a dominance of the service sector, and the formulation of the reindustrialisation postulate. Industry 4.0, which stands for digitalisation and automation, constitutes an important factor of reindustrialisation and a remedy for the growing shortage of labour force.

Nonetheless, these processes raise concern about unemployment. Another important issue is the compounding social consequences which may be difficult to assess at the moment. In the discussion about the economic effects of the new stage of the Industrial Revolution, the benefits attributable to a fast delivery of a customised product are exposed, and less attention is brought to the cost of labour and the economies of scale (the result of extending the series), which is a new thing in Poland. Additional taxation of robots and universal basic income (regardless of employment) might be a remedy for unemployment; such steps have already been considered by a few highly-developed countries. It is worth including social and economic processes in research programmes, giving due regard to the adaptation of enterprise management systems to new conditions dictated by automation, ever-accelerating technological progress in IT and the globalisation of the Internet.

Bibliography

Blung M., *Teoria ekonomii. Ujęcie retrospektywne*, transl. I. Budzyńska, Wydawnictwo Naukowe PWN, Warszawa 2000.

Götz M., Gracel J., *Przemysł czwartej generacji*, "Kwartalnik Naukowy Uczelni Vistula" 2017, 1 (51).

Kiełczewski D., *Uwagi o serwicyzacji gospodarki*, "Optimum. Studia Ekonomiczne" 2012, 4 (58).

Olender-Skorek M., *Czwarta rewolucja przemysłowa a wybrane aspekty teorii ekonomii*, "Nierówności Społeczne a Wzrost Gospodarczy" (Uniwersytet Rzeszowski) 2017, 3 (51).

Raport "Internet of Things i Artificial Intelligence w Polsce," ed. by B. Michałowski, Instytut Sobieskiego, Warszawa 2018.

Schab K., *The Fourth Industrial Revolution*, World Economic Forum 2016, Penguin Random House, London 2017.

Strategia na rzecz odpowiedzialnego rozwoju, Rada Ministrów, Warszawa 2016.

Tadeusiewicz R., *Odkrywanie właściwości sieci neuronowych przy użyciu programów w języku C#*, Polska Akademia Umiejętności, Kraków 2007.

Toffler A., *Future Shock*, Bantam Books, New York 1970, Polish edition: *Szok przyszłości*, transl. W. Osiatyński, E. Grabczak-Ryszka, E. Woydyłło, Zysk i S-ka, Poznań 1998.

Toffler A., *The Third Wave*, Bantam Books, William Morrow & Co., New York 1980, Polish edition: *Trzecia fala*, transl. E. Woydyłło, PIW, Warszawa 1986, 1997.

Ideology, Trust, and Spirituality: A Framework for Management Control Research in the Era of Industry 4.0

Roman Lewandowski, Ph.D.   https://orcid.org/0000-0002-9589-0629
University of Social Sciences, Łódź, Poland

Prof. Anatoliy G. Goncharuk, Ph.D.   https://orcid.org/0000-0001-9870-4679
International Humanitarian University, Odessa, Ukraine

Prof. Jarosław J. Fedorowski, M.D., Ph.D., MBA
University of Warmia and Mazury, College of Medicine, Olsztyn, Poland

Abstract

The forthcoming era of Industry 4.0 will bring new challenges for management control (MC) research and practice. Extant studies demonstrate that organisations characterised by a high level of technological complexity and innovation capability need control forms based more on social than on cybernetic mechanisms. Although many frameworks concerning MC research have been developed over the last half century, they have not included important forms of social control, such as ideology, trust, and spirituality. Thus, the study is going to fill the gap and propose a renewed framework for management control research. This framework contributes to the MC literature by supplying a more thorough and unequivocal description of normative control modes, such as trust, ideology, and spirituality as well as of the relationships among them.

Keywords: management control, Industry 4.0, framework, MC research, spirituality, ideology

Introduction

Managerial control (MC) has been present in management literature for over a century, and with time, the phenomenon has covered more and more types of organisations and dimensions of organisational activities. In the beginning, there were two different, although interwoven streams of research, one concerning control in industrial organisations conducted by such researchers as F. W. Taylor, H. Emerson, H. Ford or H. Fayol, and the second in bureaucracy, initialised by M. Weber.[1] In these approaches, direct supervision of employee behaviour or precise measurement of their output, as well as authority and hierarchy, were the main mechanisms of control in the industry and in administration. In organisations populated by professionals, like hospitals and universities, whose performance is hardly measurable, both individual professionals and whole organisations are coordinated and controlled differently, based on collegial and trust mechanisms.

With time, however, control practices from industrial and bureaucratic organisations were also applied to professional organisations, mainly to hospitals, as the biggest and most complex entities. The introduction of "corporatist managerialism" based on simple bureaucratic control modes into public-sector service organisations in the United Kingdom during the 1970s as a response to increasing organisational complexity, left trust-based professional autonomy largely intact but did not bring a substantial effect.[2] Therefore, during the 1980s and 1990s, in the UK, Sweden, the US, Poland and other countries, a new wave of "entrepreneurial governance" or "new managerialism" was introduced in public-sector service organisations. In hospitals, for example, it was realized mostly by employing professional managers as leaders of organisations.[3] That evoked substantial restructuring of trust-control relations in favour of managerial control regimes, subjecting many semi-autonomous professional groups to much more intrusive, intensive, and extensive surveillance technologies.[4]

At the same time, many changes also occurred in industrial organisations, transforming them into more complex and populated in a more considerable extent by highly educated professionals. In the forthcoming era of Industry 4.0, when not only production but also decision-making activities will be taken over by cyber-physical systems,[5] employees will have to be shifted to more and more creative activities. The primary demand for them will not be the productivity but creative problem-solving and innovativeness. Thus, after a century, control demands in industrial and healthcare organisations are getting more and more similar. In the former, employees have to investigate and creatively solve problems of cyber-physical systems, while in the latter ones—of human beings in health needs. This means that industrial organisations,

[1]   More in: R. A. Lewandowski, J. Sasak, A. Kożuch, *Kontrola zarządcza w placówkach ochrony zdrowia*, Wolters Kluwer, Warszawa 2018, pp. 118–130.

[2]   J. Lawler, J. Hearn, *UK Public Sector Organizations: The Rise of Managerialism and the Impact of Change on Social Services Departments*, "International Journal of Public Sector Management" 1995, 8 (4), pp. 7–16.

[3]   M. von Knorring, A. de Rijk, K. Alexanderson, *Managers' Perceptions of the Manager Role in Relation to Physicians: A Qualitative Interview Study of the Top Managers in Swedish Healthcare*, "BMC Health Services Research" 2010, 10 (1), p. 2.

[4]   P. du Gay, *Colossal Immodesties and Hopeful Monsters: Pluralism and Organizational Conduct*, "Organization" 1994, 1 (1), pp. 125–148.

[5]   R. Y. Zhong et al., *Intelligent Manufacturing in the Context of Industry 4.0: A Review*, "Engineering" 2017, 3 (5), p. 616.

similarly to healthcare settings, could not be managed on a command and control basis.[6] However, the departure from command and control management cannot mean a lack of control, since no organiaation could survive without it.[7] Therefore, MC has to balance tensions between autonomy and constraint, between empowerment and accountability, between top-down direction and bottom-up creativity, between experimentation and efficiency.[8] But this does not mean that traditional modes of control should be dismissed and, for example, empowerment could replace accountability. Both are needed in the organisation and should create a positive and negative control system. Positive controls should reward, motivate, guide, promote learning and innovation, while negative should punish, coerce, impose, and require. Positive and negative controls are opposing forces that need to coexist to create dynamic tensions, which, in turn, ensure effective control.[9]

A single control form cannot fulfill these multiple roles, it requires a system or a package of tools. In this vein, Merchant and Van der Stede[10] claim that MC "should include all the devices or systems that managers have at their disposal to ensure the behaviors and decisions of their employees are consistent with the organization's objectives and strategies." Such a broad analytical conception, to be studied empirically according to Malmi and Brown[11] demands the elaboration of a sufficiently broad, yet parsimonious framework. These existing in the literature[12] either omit essential types of control that managers have at their disposal, or do not clearly distinguish the differences between them. They mainly do not include forthcoming changes due to the

---

[6]   A. Fried, *Terminological Distinctions of "Control": A Review of the Implications for Management Control Research in the Context of Innovation*, "Journal of Management Control" 2017, 28 (1), p. 6.

[7]   K. A. Merchant, V. A. Van der Stede, *Management Control Systems: Performance Measurement, Evaluation and Incentives*, 4th ed., Pearson Education, Harlow, United Kingdom 2017, p. 1.

[8]   R. Simons, *Levers of Control: How Managers Use Innovative Control Systems to Drive Strategic Renewal*, Harvard Business Press, Cambridge 1995, p. 4.

[9]   J.-F. Henri, *Management Control Systems and Strategy: A Resource-Based Perspective*, "Accounting, Organizations and Society" 2006, 31 (6), p. 533.

[10] K. A. Merchant, V. A. Van der Stede, *Management Control...*, p. 8.

[11] T. Malmi, D. A. Brown, *Management Control Systems as a Package—Opportunities, Challenges and Research Directions*, "Management Accounting Research" 2008, 19 (4), p. 288.

[12] E.g. W. G. Ouchi, *A Conceptual Framework for the Design of Organizational Control Mechanisms*, "Management Science" 1979, 25 (9), pp. 833–848; idem, *Markets, Bureaucracies, and Clans*, "Administrative Science Quarterly" 1980, pp. 129–141; E. G. Flamholtz et al., *Toward an Integrative Framework of Organizational Control*, "Accounting, Organizations and Society" 1985, 10 (1), pp. 35–50; R. Simons, *Levers of Control...*; D. Otley, *Performance Management: A Framework for Management Control Systems Research*, "Management Accounting Research" 1999, 10 (4), pp. 363–382; K. S. Herath, *A Framework for Management Control Research*, "Journal of Management Development" 2007, 26 (9), pp. 895–915; T. Malmi, D. A. Brown, *Management Control Systems...*; A.-M. Kruis, *Management Control System Design and Effectiveness*, Nyenrode Business Universiteit, The Netherlands 2008, https://papers.ssrn.com/sol3/papers.cfm?abstract_id=1441243 (access: 15 May 2019); J. Hutzschenreuter, *Management Control in Small and Medium-Sized Enterprises*, Gabler, Wiesbaden 2009; A. Ferreira, D. Otley, *The Design and Use of Performance Management Systems: An Extended Framework for Analysis*, "Management Accounting Research" 2009, 20 (4), pp. 263–282; K. A. Merchant, V. A. Van der Stede, *Management Control...*

implementation of Industry 4.0. This research is going to fill the gap. There is especially a lack of a comprehensive framework, which would also embrace such phenomena as trust, ideology, and spirituality. These phenomena can also serve as an effective form of control in organisations, where other forms, such as cybernetic and administrative, are ineffective. Thus, the study aims to elaborate on a comprehensive framework for management control research including trust, ideology, and spirituality.

Our study contributes to the control literature in many ways. First, the study extends the MC literature by supplying a more thorough and unequivocal description of normative control modes, such as trust, ideology, and spirituality. Second, the theoretical analysis demonstrates that the implementation of singular control modes in isolation and without thorough knowledge about the relationships with other control practices may not be beneficial. It suggests that relying on the results of independent analyses of MC practices alone is insufficient for understanding the constitution of effective MC packages.[13] Finally, this study adds to the emerging body of research by theoretically investigating and describing interdependencies among different normative MC practices.

Generic control variables: outcome and behaviour

There are only two variables concerning members of every organisation that could be controlled, namely their behaviour and results (output) of their work.[14] Based on Ouchi studies, Eisenhardt[15] claimed that which variable can be monitored depends on the complexity and programmability of tasks, as well as the ability to measure results. When knowledge about the transformation process is high, the behaviour leading to satisfactory results can be defined unambiguously. As this knowledge decreases, since tasks become less susceptible to programming, i.e., there may be many non-standard situations that require making autonomous decisions based on several variables—behaviour control becomes more and more difficult, because it is impossible to determine the effective behaviour. In such a case, only the final result of the performed task can be used as the control strategy. A salesman could be an example. If, on the other hand, the measurement of results is ambiguous, but the tasks are programmable, then the only available control option is the evaluation of behaviuor, like in the case of night guards. They have to remain on site, watch CCTV and call the intervention group when seeing something suspicious. Their work cannot be evaluated according to how

13 D. S. Bedford et al., *Management Control Effectiveness and Strategy: An Empirical Analysis of Packages and Systems*, "Accounting, Organizations and Society" 2016, 51, p. 13.

14 W. G. Ouchi, *The Relationship between Organizational Structure and Organizational Control*, "Administrative Science Quarterly" 1977, 22 (1), p. 97.

15 K. M. Eisenhardt, *Control: Organizational and Economic Approaches*, "Management Science" 1985, 31 (2), p. 135.

many suspicious situations they reveal since this is beyond their control. In a situation where both the measurement of results is ambiguous, and the tasks are complex and non-programmable, i.e., neither results nor behaviour control can be carried out—only ceremonial or ritual forms of control are possible.[16] The above distinctions are fundamental for the whole MC research and practice.

Extant control frameworks

Ouchi[17] distinguished three generic forms of control: market, bureaucracy, and clan. Each of these forms could be applied depending on the degree of goal congruence between the cooperating parties and the possibility of an unambiguous assessment of work performance.[18] Market control can be effective when the assessment of work performance is unambiguous, regardless of the difference in goal congruence between parties. Bureaucratic control can be effective when both the discrepancy of goals and the difficulty in assessing work performance are at a moderate level. Clan control can be effective, despite the lack of possibility to assess work performance, provided that the goals of the parties are congruent. This means that an organisation can function effectively, when the results of individual work can be precisely measured, or when people can trust that none of them will behave opportunistically.

This framework refers to the assumption that every cooperation, including that within an organisation, is based on some form of transaction, in which something valuable is exchanged between the parties. For example, one person gives work and effort, and the other gives money in return. Thus, output and behaviour control could be implemented through market, bureaucracy, or clan control. It has to be remembered, however, that the clan mode of control is unable to implement any explicit form of monitoring and evaluation of anything but attitudes, values, norms and beliefs.[19] The Ouchi framework was further developed in other scholarship, which refers to market, bureaucracy, and clan, for example as price, authority/hierarchy, and norms.[20]

Some authors[21] proposed a framework of MC consisting of nine elements. Three contextual elements were external environment, organizational culture and structure, and six core control system mechanisms included planning, operational subsystem,

---

[16]   W. G. Ouchi, *A Conceptual Framework…*, p. 844.

[17]   Idem, *Markets, Bureaucracies…*

[18]   Ibidem, p. 129.

[19]   W. G. Ouchi, *A Conceptual Framework…*, p. 844.

[20]   J. L. Bradach, R. G. Eccles, *Price, Authority, and Trust: From Ideal Types to Plural Forms*, "Annual Review of Sociology" 1989, 15, pp. 97–118; P. S. Adler, *Market, Hierarchy, and Trust: The Knowledge Economy and the Future of Capitalism*, "Organization Science" 2001, 12 (2), pp. 215–234.

[21]   E. G. Flamholtz et al., *Toward an Integrative Framework…*; E. Flamholtz, *Effective Organizational Control: A Framework, Applications, and Implications*, "European Management Journal" 1996, 14 (6), pp. 596–611.

measurement, feedback, evaluation-reward and outcome.[22] Planning includes goals and setting of standards. The operational subsystem consists of internal processes transforming inputs into outputs. The outcome element embraces performance (e.g. sales volume, productivity, profit margin), and other outcomes such as turnover and absenteeism. The measurement includes the management information system (e.g. production, inventory,) and the appraisal system of employee performance. The feedback refers to the delivery of information regarding performance compared against pre-determined goals and standards, to the operational subsystem for correction, to the planning element for goals or adjustment of standards, and to the evaluation reward element for reward administration. The evaluation reward element comprises the administration of extrinsic rewards based on the evaluation of work performance.[23]

In the framework, the core control system is embedded in a wider control context, including the organisational structure, organisational culture, and external environment. The control context may either facilitate or inhibit the effectiveness of the core control system. It may facilitate the coordination of human efforts toward the attainment of organisational goals by additional control through formalisation, centralisation, social norms in the organisational culture, or standards of professionalism found in the organisation's external environment. The control context may also inhibit the effectiveness of the core control system, if it is incompatible with the norms, values, management philosophy or practices in the larger context.[24] A similar framework was proposed by Herath.[25] She adds to Flamholtz a proposition strategy as a contextual variable and places the management information system outside the core control system.

Otley[26] proposed a performance management framework for MC systems research, which consists of questions addressing the central areas indispensable for the successful attainment of organisational objectives. These areas are: key objectives, strategies, plans and the evaluation of the level of their achievements, the processes and activities that are required for successful implementation of plans, measures and levels (targets) of performance, reward and penalty systems as well as information systems, including feedback and feed-forward loops enabling organisational learning. Ten years later, Ferreira and Otley[27] extended the framework by including contextual factors such as organisational structure (explicitly) and culture (implicitly). In the renewed framework, they also distinguished interactive and diagnostic use of control.[28]

---

[22]   E. Flamholtz, *Effective Organizational Control...*, p. 600.
[23]   E. G. Flamholtz et al., *Toward an Integrative Framework...*, p. 39.
[24]   Ibidem, p. 45.
[25]   K. S. Herath, *A Framework for Management...*, p. 905.
[26]   D. Otley, *Performance Management...*, p. 365.
[27]   A. Ferreira, D. Otley, *The Design and Use...*
[28]   R. Simons, *Levers of Control...*, p. 7.

It is important to clarify the dyadic role of planning and information in organisations. Planning as a function of management consists of ex-ante decision-making, however, as a form of control, it should create goal congruence within an organisation. Thus, planning as a control mechanism involves the setting of work goals and the establishment of standards (targets) for each goal to direct effort and behaviour. Planning is an ex-ante form of control since it provides the information necessary to direct or guide individuals and groups and promote goal congruence between the individual and the organisation to ensure they are in line with desired organisational outcomes. Information could be used either as a decision-support system or as a control mechanism. In the control function, information serves as a vehicle to influence behaviour, while in the decision function—just as a support in the decision-making process. A different situation appears, when we consider not just information, as, for example, information about the external environment, but also feedback information. This means information about work behaviours and outcomes as a result of previous decisions, plans, and organisational processes. When feedback information is used for corrective actions of work behaviour, this is the traditional cybernetic control called by Simons "diagnostic control."[29] When feedback information is used to change the underlying decisions and plans, then there is an "interactive control."[30]

Speklé, based on four contingency variables (structure, standardisation, monitoring and performance evaluation, and reward and incentive structure), proposed five types of control: arm's length control, machine control (result oriented), machine control (action oriented), exploratory control, and boundary control.[31] Hutzschenreuter[32] divided MC into four categories according to the degree of interaction with employees: behaviour control, results control, personnel control, and cultural control. More recently Merchant and Van der Stede[33] published their refined framework dividing MC into four categories: result and action control, which refers to cybernetic control of results and behaviour, and personnel and cultural control, referring to shared values and norms.

Malmi and Brown[34] proposed a framework of MC, which embraces most of the elements present in the frameworks mentioned above. Their framework embraces five types (systems) of control: planning, cybernetic, reward and compensation, administrative, and cultural controls[35] (Figure 1).

---

[29]   Ibidem, p. 59.
[30]   Ibidem, p. 91.
[31]   R. Speklé, A.-M. Kruis, *Management Control...*, p. 21.
[32]   J. Hutzschenreuter, *Management Control...*, p. 47.
[33]   K. A. Merchant, V. A. Van der Stede, *Management Control...*, p. 19.
[34]   T. Malmi, D. A. Brown, *Management Control Systems...*
[35]   Ibidem, p. 291.

Cultural Controls					
Clans		Values		Symbols	

Planning		Cybernetic Controls			Reward and Compensation
Long range planning / Action planning	Budgets	Financial Measurement Systems	Non Financial Measurement Systems	Hybrid Measurement Systems	

Administrative Controls		
Governance Structure	Organization Structure	Policies and Procedures

Figure 1. Framework of management control research

Source: T. Malmi, D. A. Brown, *Management Control Systems as a Package–Opportunities, Challenges and Research Directions*, "Management Accounting Research" 2008, 19 (4), p. 291.

According to Malmi and Brown[36] their framework "was developed by analysing and synthesising nearly four decades of MCS research," and "this analytical conception of MCS as a package provides a sufficiently broad, yet parsimonious, approach for studying the phenomenon empirically."[37] Since this is maybe the most widely cited and best-received framework by researchers in the last decade, it is worth taking a critical look at it and improving it.

Improved framework for MC research

Although the framework elaborated by Malmi and Brown[38] includes most of the fundamental forms of control, it has inherited some weaknesses from extant works and also introduced some new ones. Firstly, in cybernetic controls, the authors include somehow overlapping categories such as Financial Measurement System, Non-Financial Measurement System, and Hybrid Measurement System. The Hybrid Measurement System already includes financial and non-financial measures, and it is rather the development of Financial Measurement System than a different element of a control system. Secondly, the framework places different levels of controls in the same section like Budgets and Financial, Non-Financial and Hybrid Measurement Systems. In many organisations, the budget is the main and universal control tool thanks to its ability to

---

[36]   Ibidem.
[37]   Ibidem, p. 291.
[38]   Ibidem.

integrate many aspects of an organisation into a comprehensive plan that serves many different purposes, particularly performance planning and ex-post evaluation of actual performance in relation to the plan.[39] Hence, the budget is not on the same conceptual level as a financial or non-financial measurement system, since it is a wide-ranging, complete technique, whereas financial or non-financial measurement systems can be used in a limited fashion in target-setting. The budget is not only a higher level control system, because it embraces financial performance measurement, but it also contains planning, which is distinguished as a separate form of control in the framework in question (Figure 1).

Due to these inconsistencies in the revised framework (Figure 2), the cybernetic control section should be changed. Previous elements should be replaced by such basic controls systems as management information systems, feedback, and links between goals and rewards.

Management information systems embrace the three previously separated systems and could be defined as an integrated structure of databases and information flow over all levels of an organisation enabling an efficient collection, transfer, and presentation of information according to the needs of the organisation.[40] Especially important is the measurement of individual or group performance since the measurement could serve as a separate form of control per se. The very fact that something is the subject of measurement tends to influence the behaviour of people in organisations. Thus, the process of measurement is a stimulus in itself.[41]

Feedback. Information is also critical for other components of the cybernetic control system. The feedback element consists of information about operations and employees behaviour compared to their results. It could be corrective and evaluative feedback. Corrective feedback serves to improve organisational performance, while evaluative feedback consists of information about how well employees are doing and provides a basis for performance evaluation, as well as the administration of rewards.[42]

Links between goals and rewards. Organisations usually collect information about many aspects of performance, which are not equally important for their success. As the measurement per se could be a stimulus, organisations have to show employees which goals and targets are the most important. Thus, links between goals and rewards strengthen the stimuli and direct the effort of employees in particular directions.

---

[39]   S. C. Hansen et al., *Practice Developments in Budgeting: An Overview and Research Perspective*, "Journal of Management Accounting Research" 2003, 15 (1), p. 96.

[40]   K. S. Herath, *A Framework for Management...*, p. 909.

[41]   E. Flamholtz, *Effective Organizational Control...*, p. 601.

[42]   Ibidem.

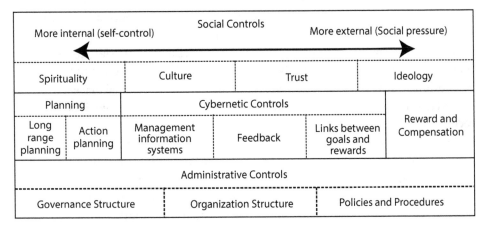

Figure 2. Revised framework of management control research

Source: authors' own elaboration.

Finally, the framework similarly like the others, has omitted broad and essential types of social controls such as spirituality, trust, and ideology (Figure 2).

Extending the exploration of social controls is driven by the recent research, which indicates that high levels of technological complexity and innovation capability are expected to be negatively associated with the application of results and action control, which are similar to cybernetic control (monitoring and rewarding outputs and behaviors) whereas personnel and cultural control seem to be more appropriate for organisations with high levels of technological complexity as well as innovation capability.[43] High levels of technological complexity and innovation capability are the features, which may characterise Industry 4.0 organisations, as well as hospitals.

Trust as the control mechanism

"Trust serves as a powerful control mechanism, just as price and authority do."[44] Authority is the prime coordination mechanism in hierarchical relationships (administrative controls), and price (material incentives) is the central control mechanism in cybernetic controls. Trust is not only a control form per se but is also an ingredient of other control modes and can create "hybrid" forms of control.[45] Trust represents

---

[43] E. Haustein et al., *Management Control Systems in Innovation Companies: A Literature Based Framework*, "Journal of Management Control" 2014, 24 (4), p. 372.

[44] J. L. Bradach, R. G. Eccles, *Price, Authority, and Trust...*, p. 110.

[45] *Handbook of Trust Research*, ed. by R. Bachmann, A. Zaheer, Edward Elgar Publishing, Cheltenham 2006, p. 2.

a coordinating mechanism based on shared moral values and norms supporting collective co-operation and collaboration within uncertain environments.[46]

In the MC literature trust is usually associated with the cultural (clan) control mode, however, after more thorough analysis it appears that it is also present in the market and administrative (bureaucratic) modes of control. Ouchi[47] claimed that each form is related to some social and informational prerequisites. The market requires a norm of reciprocity. A bureaucracy cannot exist not only without a norm of reciprocity but also without an agreement on legitimate (legal) authority. A clan demands not exclusively a norm of reciprocity and the idea of legitimate authority (preferably the "traditional" than the "legal" form) but also social agreement on a broad range of values and beliefs.[48] The norm of reciprocity is slightly different for each form of control. On the market, the norm of reciprocity assures that when one party would cheat another, then the cheater, if discovered, would be punished by all members of the social system, not only by the victim. In the bureaucracy, the norm is reflected by the unbiased assessment of one's input to the organisational outcome and could be reflected in the notion of "an honest day's work for an honest day's pay."[49] In the clan, the norm of reciprocity guarantees that cooperating parties behave according to shared values and beliefs.

Hence, the norm of reciprocity related to each control form includes an element of trust. On the market, when there is no explicit information about cheating, a party would trust that the transaction is going to be fair. In an administrative form, a member of the organisation must trust that their contribution is rightly assessed. In the culture (clan), having no possibility to measure one's output or individual input to the group's output, colleagues must trust each other that no one behaves opportunistically; otherwise, they will not make adequate effort to contribute to the organisation's/clan's outcome.

Trust is also present in planning, cybernetic, evaluation and compensation forms of control, mainly through the information they require to be effective. Managers setting goals and standards, taking corrective actions, and evaluating the performance of subordinates must trust information, which is the basis of these activities. Information is not only acquired from technical and objective sources, like accounting systems, which are rather trustworthy, but some information has to be also collected directly from employees. This requires trust since people are willing to share information, even unfavourable to their personal interests only when they trust each other.[50] Thus, trust is essential, since the presence of invalid data in information systems has

---

[46]   M. I. Reed, *Organization, Trust and Control: A Realist Analysis*, "Organization Studies" 2001, 22 (2), p. 201.

[47]   W. G. Ouchi, *Markets, Bureaucracies…*

[48]   Ibidem, p. 137.

[49]   W. G. Ouchi, *A Conceptual Framework…*, p. 838.

[50]   K. T. Dirks, *Three Fundamental Questions Regarding Trust in Leaders* [in:] *Handbook of Trust Research*, ed. by R. Bachmann, A. Zaheer, Edward Elgar Publishing, Cheltenham 2006.

been recognised for decades as a major problem for the design and administration of organisational control systems.[51] Also, the effectiveness of reward and compensation systems may depend on trust. Employees, in order to increase their effort, must trust their superiors that they will reward them adequately, not only in the short run but also in the longer term. This means that managers do not increase their targets too quickly.

From the short analysis, it appears that trust is an ingredient of almost every control form and that the "combinations" of different control forms serve as building blocks for complex social structures so common in organisational life.[52] However, we must distinguish trust as a form of control from trust as believing in someone's good intentions, similarly as we distinguish planning as setting directions and information as decision-making support, from planning and information as a control mechanism. Trust as a form of control, impacts people's behaviour in two ways. First, people trust that others are behaving non-opportunistically and contribute to the achievement of organisational goals, so they are also motivated to support the common good. Secondly, as trust is an ingredient of every organisational relation and social structure, people may be afraid that their opportunistic behaviour could be revealed, and they would lose their trustworthiness bringing serious negative consequences to them. Trust could be a strong control mechanism even in situations, when the probability of revealing opportunistic behaviour is low, since repairing trust is more difficult than building trust initially. The party, which loses trust, has to firstly overcome distrust before it would be able to re-establish the previous level of trust.[53] Trust is especially important in hospitals, where complex relations are present not only among staff members but also between staff and the patients, who are actually clients of the organisation.

Culture and ideology

In MC literature, culture is widely recognised as the phenomenon, which is able to increase congruence of attitudes, values and beliefs and even goals among parties within an organisation.[54] Control through culture can be anchored in broader, historically-derived[55] collective patterns involving attitudes, beliefs and values that obtain

---

[51] E. G. Flamholtz et al., *Toward an Integrative Framework...*, p. 40.

[52] J. L. Bradach, R. G. Eccles, *Price, Authority, and Trust...*, p. 98.

[53] K. T. Dirks, *Three Fundamental Questions...*, p. 25.

[54] E.g. W. G. Ouchi, *Markets, Bureaucracies...*; idem, *A Conceptual Framework...*; E. G. Flamholtz et al., *Toward an Integrative Framework...*; R. Simons, *Levers of Control...*; D. Otley, *Performance Management...*; K. S. Herath, *A Framework for Management...*; T. Malmi, D. A. Brown, *Management Control Systems...*; R. Speklé, A.-M. Kruis, *Management Control System...*; J. Hutzschenreuter, *Management Control...*; A. Ferreira, D. Otley, *The Design and Use...*; K. A. Merchant, V. A. Van der Stede, *Management Control...*

[55] G. Hofstede et al., *Measuring Organizational Cultures: A Qualitative and Quantitative Study Across Twenty Cases*, "Administrative Science Quarterly" 1990, 35 (2), p. 286.

legitimacy in an organisation.[56] The legitimacy of norms and values means that both managerial and employee actions can only take place within these patterns, and not outside of them. Lebas and Weigenstein[57] argued that:

> Culture . . . removes the need for personal supervision . . . It establishes a system of norms and informal rules which spells out how people are to behave most of the time and allows them to extrapolate in new situations and act quickly, because even if the situation is new, the values are clear. Culture is thus an especially desirable control approach where the causal model is unclear, uncertainty is high, communication is difficult with other actors, and the cycle of action and consequence is compressed.

This means that culture offers one of the ways to broaden, improve and automate the correction of behaviour: when goals, rules, and procedures are internalised, then members of the culture will correct their behaviour as part of the self-control process, without the interference of managers. For employees, acting in accordance with the surrounding culture is comfortable, because it allows coordinating their actions in response to various information and events with activities as well as the expectations of others, thus allowing them to gain acceptance of the environment and bringing a sense of security and comfort. On the other hand, the lack of conformity between the values and norms held by the employee and the resulting activities with the organisation's culture, are the reason for the sense of alienation and the lack of social acceptance. This discrepancy impedes effective work, because it is challenging to expect involvement in activities that the employee either does not understand or even does not accept.[58]

The culture has some characteristics, which undermine its usability as a control form in a quickly changing environment that is going to be a prevailing feature in the contemporary world. In his review, Guldenmund[59] found that culture is relatively stable; its period of stability is at least five years. This stability is due to the fact that culture is based on behavioural regularities when people interact (language, customs and traditions, rituals), group norms, espoused values, habits of thinking, mental models, linguistic paradigms, shared meanings and metaphors, or integrating symbols—all these characteristics are difficult to instill in a short time and hard to manage.[60]

---

[56]   M. Alvesson, H. Willmott, *Identity Regulation as Organizational Control: Producing the Appropriate Individual*, "Journal of Management Studies" 2002, 39 (5), p. 636.

[57]   M. Lebas, J. Weigenstein, *Management Control: The Roles of Rules, Markets and Culture*, "Journal of Management Studies" 1986, 23 (3), p. 265.

[58]   C. Sikorski, *Znaczenie kultury organizacyjnej w szpitalu* [in:] *Kulturowe determinanty zarządzania szpitalami w Polsce*, ed. by Ł. Sułkowski, R. Seliga, Difin, Warszawa 2012, p. 21.

[59]   F. W. Guldenmund, *The Nature of Safety Culture: A Review of Theory and Research*, "Safety Science" 2000, 34 (1–3), p. 222.

[60]   Ibidem, p. 225.

There are two methods that an organisation can use to make employees, values more congruent with those preferred by the organisation. Firstly, an organisation can recruit individuals that have particular types of values matching those of the organisation, and secondly, an organisation may socialise individuals to influence their values.[61] The first method is restrained since it would be difficult to exchange a significant part of the staff when organisational values change. Hence, an organisation has to rely mostly on the socialisation process. However, the effectiveness of socialisation may depend on the level of internalisation of previous values and susceptibility to change the previous values by organisational members. An example of extremely deep value internalisation could be observed in spiritual people.

Spirituality

Spirituality in an organisational context is usually not interpreted as being the same as religion; it is recognised as immateriality, transcendence, self-perfection, and a belief in a higher power.[62] It relates to such existential questions as: "Why am I doing this work? What is the meaning of the work I am doing? Where does this lead me to? Is there a reason for my existence and the organisation's?"[63] More recently, scholars have noted that a common definition of workplace spirituality has emerged around three primary dimensions: the inner life, meaningful and purposeful work, and a sense of community and connectedness. Some also add such dimensions as organisational values, mindfulness, and compassion.[64]

The most important feature of this phenomenon is its loose connection with the rationality of cause and effect. For "spiritual actors" the time span between cause and effect is extended in a spiritual worldview to the point that learning about the consequences of one's actions from one's experience becomes difficult or impossible.[65] The distance between cause and consequence guarantees that one does not need to worry if a rationale for one's reasoning is present or not, because it can reveal itself later (even after one's death). Besides, even if something appears clearly false, it may merely be due to the inherent incompleteness of our worldview, thus no explanation is ever really complete.[66] Therefore, the logic of organisational spirituality's conceptual

---

[61]   T. Malmi, D. A. Brown, *Management Control Systems...*, p. 294.

[62]   M. Izak, *Spiritual Episteme: Sensemaking in the Framework of Organizational Spirituality*, "Journal of Organizational Change Management" 2012, 25 (1), p. 28.

[63]   S. Krishnakumar, C. P. Neck, *The "What", "Why" and "HOW" of Spirituality in the Workplace*, "Journal of Managerial Psychology" 2002, 17 (3), p. 156.

[64]   J. D. Houghton et al., *The What, Why, and How of Spirituality in the Workplace Revisited: A 14-Year Update and Extension*, "Journal of Management, Spirituality & Religion" 2016, 13 (3), p. 181.

[65]   M. Izak, *Spiritual Episteme...*, p. 33.

[66]   Ibidem, p. 37.

framework is vastly inconsistent with rationalism, which underpins most control strategies. The negative correlation between focus on materiality and spiritual fulfillment and the displacement of focus from living in the "having" mode, towards the "being" mode of life[67] influence the behaviour of employees in this way, that control strategies based on material rewards are hardly effective. Normative controls should be reshaped, as negotiating space is heavily constrained.

Although control over the behaviour of spiritual people is sophisticated, it is difficult to escape from this duty, since a significant part of the society experience spiritual needs, and spiritual people achieve a higher level of performance, higher job satisfaction, job involvement, lower intentions to quit, and more frequently present organisational citizenship behaviour than their non-spiritual colleagues.[68] Krishnakumar and Neck[69] claimed that "the experience of spirit at work is linked with increased creativity, honesty, trust, and commitment in the workplace, along with an enhanced sense of personal fulfillment of employees." Spirituality also reduces career and social costs encountered by women in the workplace[70] and Machiavellian behaviours, as well as aggressive and counterproductive work behaviours.[71]

Therefore, using culture as a form of control in an unstable environment, when fundamental organisational objectives could relatively frequently be changed is rather difficult. The problem is augmented by the fact that probably there is a trade-off relationship between strong culture characterised by deep internalisation of values and the effectiveness of cultural control. The deeper is the internalisation of values, the more effective the control based on the values. The phenomenon that appears to be able to help culture become more effective in the control function is ideology.

Ideology

Ideology has some similarities with culture since it also operates on values and norms. Culture, however, produces and spreads values, while ideology explains reality and affects the perception of the world and value system.[72] Ideology is a set of ordered views, ideas, principles, and standards. It is the worldview supplemented with guidelines as

---

67   Cf. E. Fromm, *To Have or To Be?*, Bloomsbury Publishing, London 2013, pp. 59–72.

68   J. D. Houghton et al., *The What…*, pp. 188–191.

69   S. Krishnakumar, C. P. Neck, *The "What"…*, p. 156.

70   M. Stout et al., *Reframing Workplace Spirituality to Reduce Career and Social Costs to Women*, "Public Integrity" 2015, 17 (2), pp. 143–164.

71   S. Krishnakumar, M. D. Robinson, *Maintaining an Even Keel: An Affect-Mediated Model of Mindfulness and Hostile Work Behavior*, "Emotion" 2015, 15 (5), p. 582.

72   G. Therborn, *The Ideology of Power and the Power of Ideology*, Verso Editions and NLB, London 1980, p. 18.

to which action should be taken and how.[73] Ideologies influence people by telling them what exists, and the corollary of that, namely what does not exist, what is real, true, good, right, just, beautiful, attractive, enjoyable, and its opposites. Thus, ideology by distributing spotlights, shadows, and darkness explains the world and people's place in it.[74] Ideologies are openly presented and promoted, while value systems related to culture are more hidden and less tangible, hence ideologies can be more effectively used to control people than cultures, which are more difficult to convey and instill.[75] Ideologies may be an effective control device, since they not only make some values and beliefs more conspicuous and other less visible, but they are an efficient tool of group differentiation. They are "foundational beliefs that underlie the shared social representations of specific kinds of social groups. These representations are, in turn, the basis of discourse and other social practices."[76]

Ideologies are most effective when they question the current system of values or a worldview (the current competitive ideology), because then they are debated and contested.[77] In this situation, discursive explanations focus on describing the other ideology or its believers in a negative light while own group members in a positive one. These can be a fuel for social ostracism and open critique, forcing people to behave according to the organisational ideology.

Czarniawska-Joerges[78] indicated that ideological control acts on the perception of reality by offering attractive targets and convincing interpretations. Ideologies are both objectives and means of control: new ideologies should replace the old, and organisational ideologies ought to substitute individual ones. Being in harmony with the "right" ideology is the source of many social and psychological rewards: social acceptance, a sense of belonging, the reduction of uncertainty. Deviations from the correct ideology call for appropriate punishment: a sense of isolation, cognitive dissonance, and the possibility of exposure to open criticism.[79]

Thus, the differences between culture and ideology as forms of control are twofold. First, culture operates on internalised values and beliefs, while ideology rather interprets these values and beliefs according to actual organisational needs, since ideologies operate as "a set (system) of ideas describing the organization-relevant reality, projecting a desired state of affairs, and indicating possible ways of reaching the desired states."[80]

---

[73]   R. A. Lewandowski, *Ideological Control in Public and Business Organizations*, "Nowoczesne Systemy Zarządzania" 2017, 12 (2), p. 21.

[74]   G. Therborn, *The Ideology of Power...*, p. 18.

[75]   R. A. Lewandowski, *Ideological Control...*, p. 21.

[76]   T. A. Van Dijk, *Ideology and Discourse Analysis*, "Journal of Political Ideologies" 2006, 11 (2), p. 120.

[77]   R. A. Lewandowski, *Ideological Control...*, p. 21.

[78]   B. Czarniawska-Joerges, *Ideological Control in Nonideological Organizations*, Praeger Publishers, New York 1988.

[79]   Ibidem, p. 10.

[80]   Ibidem, p. 7.

Second, the cultural form of control refers rather to the self-control mechanism, while ideological control to external social pressure.

Summary

In the framework presented in Figure 1 at the top are social controls instead of cultural controls proposed by Malmi and Brown.[81] This may be regarded as an essential improvement, since decades of research have proven that there are more socially related controls, than only the culture and its sub-elements like clans, values, and symbols. In the new framework, spirituality, trust, and ideology are added as forms of social control. They create a continuum from controls more based on self-control and internal rewards and punishments like spirituality, to controls dependent rather on external social pressure and external rewards and punishments, like ideology. Spiritual persons do not anticipate rewards or punishments for behaviour consistent with internalised values in a predictable time, and they can accept them "even after one's death."[82] This is similar to a conscience clause in healthcare. On the other side of the continuum, ideological control influences people's behaviour by group segregation, social ostracism, and the possibility of being subjected to open criticism.[83] The fact that a form of control is on the other side of the continuum does not mean that it does not also work through self-control or external social control. It is a matter of proportions.

In the middle of Figure 2 are the planning, cybernetic, and reward and compensation controls, which nowadays constitute the core control vehicle in most complex organisations. Here, the framework draws attention to the importance of goals and standards setting, management information systems, feedback and links between goals and rewards as fundamental elements of cybernetic control. Although the separation of planning, and reward and compensation from cybernetic controls is artificial, it is not changed compared[84] to the framework because of two reasons. The study aims to refine the framework already accepted in the scientific community and adjust it to the changing environment, including the implementation of Industry 4.0, instead of building a totally new one. To meet this goal, all reasonable explanations of previous authors have been accepted, like: "As planning may have a major role in directing employee behavior, we treat it as a separate system in our MCS typology"[85] and "Although rewards are often linked to cybernetic controls, organizations also provide rewards and compensation for other reasons. These include retaining employees and encouraging

---

[81]   T. Malmi, D. A. Brown, *Management Control Systems...*
[82]   M. Izak, *Spiritual Episteme...*, p. 37.
[83]   B. Czarniawska-Joerges, *Ideological Control...*, p. 10.
[84]   T. Malmi, D. A. Brown, *Management Control Systems...*
[85]   Ibidem, p. 292.

cultural control, via group rewards."[86] For that same reason also administrative controls remained untouched.

The main focus in this revision of the extant framework is placed on social controls since, as it is mentioned in the introduction, in the forthcoming Industry 4.0 era, management control will have to cope with problems concerning creativity and innovation. In the new era, routine tasks and decisions will be accomplished by cyber-physical systems[87] and organisations will employ more and more well-educated and autonomous professionals demanding much more from organisations than only a decent salary, which has always been present in healthcare.[88] Therefore, organisations will have to give employees more meaning to their work, and convince them that by working for a particular organisation or doing a specific task they "make the world a better place."

The revised framework presented in Figure 2 may help researchers and also managers to better understand the variety of control forms and to give them the base for questioning the potential linkages among control modes in both commercial and social organisations. Finally, it should stimulate discussion and research in this area for the forthcoming era of Industry 4.0.

Bibliography

Adler P. S., *Market, Hierarchy, and Trust: The Knowledge Economy and the Future of Capitalism*, "Organization Science" 2001, 12 (2).

Alvesson M., Willmott H., *Identity Regulation as Organizational Control: Producing the Appropriate Individual*, "Journal of Management Studies" 2002, 39 (5).

Bedford D. S., Malmi T., Sandelin M., *Management Control Effectiveness and Strategy: An Empirical Analysis of Packages and Systems*, "Accounting, Organizations and Society" 2016, 51.

Bradach J. L., Eccles R. G., *Price, Authority, and Trust: From Ideal Types to Plural Forms*, "Annual Review of Sociology" 1989, 15.

Czarniawska-Joerges B., *Ideological Control in Nonideological Organizations*, Praeger Publishers, New York 1988.

Dirks K. T., *Three Fundamental Questions Regarding Trust in Leaders* [in:] *Handbook of Trust Research*, ed. by R. Bachmann, A. Zaheer, Edward Elgar Publishing, Cheltenham 2006.

Eisenhardt K. M., *Control: Organizational and Economic Approaches*, "Management Science" 1985, 31 (2).

Ferreira A., Otley D., *The Design and Use of Performance Management Systems: An Extended Framework for Analysis*, "Management Accounting Research" 2009, 20 (4).

---

[86] Ibidem, p. 293.
[87] R. Y. Zhong et al., *Intelligent Manufacturing…*, p. 616.
[88] A. G. Goncharuk, *Exploring a Motivation of Medical Staff*, "The International Journal of Health Planning and Management" 2018, 33 (4), pp. 1013–1023.

Flamholtz E., *Effective Organizational Control: A Framework, Applications, and Implications*, "European Management Journal" 1996, 14 (6).

Flamholtz E. G., Das T. K., Tsui A. S., *Toward an Integrative Framework of Organizational Control*, "Accounting, Organizations and Society" 1985, 10 (1).

Fried A., *Terminological Distinctions of "Control": A Review of the Implications for Management Control Research in the Context of Innovation*, "Journal of Management Control" 2017, 28 (1).

Fromm E., *To Have or To Be?*, Bloomsbury Publishing, London 2013.

Gay P. du, *Colossal Immodesties and Hopeful Monsters: Pluralism and Organizational Conduct*, "Organization" 1994, 1 (1).

Goncharuk A. G., *Exploring a Motivation of Medical Staff*, "The International Journal of Health Planning and Management" 2018, 33 (4).

Guldenmund F. W., *The Nature of Safety Culture: A Review of Theory and Research*, "Safety Science" 2000, 34 (1–3).

Handbook of Trust Research, ed. by R. Bachmann, A. Zaheer, Edward Elgar Publishing, Cheltenham 2006.

Hansen S. C., Otley D. T., Van der Stede W. A., *Practice Developments in Budgeting: An Overview and Research Perspective*, "Journal of Management Accounting Research" 2003, 15 (1).

Haustein E., Luther R., Schuster P., *Management Control Systems in Innovation Companies: A Literature Based Framework*, "Journal of Management Control" 2014, 24 (4).

Henri J.-F., *Management Control Systems and Strategy: A Resource-Based Perspective*, "Accounting, Organizations and Society" 2006, 31 (6).

Herath K. S., *A Framework for Management Control Research*, "Journal of Management Development" 2007, 26 (9).

Hofstede G., Neuijen B., Ohayv D. D., Sanders G., *Measuring Organizational Cultures: A Qualitative and Quantitative Study Across Twenty Cases*, "Administrative Science Quarterly" 1990, 35 (2).

Houghton J. D., Neck C. P., Krishnakumar S., *The What, Why, and How of Spirituality in the Workplace Revisited: A 14-Year Update and Extension*, "Journal of Management, Spirituality & Religion" 2016, 13 (3).

Hutzschenreuter J., *Management Control in Small and Medium-Sized Enterprises*, Gabler, Wiesbaden 2009.

Izak M., *Spiritual Episteme: Sensemaking in the Framework of Organizational Spirituality*, "Journal of Organizational Change Management" 2012, 25 (1).

Knorring M. von, Rijk A. de, Alexanderson K., *Managers' Perceptions OF THE Manager Role in Relation to Physicians: A Qualitative Interview Study of the Top Managers in Swedish Healthcare*, "BMC Health Services Research" 2010, 10 (1).

Krishnakumar S., Neck C.P ., *The "What", "Why" and "How" of Spirituality in the Workplace*, "Journal of Managerial Psychology" 2002, 17 (3).

Krishnakumar S., Robinson M. D., *Maintaining an Even Keel: An Affect-Mediated Model of Mindfulness and Hostile Work Behavior*, "Emotion" 2015, 15 (5).

Lawler J., Hearn J., *UK Public Sector Organizations: The Rise of Managerialism and the Impact of Change on Social Services Departments*, "International Journal of Public Sector Management" 1995, 8 (4).

Lebas M., Weigenstein J., *Management Control: The Roles of Rules, Markets and Culture*, "Journal of Management Studies" 1986, 23 (3).

Lewandowski R. A., *Ideological Control in Public and Business Organizations*, "Nowoczesne Systemy Zarządzania" 2017, 12 (2).

Lewandowski R. A., Sasak J., Kożuch A., *Kontrola zarządcza w placówkach ochrony zdrowia*, Wolters Kluwer, Warszawa 2018.

Malmi T., Brown D. A., *Management Control Systems as a Package—Opportunities, Challenges and Research Directions*, "Management Accounting Research" 2008, 19 (4).

Merchant K. A., Van der Stede W. A., *Management Control Systems: Performance Measurement, Evaluation and Incentives*, 4th ed., Pearson Education, Harlow, United Kingdom 2017.

Otley D., *Performance Management: A Framework for Management Control Systems Research*, "Management Accounting Research" 1999, 10 (4).

Ouchi W. G., *The Relationship between Organizational Structure and Organizational Control*, "Administrative Science Quarterly" 1977, 22 (1).

Ouchi W. G., *A Conceptual Framework for the Design Of Organizational Control Mechanisms*, "Management Science" 1979, 25 (9).

Ouchi W. G., *Markets, Bureaucracies, and Clans*, "Administrative Science Quarterly" 1980.

Reed M. I., *Organization, Trust and Control: A Realist Analysis*, "Organization Studies" 2001, 22 (2).

Sikorski C., *Znaczenie kultury organizacyjnej w szpitalu* [in:] *Kulturowe determinanty zarządzania szpitalami w Polsce*, ed. by Ł. Sułkowski, R. Seliga, Difin, Warszawa 2012.

Simons R., *Levers of Control: How Managers Use Innovative Control Systems to Drive Strategic Renewal*, Harvard Business Press, Cambridge 1995.

Speklé R., Kruis A.-M., *Management Control System Design and Effectiveness*, Nyenrode Business Universiteit, The Netherlands 2008, https://papers.ssrn.com/sol3/papers.cfm?abstract_id=1441243 (access: 15 May 2019).

Stout M., Tower L. E., Alkadry M. G., *Reframing Workplace Spirituality to Reduce Career and Social Costs to Women*, "Public Integrity" 2015, 17 (2).

Therborn G., *The Ideology of Power and the Power of Ideology*, Verso Editions and NLB, London 1980.

Van Dijk T. A., *Ideology and Discourse Analysis*, "Journal of Political Ideologies" 2006, 11 (2).

Zhong R. Y., Xu X., Klotz E., Newman S. T., *Intelligent Manufacturing in the Context of Industry 4.0: A Review*, "Engineering" 2017, 3 (5).

Renewable Energy through Industry 4.0 on the Example of Photovoltaic Development in Selected European Countries

Prof. Piotr Buła, Ph.D.   https://orcid.org/0000-0001-8741-8327
Cracow University of Economics
University of Johannesburg

Tomasz Schroeder, M.Sc. Eng.   https://orcid.org/0000-0003-1562-1398
Cracow University of Economics

Monika Ziółko, Ph.D.   https://orcid.org/0000-0003-3229-3509
Cracow University of Economics

Abstract

The fourth industrial revolution, known as Industry 4.0, is changing the face of business through the integration of digital and physical systems. The emerging cyber-physical systems, together with artificial intelligence, offer completely new possibilities for exploiting the potential of this change. Progressive digitisation and technological progress require equally progressive electrification. The Industry 4.0 influences the use of renewable energy sources not only because of the increased demand, but also because of the many opportunities that renewable energy sources provide. Digital business needs stable and cheap electricity, which solar farms are able to provide. The industrial revolution is an opportunity for the development of industries and the economy, so it is crucial to adopt the right strategy and the right approach, favouring new business models and innovative technologies. They may contribute to reindustrialisation and improvement of the competitive position of the industry in individual countries, including those analysed. Therefore, the aim of the article is to evaluate the possibilities and level of development of solar energy, mainly industrial, in selected European countries: Poland, Germany, Romania, and Ukraine. In the first part of the study the main assumptions of Industry 4.0 are presented. Then the issues related to renewable energy sources, including solar energy, are embedded in them. In the following part of the article, the amount and structure of installed photovoltaic power in the countries surveyed are analysed. In the last part of the study, the level of development of solar energy in the analysed countries is assessed and on this basis the level of implementation of the assumptions included in the Industry 4.0 strategy in the field of energy security is determined.

Keywords: renewable energy sources, photovoltaic, Industry 4.0, industrial revolutions, Internet of Things, smart grid

Background

Observing new trends in technology development, the fourth industrial revolution, referred to as Industry 4.0, has a huge impact on changes in business. The accelerated pace of the digitisation process is changing the face of business and is contributing to an even more dynamic environment and market structure.[1] The first Industrial Revolution in the use of steam and hydropower revolutionised mechanisation processes. The second one, related to electrification, provided new opportunities that were used in mass production. Another industrial revolution is the use of computers and IT tools in the broadly understood automation. The fourth, ongoing revolution is the use of the network, the Internet and Big Data[2] resources in cyber-physical systems.[3] CPS (Cyber-Physical System) is a mechanism through which physical objects and software are closely intertwined, enabling different components to interact with each other in a myriad of ways to exchange information.[4] The changes are certainly affecting businesses through technological development, in particular by increasing the computing power of computers and the size of the available databases. The industry is facing rapid changes in the use of IT tools and communication. The pace of technological change is definitely the fastest in history. With the increasing use of computer technology, most of the recorded information became digital. In 1993 only 3% of the world's recorded information was digitally stored, while by 2007 this number had risen to 94%.[5] This phenomenon is not separated from industrial change. As technology develops, Artificial Intelligence can be used to analyse Big Data resources. Analysis of such resources can be particularly valuable as it can lead to the acquisition of new knowledge. The use of AI for data resources analysis can support decision-making processes, which in turn can have an impact on industrial enterprise strategies. The possibilities of artificial intelligence analysis far exceed those of other analysis tools and allow to obtain a solution based on a general determinant, obtained from the many taken into account. This can be done by using an approach that combines classic decision-making problem-solving with the fuzzy set theory, in which case the use of artificial intelligence tools is based on the assumption that objectives and limitations take the form of sets.[6] This approach expands the possibilities of data analysis, because it allows to describe phenomena in

---

[1] Y. Kayikci, *Sustainability Impact of Digitization in Logistics*, 15th Global Conference on Sustainable Manufacturing, "Procedia Manufacturing" 2018, 21, p. 782.

[2] Big Data is a term used to refer to large data sets that are variable and heterogeneous.

[3] L. S. Dalenogare, G. B. Benitez, N. F. Ayala, A. G. Frank, *The Expected Contribution of Industry 4.0 Technologies for Industrial Performance*, "International Journal of Production Economics" 2018, 204, p. 384.

[4] R. Y. Zhong, X. Xu, E. Klotz, S. T. Newman, *Intelligent Manufacturing in the Context of Industry 4.0: A Review*, "Engineering" 2017, 3 (5), p. 620.

[5] Y. Kayikci, *Sustainability Impact...*, p. 783.

[6] P. Wappa, *Using of Artificial Intelligence Methods in Logistics*, "Economy and Management" 2011, 4, p. 110.

a wider perspective, and the use of bivalent logic is only a part of the description of events occurring in the decision-making space. Industry 4.0 relies on the adoption of digital technologies to gather data in real time and to analyse it, providing useful information to the manufacturing system.[7]

Table 1. Four industrial revolutions: The main assumptions

1.0	2.0	3.0	4.0
The end of the 18th century	The turn of the 19th and 20th centuries	The 1970s	Currently
Introduction of mechanisation in production through steam energy	Introduction of division of labour and mass production through electricity	Use of electronics and IT for further automation of production	Integration of digital and physical systems
• Mechanised weaving workshop • Development of iron production using coal	• Progress in steel production • Series production of machines • Series manufacturing of machines	• Development of polymer production • Automated industrial robots • Improvement of energy and material efficiency after the oil crisis	• Internet of Things, cyber-physical systems • Dynamic data processing • Economy on demand • Renewable Energy Sources • Closed circuit in the economy

Source: prepared by the authors, based on: *Gospodarka 4.0. Czas zmiany dla biznesu*, Raport PKN Orlen, Warszawa 2017, p. 10.

Progressive digitalisation does not only affect the virtual world, but also the real world. Technology provides us with tools that we can use in business operations. Technological progress can mean a number of opportunities and can be a threat due to rapid progress and the need to implement new solutions. Certainly Industry 4.0 will influence the use of renewable energy sources (Table 1), also affecting the production of fossil fuel energy. Progressive digitalisation requires progressive electrification. Nowadays, new technologies such as machines communicating with each other, the example of which is the Internet of Things, are being developed. The Internet of Things (IoT) is a network of physical objects—devices, vehicles, buildings and other objects—that are connected to electronics, software, sensors and network enabling them to collect and exchange information[8]. Artificial intelligence algorithms such as Deep Learning can be used to

---

[7]   A. G. Frank, L. S. Dalenogare, N. F. Ayala, *Industry 4.0 Technologies: Implementation Patterns in Manufacturing Companies*, "International Journal of Production Economics" 2019, 210, p. 15.

[8]   A. Rakotonirainy, O. Orfila, D. Gruyer, *Reducing Driver's Behavioural Uncertainties Using an Interdisciplinary Approach: Convergence of Quantified Self, Automated Vehicles, Internet of Things and Artificial Intelligence*, "IFAC-Papers Online" 2016 (49–32), p. 78.

analyse or classify the data flowing from IoT.[9] The IoT which refers to machine-to-machine interaction without human intervention is a network of devices connected to the system (smart system) and this is what has led to the industrial revolution known as Industry 4.0.[10] Improving the data collection process, e.g. by smart sensors, also requires the correct processing of these data in order to ensure the right information at the right time.

The relationship between Industry 4.0 and renewable energy sources

Not only artificial intelligence, but also the servers themselves, which collect data, need electricity. Industry 4.0 therefore influences the use of renewable energy sources not only due to the increased demand, but also because of the many opportunities provided by renewable energy sources. New technologies of Industry 4.0 may affect the development of RES in terms of:

- photovoltaics: new material technologies (e.g. perovskites), electric cars,[11] energy storage, new generation inverters, teleautomation, solar trackers, RES energy infrastructure management;
- geothermal energy: new technologies for drilling, geotechnical and geological surveys, new technologies for land surveys for exploration and resource assessment (seismic methods, electro-resistive methods);
- wind energy:[12] new material technologies (composites, mechanics, automation, control).

On the other hand, apart from the wide use of new technologies for the development of renewable energy sources, the development of RES alone can positively influence Industry 4.0 through:

- supply of electricity (stable, possibility of dispersed deliveries in the places of energy production);
- storage of electricity (safety of production lines and management systems);
- electricity transmission (new technologies to reduce energy transmission losses).

Digital business needs stable electricity, which can be supplied by solar and wind farms as well as geothermal energy. Technological progress constantly reduces the cost of producing and storing renewable energy at zero primary energy cost. Low and

---

[9]   Ibidem.

[10]   S. S. Kamble, A. Gunasekaran, S. A. Gawankar, *Sustainable Industry 4.0 Framework: A Systematic Literature Review Identifying the Current Trends and Future Perspectives*, "Process Safety and Environmental Protection" 2018, 117, pp. 408–409

[11]   N. Chowdhury, C. A. Hossain, M. Longo, W. Yaïci, *Optimization of Solar Energy System for the Electric Vehicle at University Campus in Dhaka, Bangladesh*, "Energies" 2018, 11, p. 2433.

[12]   J. A. Sainz, *New Wind Turbine Manufacturing Techniques*, "Procedia Engineering" 2015, 132, p. 884.

predictable energy costs and investment outlays are very important from the economic point of view of companies.

However, the use of electricity produced from renewable energy sources depends on the weather conditions. This is a major difference compared to conventional power plants. Differences in demand and supply can be bridged by the "uberisation" of the energy network. In the near future, an alternative model of functioning on the virtual power plant market may become popular, in which companies will move away from owning generation units to renting them, thus developing a market of aggregators, which will concentrate many small and private installations (mainly RES) and manage them as one large virtual power plant.[13] The development of virtual power plants may reduce the interest of investors in traditional power units, and dispersed and flexible producers of energy obtained from RES will be able to supply cheap energy in a competitive manner. Devices operating in Industry 4.0 will automatically send information to a virtual power plant about the demand for energy that they will receive in the most efficient and cost-effective way. The best effect would be to integrate all solutions through economy 4.0 technologies and create a "smart grid"—low and medium voltage electricity grids that are able to respond to local shifts in the demand and supply of electricity.[14] Solar and wind farms can be intelligent energy systems if new technologies such as the Internet of Things are used in combination with artificial intelligence. Robotisation, which increasingly concerns transport and logistics itself, also requires energy, for example, autonomous vehicles that can only be powered by electricity.

Industry 4.0 may be beneficial for the development of Polish enterprises provided that appropriate implementation of new technologies and active action in the area of innovation are carried out. Potential opportunities and threats of Industry 4.0 for Poland are presented in Table 2. Taking advantage of the opportunities offered by Industry 4.0 depends on the implementation of new technologies, especially Big Data and the Internet of Things. The benefits resulting from the development of new sectors, productivity growth and the creation of new jobs with high added value are achievable through an appropriate system of education of specialists and the use of tools offered by Industry 4.0. Another important factor in the implementation of new technologies is access to infrastructure that will ensure stable and low-cost energy supply and access to broadband Internet. Lack of action in this area may reinforce the risks associated with the fourth industrial revolution. Rapid growth of Industry 4.0 in Western countries can result in the relocation of part of the production outside the country. The competitiveness of Polish companies will change due to the reduction of their cost advantage. An additional significant threat is the possibility of structural unemployment with the simultaneous emergence of new jobs through the misalignment of workers' qualifications to new market needs.

---

[13]　*Gospodarka 4.0. Czas zmiany dla biznesu*, Raport PKN Orlen, Warszawa 2017, p. 42.
[14]　Ibidem.

Table 2. Potential opportunities and threats of Industry 4.0 for Poland

Opportunities	• Better meeting consumers' needs	Products designed for individual orders, manufactured in small batches (mass customisation)
	• Productivity growth	Industry 4.0 allows for optimisation of the production process, shortening of downtime, better allocation of resources and creation of new products
	• New high value-added jobs	New jobs focused on automation and IT as well as new industries related to the cooperation of robots with people are also being created
	• Innovative economy	The economy is becoming more and more innovative, also enabling the expansion of technology abroad
	• Attractiveness for investors	High competence of employees and dynamically developing innovative economy, with appropriate mechanisms, attracts investors
	• Development of new industries	Development of new industries thanks to suppliers of Industry 4.0 solutions and companies implementing these solutions
	• Decrease in production costs	Improving product quality and reducing inventory cuts production costs
	• Efficient use of materials and energy	Rational use of materials and improved energy efficiency go hand in hand with sustainability
Threats	• Job losses	Industry 4.0 can result in workers being replaced by new solutions (e.g. robots); their reemployment requires new skills
	• Inadequacy of staff qualifications	Industry 4.0 creates jobs with skills other than those it replaces; without proper training there is a high risk of co-existence of vacancies and structural unemployment
	• Outflow of a part of the industry from Poland	Implementation of solutions in other countries may make it beneficial for companies to relocate production back to, e.g. Western Europe (lower labour costs in Poland less important)
	• Decreasing the competitiveness of Polish companies	Polish companies, currently with a strong position on export markets due to cost advantages, may lose their competitiveness
	• Advantage of foreign providers of 4.0 solutions	Later development of Industry 4.0 than in developed countries may mean a significant advantage of foreign technology suppliers from the very beginning

Source: *Przemysł 4.0 PL. Szansa czy zagrożenie dla rozwoju innowacyjnej gospodarki?*, The Boston Consulting Group, 2016, p. 25.

In recent years, the innovativeness of the Polish economy has increased, as has the ability to think about innovations. Examples of the effects of such a change include, among others, the construction of a new R&D infrastructure and strengthening of the competences of staff implementing innovative projects. Adequate human capital is crucial for the development of innovativeness of enterprises through the creation of products and services with high added value, which in turn affects the competitiveness of enterprises. The development of the fourth industrial revolution may help to build a competitive advantage at the level of the whole country and individual regions. In this process, it is important to have adequate human capital (educated specialists), access to infrastructure enabling the use of new technologies and stable and cheap energy supplies. Industry 4.0 enables large-scale direct trade through Internet-based communication.

The photovoltaic solution to the needs of the Industry 4.0

Solar energy is one of the main sources of renewable energy on which the modern and future industry will be based. In addition to energy security issues—energy, which they provide in the event of interruptions in its supply from power plants based on conventional sources—it also has many positive aspects such as reducing losses associated with energy transmission, supplying energy to regions where it is lacking or the cost of bringing energy from traditional sources is too expensive. It should also be remembered that solar energy is the most abundant renewable energy source in the world, because solar radiation, with varying intensity, reaches everywhere. The potential for direct conversion of solar energy into electricity,[15] without contaminating the environment, is also great, which is not the case with the production of electricity from traditional fossil fuels.

Photovoltaics finds application in virtually every area of human life and business. From powering small, several-watt electronic devices, such as watches, calculators and mobile phones, through autonomous systems supplying street traffic lights and installations in private residential buildings, with solar farms from a few kW up to several dozen or even several hundred megawatts.[16]

The installed capacity in solar energy increases regularly every year. According to data published by the International Energy Agency Photovoltaic Power System Program (IEA-PVPS), the capacity installed in solar farms worldwide in 2018 exceeded 500 GW.[17] Figure 1 shows the results in this regard in 2000–2018.

With every year a dynamic increase in the power installed in solar farms can be observed. A large increase was recorded especially after 2007, in which 8.31 GW of capacity was installed, and a year later this result was increased by as much as 74%. China, where the largest number of solar cells and modules is produced, has had the largest share in this area for many years. In 2018 there was 176.1 GW of solar power installed in the country.[18]

---

[15] M. Ziółko, *Rozwój fotowoltaiki w Polsce na tle innych krajów Unii Europejskiej* [in:] *Energetyka solarna w badaniach naukowych*, ed. by P. Kwiatkiewicz, Fundacja na rzecz Czystej Energii, Poznań 2018, p. 39.
[16] M. Sibiński, K. Znajdek, *Przyrządy i instalacje fotowoltaiczne*, Wydawnictwo Naukowe PWN, Warszawa 2016, p. 85.
[17] http://www.iea-pvps.org (access: 26 July 2019).
[18] Ibidem (access: 27 May 2019).

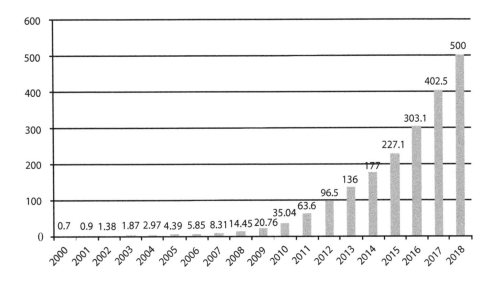

Figure 1. Cumulated capacity installed in solar farms worldwide in the years 2000–2018 in GW

Source: prepared by the authors, based on: http://www.iea-pvps.org (access: 26 July 2019).

Photovoltaic development in European countries

Germany is the leader on the European market of renewable energy sources. It is a country with very similar sunlight conditions to Poland. Wind farms and other energy sources that do not emit environmental pollution also play an important role in energy management there. Northern Europe, due to the proximity of the Pole, on a European scale has a lower value of energy obtained from solar radiation. It remains at the level of 900–1000 kWh/m²/year. The largest sun exposure occurs in the southern part of the continent, where this value can reach up to 2000 kWh/m²/year in the Mediterranean region.[19]

In the conducted research, outside of Poland, countries such as Germany, Romania and Ukraine will serve as an example of photovoltaic development. These countries are located a short distance from each other, which translates into comparable climatic conditions. This has indisputable impact on the possibilities of photovoltaic development. Three of the analysed countries (Poland, Germany, Romania) are members of the European Union, which gives them similar opportunities in the use of financial resources that the Community allocates to the development of renewable energy. This is also associated with similar restrictions in the field of low carbon economy to which

---

[19]   K. Mientus, *Energia Słońca – aspekty ekologiczne i ekonomiczne*, Politechnika Opolska, Opole 2011, p. 3.

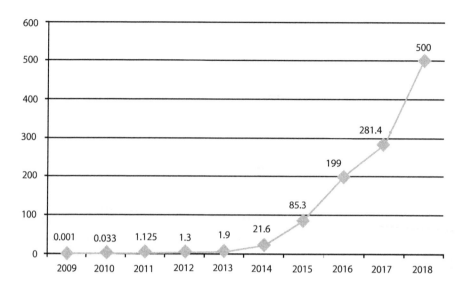

Figure 2. Cumulated PV power installed in Poland in the years 2009–2018 including micro-installations in MW

Source: prepared by the authors, based on: http://www.iea-pvps.org (access: 26 July 2019); https://www.ure.gov.pl/pl/rynki-energii/energia-elektryczna/odnawialne-zrodla-ener/potencjal-krajowy--oze/5753,Moc-zainstalowana-MW.html (access: 29 June 2019); http://gramwzielone.pl/energia--sloneczna/21522/w-2015-r-przylaczono-74-mwp-nowych-mocy-w-fotowoltaice (access: 8 July 2019); http://ieo.pl/pl/aktualnosci/1181-raport-rynek-fotowoltaiki-w-polsce-2018 (access: 8 July 2019); http://ieo.pl/pl/projekty/raport-rynek-fotowoltaiki-w-polsce-2018 (access: 8 July 2019); https://magazynfotowoltaika.pl/moc-fotowoltaiki-zainstalowana-w-polsce-raport/ (access: 10 July 2019); https://ieo.pl/pl/projekty/raport--rynek-fotowoltaiki-w-polsce-2019 (access: 1 August 2019).

the Member States are subject. To compare this aspect, an example of Ukraine was presented, which, despite not using EU support, has installed a capacity much higher than that of many Member States. An interesting aspect in the selection of the countries surveyed is their level of economic development, which further enriches the analysis with diversity and uncertainty about the expected results.

Poland is the first analysed country, it does not belong to countries with very sunny weather; its sunshine duration varies from 1400 to 1900 h per year.[20] The Polish solar market has a huge, but still untapped potential for development. The total capacity installed in solar energy in Poland at the end of 2018 was about 500 MW, while in May 2019 it exceeded 700 MW.[21] The increase of installed power in photovoltaics over the last 10 years is shown in Figure 2.

---

[20] S. Leszczycki, R. Domański, *Geografia Polski społeczno-ekonomiczna*, PWN, Warszawa 1992, p. 100.
[21] https://ieo.pl/pl/projekty/raport-rynek-fotowoltaiki-w-polsce-2019 (access: 1 July 2019).

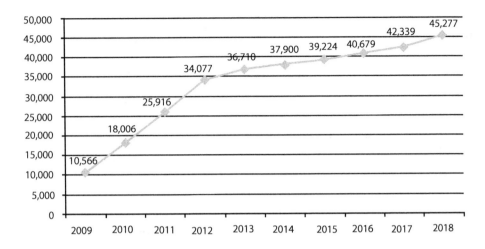

Figure 3. Cumulated power installed in solar farms in Germany in the years 2009–2018 (MW)

Source: prepared by the authors, based on: https://www.umweltbundesamt.de/sites/default/files/medien/376/publikationen/180315_uba_hg_eeinzahlen_2018_bf.pdf (access: 8 July 2019); https://www.umweltbundesamt.de/sites/default/files/medien/1410/publikationen/uba_hgp_eeinzahlen_2019_bf.pdf (access: 28 July 2019).

Currently in Poland micro-installations have a large share in the total installed capacity in photovoltaics—about 350 MW (as of February 2019). A significant part of photovoltaic micro-installations (about 75% of capacity) are those with up to 50 kW (in practice up to 10 kW) implemented by individual prosumers, i.e. household investments. The remaining are micro-installations in local governments and enterprises with 10–50 kW (the so-called business prosumer). In recent years, the increase in new installations is very dynamic,[22] probably due to the auction system introduced in 2015.[23]

Germany is the second country analysed. Total radiation in this country oscillates around 900–1200 kWh/m²/year.[24] For example, for Berlin, the average value is 1050 kWh/m²/year.[25] Germany is the unquestioned European leader in the field of photovoltaics and one of the countries at the forefront in terms of installed capacity in solar energy. In 2018, the total accumulated power installed in solar farm was 45,277 MW[26] (Figure 3).

---

[22]   https://ieo.pl/pl/projekty/raport-rynek-fotowoltaiki-w-polsce-2019 (access: 7 July 2019).

[23]   M. Trela, A. Dubel, *Porównanie systemów wsparcia odnawialnych źródeł energii w Polsce: zielone certyfikaty vs system aukcyjny, na przykładzie instalacji PV*, "Polityka Energetyczna – Energy Policy Journal" 2017, 20 (2), p. 108.

[24]   http://www.imn.htwk-leipzig.de/~stich/Bilder_UCH/II.II.pdf (access: 6 July 2019).

[25]   *Neutronenaktivierungsanalyse in Archäometrie und Solarenergieforschung*, https://publications.ub.uni-mainz.de/theses/volltexte/2016/100000548/pdf/100000548.pdf (access: 6 July 2018).

[26]   https://www.umweltbundesamt.de/sites/default/files/medien/1410/publikationen/uba_hgp_eeinzahlen_2019_bf.pdf (access: 28 July 2019).

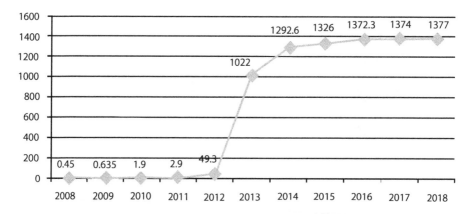

Figure 4. Cumulated PV capacity installed in Romania in the years 2008–2018 (MW)

Source: prepared by the authors, based on: https://www.eurobserv-er.org/category/all-photovoltaic-
-barometers/(access: 8 July 2019).

The largest increase in power can be observed in 2010–2012. During this period, the largest photovoltaic farms with capacities exceeding 100MW[27] were created in Germany. At the end of 2018, installations with a capacity above 500 kW accounted for about 32% in Germany, installations with a capacity of 100 to 500 kW accounted for 14%, while smaller installations with a capacity of 10 to 100 kW and below 10 kW accounted for 40% and 14% respectively.[28]

The photovoltaic industry in Germany has developed and systematically increased the capacity installed in solar power plants each year, mainly thanks to state support and EU funds.

In the next studied country, Romania, the average annual sunshine duration varies from 2200 hours in most areas of the country to 1800 hours in the mountains.[29] The largest number of sunny days here falls in July—280.7, while the least in December—58.[30] The highest annual values are recorded on the coast of the Black Sea and reach over 2300 hours per year.[31] In 2018, Romania had a total installed capacity of approximately

[27]   http://sunenergysite.eu/en/pvpowerplants/top50pv.php (access: 27 June 2019).

[28]   F. Klausmann, L. Zhu, *Technologiestudie Microgrid Markt- und Technologieübersicht für Komponenten eines Microgrids,* Fraunhofer-Institut für Arbeitswirtschaft und Organisation IAO in Stuttgart, Stuttgart 2018, p. 11, https://www.iat.uni-stuttgart.de/dokumente/smales/Technologiestudie-Microgrid_final_190221.pdf (access: 30 July 2019).

[29]   A. G. Lupuiinni, *SWOT Analysis of the Renewable Energy Sources in Romania—Case Study: Solar Energy,* 7th International Conference on Advanced Concepts in Mechanical Engineering, "Materials Science and Engineering" 2016, 147, p. 5.

[30]   E. Erhan, *Nebulozitatea și durata de strlucire a Soarelui la Iași în ultimie 50 de ani,* Lucrările Seminarului Geografic "Dimitrie Cantemir" 1993–1994, 13–14, p. 47.

[31]   http://www.vremea.ro/gt/durata-de-stralucire-a-soarelui/ (access: 7 July 2019).

1377 MW.[32] Figure 4 summarises the power installed in solar energy in Romania over the years 2009–2018.

In the years 2010–2013, there was a very dynamic development of investments in renewable energy structures in Romania, caused by the creation by the Government of Romania of "Certificateverzi"—green certificates, that is the investment support system in renewable energy sources.[33] This also translated into increased interest in solar energy in this country, which experienced a kind of "boom" mainly in 2013. A very generous system of support from the state for companies producing electricity from renewable sources, in a short time meant that more than 1500 windmills were installed in the country, and hectares of land were covered with solar panels.[34] The year 2013 brought the largest investments in solar energy, at that time the largest solar farms in the country were created, with an installed capacity above 50MW each.[35] Due to the pressure of large entities producing electricity,[36] in June 2013 the Romanian government issued a regulation in which it decided to suspend the issuing of green certificates to entrepreneurs producing renewable energy.[37] The effects of the abolition of support are noticeable in the annual increase in installed capacity in Romania shown in Figure 4. The effect of the support mechanisms used is also participation in the Romanian photovoltaic potential of micro-installations. Currently, almost 100% of the capacity installed in Romanian solar energy are systems included in the industrial segment. No other European Union country has such a large share of industrial solar farms in the total share of solar farms, but thanks to the support mechanisms of smaller PV producers now implemented, this situation will probably change in the near future.[38]

Ukraine is the last analysed country. The average annual sunshine duration is around 2347 h.[39] Insolation values increase from northwest to southeast and south from 1700 to 2400 h. The lowest rates are observed in northern Ukraine (1720–1800 h). The most sunny hours are recorded on the shores of the Black and Azov Seas (2300–2400 h), and on the southern slopes of Crimea (over 2400 h).[40] In 2018, the installed capacity of solar farm exceeded 2000 MW. The increase of available power in 2008–2019, according to

---

[32] https://www.eurobserv-er.org/category/all-photovoltaic-barometers (access: 8 July 2019).

[33] *Analiza rumuńskiego rynku energii 2016*, https://romania.trade.gov.pl/pl/ (access: 13 July 2019).

[34] Ibidem (access: 13 July 2018).

[35] http://www.nineoclock.ro/green-vision-seven-makes-operational-romania%E2%80%99s-largest-so-lar-farm/ (access: 30 June 2019).

[36] A. Piziak-Rapacz, *Bezpieczeństwo energetyczne Rumunii*, "Bezpieczeństwo: Teoria i Praktyka. Czasopismo Krakowskiej Szkoły Wyższej im. Andrzeja Frycza Modrzewskiego" 2014, 3 (16), p. 48.

[37] Government Regulation of June 7, 2013 concerning changes in the granting of "green certificates" to renewable energy companies, Romanian OJ, Part I, No. 335/7.

[38] *Rumuński rząd hojny dla prosumentów. Nawet 90 proc. dopłaty*, https://gramwzielone.pl/energia-slone-czna/32391/rumunski-rzad-hojny-dla-prosumentow-nawet-90-proc-doplaty (access: 26 July 2019).

[39] http://www.crimea.climatemps.com/ (access: 07 July 2019).

[40] P. A. Maslyak, P. G. Shishchenko, *Geografia Ukrainy – podręcznik*, Zodiac-ECO, Kijów 2000, p. 50.

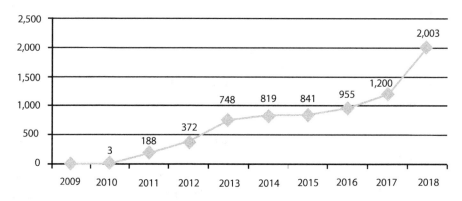

Figure 5. Cumulated capacity installed in solar farms in Ukraine in the years 2009–2018

Source: prepared by the author, based on:https://www.irena.org//media/Files/IRENA/Agency/Publication/2019/Mar/IRENA_RE_Capacity_Statistics_2019.pdf (access: 8 July 2019).

the Renewable Energy Capacity Statistics 2019 report, prepared by the International Renewable Energy Agency, is shown in Figure 5.

Since 2010, a significant increase in the installed capacity in solar farms in Ukraine can be observed. The reason for interest in solar energy in this country is probably due to high rates for the sale of energy produced in above-ground solar farms, which are among the highest in Europe. In the years 2017–2019 the tariff for the sale of energy was about 0.15 EUR/kWh, while before 2017 it was even higher and amounted to about 0.16 EUR/kWh.[41] Such rates also encouraged foreign investors to build solar power plants in Ukraine which has undoubtedly translated into an increase in installed capacity in this country in individual years covered by the analysis.

In recent years, the prosumer micro-installations segment in Ukraine has grown more and more dynamically due to financial incentives in the form of the introduction of the so-called net-metering system, thanks to which households can sell surplus energy produced after balancing at a price of about 0.18 EUR/kWh. This regulation includes solar systems up to 30 kW.[42] At the end of 2018, a total of 157 MW of capacity in prosumer installations (micro-installations) was installed in Ukraine.[43]

---

[41] http://biznesalert.pl/rosnie-popularnosc-fotowoltaiki-ukrainie/ (access: 9 July 2019).

[42] Ibidem.

[43] http://zora-irpin.info/za-5-rokiv-v-ukrayini-vstanovleno-7450-domashnih-sonyachnih-stantsij-zagalnoyu-potuzhnistyu-158-mvt-i-vartistyu-151-mln-yevro/ (access: 8 July 2019).

Summary

The development of Industry 4.0. is an improvement in the efficiency and speed of response to changing market needs. Progressing automation and robotisation increase the quality of manufactured goods and services with a high level of process reliability. Digitisation is an opportunity for the development of industries and the economy, which is why the key is to adopt an appropriate strategy that will use the opportunities of Industry 4.0. An innovative approach and early initiation of a change process is an important step towards the fourth industrial revolution whose development has a direct impact on renewable energy sources. New technologies will enable a cheaper and more efficient way of generating energy from solar cells with the involvement of new materials and modern ways of managing renewable energy infrastructure. The economy based on digitisation needs stable electricity which can be provided by solar farms. Technological progress constantly reduces the cost of producing and storing renewable energy at zero primary energy, and lower costs are an opportunity to increase competitiveness.

In recent years there has been a large increase in the installed capacity of solar farms, especially in the form of large solar power plants. The development of new technologies will increase the production of energy from renewable energy sources, including PV. Economies with a large share of renewable energy in the overall energy balance can gain an advantage in the process of change associated with the fourth industrial revolution.

Based on the research conducted among the analysed countries, it can be concluded that the German economy is best prepared to implement the assumptions of Industry 4.0 in the field of renewable energy, while the Polish economy has the least preparation in this respect, due to the lowest installed capacity and a small percentage of the share of this capacity in industrial installations. The list of the most important variables used for the analysis in individual countries is presented in Table 3.

Table 3. Summary of the most important data used in the analysis

Country	Insolation in h	Accumulated installed capacity in MW	Installed capacity in 2018 in MW	% of installed capacity in industrial installations
Poland	about 1,600	about 500	about 219	30
Germany	about 1,050	about 45,277	about 2,938	46*
Romania	about 2,000	about 1,377	about 4	99
Ukraine	about 2,347	about 2,003	about 803	92

* installations with a capacity over 100kW
Source: prepared by the authors.

Industry 4.0 is not only new technologies, but also a new way of functioning on the market. The development of virtual power plants can revolutionise energy supplies, and distributed and flexible renewable energy producers will be able to provide cheap energy in a competitive way. The stability of electricity supply and the possibility of distributed supply in places of energy production is important for the development of Industry 4.0. Integrating all solutions through Industry 4.0 technologies and creating a smart grid will allow to respond to local shifts in electricity demand and supply. The potential for direct conversion of solar energy into electricity without environmental pollution is also great. As results from the conducted analysis, the level of sunshine in a given country is not the main determinant of the choice of solar plant location. The best example of this is Germany, which according to research has the lowest average annual sunshine (Table 3), yet owns the largest power installed in solar farms among the countries studied.

Appropriate development in the realities of Industry 4.0 also depends on regulations that favour new business models and innovative technologies, and the forms of support in individual countries affect the emergence of new investments in renewable energy. Based on the research carried out, it can be seen that in countries where state aid is higher, the percentage of solar industrial installations in the total installed capacity in solar farms is also greater. This type of investment is more profitable for a potential investor. Various types of support also attract foreign investors, and thus new investments. Therefore, states should adapt regulations to take into account the needs of enterprises and consumers. The right approach could contribute to the reindustrialisation and improvement of the competitive position of the industry in individual countries. By creating the right framework for economic policy, including ensuring adequate preparation of the labour market, it is possible to positively influence the benefits of the fourth industrial revolution.

Bibliography

Analiza rumuńskiego rynku energii 2016, https://romania.trade.gov.pl/pl/ (access: 13 July 2019).

Chowdhury N., Hossain C. A., Longo M., Yaïci W., *Optimization of Solar Energy System for the Electric Vehicle at University Campus in Dhaka, Bangladesh*, "Energies" 2018, 11.

Dalenogare L. S., Benitez G. B., Ayala N. F., Frank A. G., *The Expected Contribution of Industry 4.0 Technologies for Industrial Performance*, "International Journal of Production Economics" 2018, 204.

Erhan E., *Nebulozitatea și durata de strlucire a Soarelui la Iași în ultimie 50 de ani*, Lucrările Seminarului Geografic "Dimitrie Cantemir" 1993–1994, 13–14.

Frank A. G., Dalenogare L. S., Ayala N. F., *Industry 4.0 Technologies: Implementation Patterns in Manufacturing Companies*, "International Journal of Production Economics" 2019, 210.

Gospodarka 4.0. Czas zmiany dla biznesu, Raport PKN Orlen, Warszawa 2017.

Government Regulation of June 7, 2013 concerning changes in the granting of "green certificates" to renewable energy companies, Romanian OJ, Part I, No. 335/7.

Kamble S. S., Gunasekaran A., Gawankar S. A., *Sustainable Industry 4.0 Framework: A Systematic Literature Review Identifying the Current Trends and Future Perspectives*, "Process Safety and Environmental Protection" 2018, 117.

Kayikci Y., *Sustainability Impact of Digitization in Logistics*, 15th Global Conference on Sustainable Manufacturing, "Procedia Manufacturing" 2018, 21.

Klausmann F., Zhu L., *Technologiestudie Microgrid Markt- und Technologieübersicht für Komponenteneines Microgrids,* Fraunhofer Institut für Arbeitswirtschaft und Organisation IAO im Stuttgart, Stuttgart 2018, https://www.iat.uni-stuttgart.de/dokumente/smales/Technologiestudie-Microgrid_final_190221.pdf (access: 30 July 2019).

Leszczycki S., Domański R., *Geografia Polski społeczno-ekonomiczna*, PWN, Warszawa 1992.

Lupuiinni A. G., *SWOT Analysis of the Renewable Energy Sources in Romania: Case Study: Solar Energy*, 7th International Conference on Advanced Concepts in Mechanical Engineering, "Materials Science and Engineering" 2016, 147.

Maslyak P. A., Shishchenko P. G., *Geografia Ukrainy – podręcznik*, Zodiac-ECO, Kijów 2000.

Mientus K., *Energia Słońca – aspekty ekologiczne i ekonomiczne*, Politechnika Opolska, Opole 2011.

Neutronenaktivierungsanalyse in Archäometrie und Solarenergieforschung, https://publications.ub.uni mainz.de/theses/volltexte/2016/100000548/pdf/100000548.pdf (access: 6 July 2018).

Piziak-Rapacz A., *Bezpieczeństwo energetyczne Rumunii*, "Bezpieczeństwo: Teoria i Praktyka. Czasopismo Krakowskiej Szkoły Wyższej im. Andrzeja Frycza Modrzewskiego" 2014, 3 (16).

Przemysł 4.0 PL. Szansa czy zagrożenie dla rozwoju innowacyjnej gospodarki?, Boston Consulting Group, 2016.

Rakotonirainy A., Orfila O., Gruyer D., *Reducing Driver's Behavioural Uncertainties Using an Interdisciplinary Approach: Convergence of Quantified Self, Automated Vehicles, Internet of Things and Artificial Intelligence*, "IFAC-Papers Online" 2016 (49–32).

Rumuński rząd hojny dla prosumentów. Nawet 90 proc. dopłaty, https://gramwzielone.pl/energia--sloneczna/32391/rumunski-rzad-hojny-dla-prosumentow-nawet-90-proc-doplaty (access: 26 July 2019).

Sainz J. A., *New Wind Turbine Manufacturing Techniques*, "Procedia Engineering" 2015, 132.

Sibiński M., Znajdek K., *Przyrządy i instalacje fotowoltaiczne*, Wydawnictwo Naukowe PWN, Warszawa 2016.

Trela M., Dubel A., *Porównanie systemów wsparcia odnawialnych źródeł energii w Polsce: zielone certyfikaty vs system aukcyjny, na przykładzie instalacji PV*, "Polityka Energetyczna – Energy Policy Journal" 2017, 20 (2).

Wappa P., *Using of Artificial Intelligence Methods in Logistics*, "Economy and Management" 2011, 4.

Zhong R. Y., Xu X., Klotz E., Newman S. T., *Intelligent Manufacturing in the Context of Industry 4.0: A Review*, "Engineering" 2017, 3 (5).

Ziółko M., *Rozwój fotowoltaiki w Polsce na tle innych krajów Unii Europejskiej* [in:] *Energetyka solarna w badaniach naukowych*, ed. by P. Kwiatkiewicz, Fundacja na rzecz Czystej Energii, Poznań 2018.

Employee Loyalty in the ICT Sector as a Challenge for Building Industry 4.0

Prof. Jerzy Rosiński, Ph.D.   https://orcid.org/0000-0002-8348-2839
Jagiellonian University

Abstract

Reflecting on employee loyalty in regards to persons from ICT appears to be valid at least for two reasons: firstly, as a professional group, they were (and in part of this group, will remain) the creators of Industry 4.0; secondly, the processes which are currently specific to employees of the ICT sector may, after several years, apply to larger professional groups. The text presents employee loyalty specific to employees of the ICT sector which can be described as a mercantile relationship focused on other professionals from the industry, and on one's own professional development. Conclusions on the nature of this loyalty are based on the author's own study. The text also presents the consequences of this specifically profiled loyalty of employees of the ICT sector at the organisational level, and with regard to the level of functioning of broader communities.

Keywords: employee loyalty, Industry 4.0, development, ICT sector, professional growth, organisation

Understanding loyalty

Loyalty as a concept is defined in a variety of ways. This is, on the one hand, due to the level of detail contained in the definition (from universal to detailed descriptions), while, on the other hand, loyalty is described within the bounds of different sciences, and therefore is referred to different and often overlapping areas (particularly in social sciences).

First of all, loyalty is a term defined by philosophy. For example, J. Royce[1] defines loyalty as a dedication to a given cause both in the sphere of volition and action. Dictionary definitions remain on a similar level of universalism in description, but they

---

[1]   After A. Lewicka-Strzałecka, *Lojalność pracownika: trwała wartość czy anachroniczna cnota?*, ed. by W. Banach, Adam Mickiewicz University Press, Poznań 2014, p. 149.

also include functional aspects of loyalty, as for example J. Kleinig[2] who mentions the importance of loyalty to maintain the functioning of the organisation, and maintaining the principle of reciprocity in social life.

From the definition of a universal nature we move to more detailed descriptions within individual social sciences. Thus, in psychology we can come across loyalty defined in, among others, social psychology and family psychology to the psychology of consumer behaviour.[3] The subject of loyalty, e.g. in the design of the educational system and directions of education is also undertaken by pedagogy.[4] With regard to the functioning of social groups and in a broader sense, cultural loyalty is described by sociology.[5] In terms of economy, loyalty is viewed as consumer loyalty[6] and employee loyalty.[7]

The next step towards detailed descriptions is a reference to management and employee loyalty. Yet even when narrowing the definition down to employee loyalty, we encounter a problem consisting in the fact that we identify two extremes:

- The definitions are very general, which is perhaps intended by their authors to ensure their universal character: "Loyalty is a particular attitude of the employee towards his or her employer."[8]
- The definitions are detailed and focus on one of the areas of employee loyalty, such as the employee continuing to remain in the current organisation, and his or her engaged work regardless of temporary problems in the place of employment;[9] identification with the objectives of the company, trust towards the employer, a community of values and needs;[10] speaking highly of the employer and rejecting proposals to work in other companies.[11]

---

[2]   Ibidem, pp. 152–153.

[3]   E. Aronson et al., *Psychologia społeczna – serce i umysł*, transl. A. Bezwińska, Wydawnictwo Zysk i S-ka, Warszawa 1997, p. 405; M. Bryła, *Lojalność konsumenta w aspekcie nowoczesnej psychologii*, "Marketing i Rynek" 2008, 5; E. Jerzyk, A. Disterheft, *Proces zakupu online w świetle badań okulograficznych – rola opakowania, opisu i ceny produktu*, "Studia Ekonomiczne" 2017, 342, pp. 39–51.

[4]   B. Śliwerski, *Kryzys oświatowej demokracji w świetle makropolitycznych badań pedagogicznych*, "Przegląd Pedagogiczny" 2016, 2, pp. 313–322.

[5]   P. Sztompka, *Socjologia. Analiza społeczeństwa*, Społeczny Instytut Wydawniczy Znak, Kraków 2012.

[6]   K. Kolasińska-Morawska, *E-konsument nowej generacji wyzwaniem przedsiębiorstw w XXI w.*, "Studia Ekonomiczne" 2016, 255, pp. 28–36.

[7]   D. Smarżewska, *Uwarunkowania lojalności pracowników wobec organizacji – aspekty teoretyczne*, "Przedsiębiorczość i Zarządzanie" 2018, 19 (8), part 1: *Wyzwania w zarządzaniu zasobami ludzkimi we współczesnych organizacjach. Od teorii do praktyki*, pp. 183–195; E. Studzińska, *Lojalność klienta – pojęcie, podział, rodzaje i stopnie*, Wydawnictwo Uniwersytetu Ekonomicznego we Wrocławiu, Wrocław 2015.

[8]   E. Robak, *Lojalność pracowników a zarządzanie potencjałem społecznym współczesnych organizacji*, "Zeszyty Naukowe Politechniki Częstochowskiej. Zarządzanie" 2016, 24 (2), p. 83.

[9]   A. Lipka et al., *Lojalność pracownicza. Od diagnozy typów pracowników do Zarządzania Relacjami z Pracownikami (Employee Relationship Management)*, Difin, Warszawa 2012; E. Robak, *Lojalność pracowników...*, p. 83.

[10] K. Piórkowska-Wojciechowska, *Wybrane problemy kształtowania i badania lojalności pracowniczej*, "Prace Naukowe Akademii Ekonomicznej im. Oskara Langego we Wrocławiu" 2014, 1032, p. 70.

[11] U. Bukowska, *Lojalność pracowników – ujęcie atrybutowe i procesowe* [in:] *Nauka i gospodarka w dobie destabilizacji*, ed. by J. Teczke, J. Czekaj, B. Mikuła, R. Oczkowska, Biuro Projektu Nauka i Gospodarka, Kraków 2011, pp. 26–27, after E. Robak, *Lojalność pracowników...*, p. 83.

The general attempts at a precise definition of employee loyalty are universal, however they may bring little in terms of explanation. When it comes to detailed descriptions, the definitions have certain expectations embedded in them, which one should consider as unrealistic, such as linking loyalty with a constant commitment of the employee.[12]

In order to find the best way to define employee loyalty and balance the extremes of searching for a universal nature and attention to detail, we should return to the broader context, i.e. to the social sciences mentioned earlier. A recurring motif in social sciences is describing loyalty in two aspects:

- The attitude of righteousness, truthfulness and reliability in relations with a group of people known as "we," resulting from the provisions of law and formal standards.[13]
- Bond, attachment and engagement arising from the relationship, the decision not to abuse the confidence of someone who trusts me.[14]

In both cases this may be loyalty to the company, to the people who work at that company, or it could concern customer loyalty towards the products offered by a given company. But what we have here are two sources of loyalty. In the first case, it has to do with standards external to the individual and a conformist obedience, while in the second case, it regards a personal decision resulting from a relationship.

This distinction also applies to the already mentioned philosophical reflection relating to the concept of loyalty. The above mentioned aspects are also reflected in the breakdown of loyalty into unchosen and chosen. It is the second kind of loyalty (the chosen one) that refers to the act of an informed and voluntary decision to participate in activities of a given social group.[15]

In this text, I would like to examine this second thematic area: employee loyalty resulting from a relationship, based on a decision made by the employee.

The importance of loyalty

Reflection on the importance of loyalty refers to at least several areas. For the purposes of the current analysis, the context ought to be briefly presented in relation to: the economy, the organisation, and the individual employee.

In relation to the economy, we often think beyond employee loyalty and we speak more broadly about loyalty as a component describing social capital—directly

---

[12]   Ibidem.
[13]   See: E. Studzińska, *Lojalność klienta…*, p. 196; P. Sztompka, *Socjologia…*, p. 144.
[14]   Ibidem.
[15]   See J. Kleinig, *Loyalty* [in:] *Stanford Encyclopedia of Philosophy*, http://plato.stanford.edu/entries/loyalty/ (access: 20 December 2013), after A. Lewicka-Strzałecka, *Lojalność pracownika…*, pp. 152–153.

associated with the potential of economic development.[16] Loyalty understood as "the obligation not to abuse the confidence of someone who trusts me"[17] is not a historical construct. On the contrary, in the context of the transformations of the fourth industrial revolution, the importance of trust is stressed as a key element for the development of the economy.[18]

Organisational contexts relative to the importance of loyalty reveal statements emphasising the importance of loyalty in the management of organisational transformations and achieving results in a changing environment.[19] What is also noted are the positive effects of loyalty for employee management, such as a reduced staff turnover, less sick time and a lower susceptibility to the offers of the competition, as well as greater involvement in the work and life of the company, along with increased creativity.[20] In addition to effects which are directly related to the definition of loyalty, such as increased confidence in the work team, there appear to be less clear implications as well, such as the promotion of the employer's positive image.[21]

Also in the context of how individual employees function, loyalty is described as a significant variable. In relations between co-workers, loyalty supports the principle of reciprocity, stabilising and making group relations predictable. In terms of individual functioning, it is tied to having a stable identity and conditioning a narrative life structure of a given individual. It is stressed that the absence of any loyalty means functioning from one preference to another, social alienation and difficulties in achieving individual goals.[22]

Industry 4.0

The processes of changes in technology and production known as the fourth industrial revolution are associated with profiled initiatives in different countries and regions of the world. In Europe, the fourth industrial revolution is often referred to as Industry 4.0; in the USA, the term used is Manufacturing Partnership 2.0; in China, it is called the Made in China 2025 initiative; while Japan carries out their initiatives under the

---

[16] P. Sztompka, *Kapitał społeczny. Teoria przestrzeni międzyludzkiej*, Społeczny Instytut Wydawniczy Znak, Kraków 2016.

[17] P. Sztompka, *Socjologia…*, p. 144.

[18] A. Małysa-Kaleta, *Zaufanie w relacjach rynkowych na współczesnym rynku*, Uniwersytet Ekonomiczny w Katowicach, Katowice 2015, pp. 160–161; K. Czernek et. al., *Zaufanie w gospodarce współdzielenia*, "Gospodarka Narodowa" 2018, 3 (295), pp. 24–26.

[19] A. Konieczko, *Zmiany w organizacji a lojalność pracowników*; "Edukacja Ekonomistów i Menedżerów: Problemy. Innowacje. Projekty" 2012, 1 (23), pp. 43–59.

[20] E. Robak, *Lojalność pracowników…*, p. 87.

[21] Ibidem, p. 82.

[22] A. Lewicka-Strzałecka, *Lojalność pracownika…*, pp. 152–153.

name Revitalisation—robotic strategy 2020.[23] Various national and regional initiatives differ from each other, but their common areas include: smart machines connected in networks and data exchange for the formation of the so-called smart factories understood as independent, fully automated units, continuously optimising their production environment.[24]

Although the terms "fourth industrial revolution" and "Industry 4.0" are often used interchangeably, one needs to remember that the term Industry 4.0 was originally a name invented in 2010 by the German government to outline the long-term strategy for the development of modern technologies. However, over time (despite the existence of other national initiatives in the EU) it has become a term used to describe the transformation of the fourth industrial revolution in Europe.[25] The change referred to as Industry 4.0 is defined in business in the following manner (after experts from Siemens): "The completely IT-based interaction between human, product and machine."[26] This understanding is in line with the definition of Industry 4.0 in scientific literature as the introduction of the Internet of Things and Services into the manufacturing environment.[27]

Loyalty and transformations related to Industry 4.0

It can be presumed that due to the transformation processes referred to as Industry 4.0 the meaning of loyalty will change as well. As noted by P. Sztompka,[28] late capitalism is also characterised by a crisis of political and cultural legitimacy. Imminent crises in this area easily undermine the dominion of authorities, the loyalty and involvement of citizens and their collective identity. Using a certain simplification, one can paraphrase the above findings in the form of the conclusion that the changing social reality will cause a reduced adequacy in regards to descriptions of the existing models and a need to review them.

The already ongoing transformation in which the permanence of social groups (e.g. employee groups, but also neighbour groups) decreases is having an effect on loyalty. If we change jobs, and even professions, several times in our lifetime, the groups

[23] M. Rozkwitalska, J. Slavik, *Around Learning and Industry 4.0 in Management Theory*, "International Journal of Contemporary Management" 2017, 16 (4), pp. 192–193.
[24] V. Marik et al., *National Initiative Industry 4.0*, Praha 2015, http://www.spcr.cz/images/priloha001-2.pdf (access: 22 March 2016).
[25] M. Rozkwitalska, J. Slavik, *Around Learning...*, p. 192.
[26] Ibidem, p. 194.
[27] H. Kagermann et al., *Securing the Future of German Manufacturing Industry. Recommendations for Implementing the Strategic Initiative INDUSTRIE 4.0*, Industrie 4.0 Working Group, https://www.din.de/blob/76902/e8cac883f42bf28536e7e8165993f1fd/recommendations-for-implementing-industry-4-0-data.pdf, p. 5 (access: 23 April 2019).
[28] P. Sztompka, *Socjologia...*, p. 233.

treated as "lasting for life" will be regarded as provisional, which triggers a change in engagement, identification, loyalty, and the area of carrying out life plans within these groups.[29] Changing the context of individuals' social functioning also causes the existing rules of social functioning to relax, change their importance or even disappear. For example, the normative regulation for reciprocity obligating one to return favours offered and often regardless of how much time has passed[30] was essential for functioning in stable systems. When social groups become only temporary reference points, the rules describing recognised social habits also degrade.[31]

Previously stable social groups turning temporary is becoming a common phenomenon on the job market. The generation of the so-called millennials which currently saturates the job market has different attitudes toward professional work than their parents. This is to some extent a simplification, bordering on a stereotype, but it is worth noting the tendency described by Ch. Espinoza and M. Ukleja.[32] In their reflection, they point out that the generation of baby boomers lived to work; Generation X looks for a work-life balance; while the generation of millennials works to live, and it is not uncommon to work for one year and then completely change one's activity and spend the earned money to go out in the world in search of adventure.

The increased provisional character of social groups is not only a matter of generations—a certain generation describes the scale of the phenomenon, but it does not explain its internal mechanism. For a better understanding of the nature of the transformation, it is worth attempting to clarify the "mechanics" of a single social group as well, and then refer to the scale of the phenomenon as a multiplier of "simple, single" effects. Therefore, if we are entering a new group (e.g. a group of co-workers) with the assumption that it is provisional, we will show less commitment, less identification with the group, and we will observe standards with less dedication (because we believe that "we are here for a moment"). In a self-fulfilling prophecy, such a range of behaviours increases the likelihood to leave the current group and the need to assert one's place in a new one.[33]

It can be presumed that one of the scenarios will involve a faster dissolution of the functioning of traditional social groups and give new meaning, among other things, to the concept of loyalty.

---

[29]   Ibidem, p. 148.

[30]   R. Cialdini, *Wywieranie wpływu na ludzi. Teoria i praktyka*, Gdańskie Wydawnictwo Psychologiczne, Gdańsk 2013.

[31]   P. Sztompka, *Socjologia...*, p. 67.

[32]   Ch. Espinoza, M. Ukleja, *Zarządzanie milenialsami*, Wydawnictwo Naukowe PWN, Warszawa 2018, p. 40.

[33]   Ibidem, p. 148.

Employee loyalty in the ICT sector

Focusing on the loyalty of the people employed in the ICT sector appears to be valid at least for two reasons:[34] as a professional group, they were and in part of this group will remain the creators of Industry 4.0 (a part of the group goes from being "creators" to "technical support representatives"); processes currently true for employees of the ICT sector after several years apply to larger professional groups.

A feature of loyalty which seems to be characteristic for employees of the ICT sector is directing it to their professional group rather than the organisation (see Figure 1).

The reason for such loyalty profiling when it comes to people working in the ICT sector may be the three factors which distinguish this professional group from those employed outside of the ICT sector, concerning the perception of the relationship with colleagues:[35]

- Perceiving the atmosphere between colleagues as not too friendly.
- This conviction may result from a strong competition against other people from the industry (on the open job market of ICT people), other people are considered as potential competition, hence the perceived atmosphere is not very friendly.
- Reluctance to work together within a group of professionals working in ICT and to cooperate in carrying out tasks together with other teams/departments—this reluctance intensifies with time.

The above mentioned three phenomena found in the relationships among co-workers in the ICT sector can be integrated into the following claim: employees of the ICT sector are open to cooperation with people whose specialist competences they see as high. Toward other persons they may show reserve or distance. Such an attitude towards cooperation is consistent with the concept of calculative participation in an organisation,[36] which can be summarised in the following statement: "I am willing to cooperate only with those with whom it pays off to do so, for example through such cooperation with a particular person I'll acquire new specialist competences that will increase my market value."

How to explain the paradox of focusing on one's own professional growth and at the same time being reluctant to work with persons who do similar tasks? Along with the years worked, the level of specialist competences increases, and so does the

---

[34] See J. Rosiński, *Postawy zawodowe informatyków. Jednostka, zespół, organizacja*, Wydawnictwo Uniwersytetu Jagiellońskiego, Kraków 2013.

[35] Ibidem, p. 183.

[36] A. Etzioni, *Władza, uczestnictwo i uległość w organizacjach* [in:] *Wybrane zagadnienia socjologii organizacji. Skrypty uczelniane*, ed. by A. Marcinkowski, J. B. Sobczak, Uniwersytet Jagielloński, Kraków 1985; J. Rosiński, A. Marcinkowski, *From Employee to Participant in an Organization Research Focused on IT Sector Specialists* [in:] *Organisation Management. Competitiveness, Social Responsibility, Human Capital*, ed. by D. Lewicka, AGH—University of Science and Technology Press, Kraków 2010, pp. 181–202.

value of the employee on the market. The reluctance to work with others may result from concerns about the loss of one's current status with the effect of having a unique knowledge and expertise. It can also be a simple "business calculation" in the form of the following conviction: "It does not pay off to cooperate—I won't increase my level of competences significantly, while at the same time the group will learn a lot from me." This conviction may be caused also by the standard of functioning within a professional group: competition based on having current, highly specialised knowledge. It makes one compare oneself with the group more frequently and more rigorously, so as to make sure that one continues to be part of the (elite) group. This effect can also be due to a simpler mechanism—the perception of others as potential competition on the job market. The conclusion drawn by the employee may be a strategy according to which it pays off to form lasting relationships with those thanks to whom one's market value will increase and career will develop—with people perceived as "at least as good experts as myself."

Such an arrangement of relationships with colleagues would indicate a focus on the professional environment (profession) or career (see: Figure 1) in the professional functioning of employees of the ICT sector.

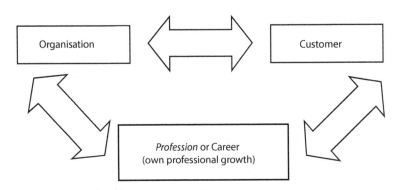

Figure 1. Directions of commitment among the audited group of IT specialists

Source: own elaboration based on N. Kinnie, J. Swart, *Committed to Whom? Professional Knowledge Worker Commitment in Cross-boundary Organizations*, "Human Resource Management Journal" 2012, 22 (1), p. 24; J. Rosiński, *Postawy zawodowe informatyków. Jednostka, zespół, organizacja*, Wydawnictwo Uniwersytetu Jagiellońskiego, Kraków 2013, p. 184.

Therefore, loyalty understood in the second of the above-mentioned meanings, as "a bond, attachment and commitment arising from the relationship," could have two aspects:

- Directing loyalty towards the professional group, without loyalty to the organisation or customers.
- Calculating the nature of loyalty linking "the decision not to abuse the confidence of someone who trusts me" with the profitability of such a decision: in the short term

directly in connection with financial benefits, or in the long term in connection with building competence, portfolio of recommendations, and project experience.

The model developed by Nicholas Kinnie and Juani Swart used in this work pointed to combining two of the three components as the most often occurring phenomenon. Therefore (according to the authors of the model), in the situation of focusing on one's professional development and while ignoring the interests of the organisation, what we should see is focus put on relationships with customers. Does the specific case of employees of the ICT sector consist in focusing solely on one element—the professional career? It is difficult to find a clear answer: ICT employees care about their relations with customers to the same extent as people from outside the industry.[37] This can be interpreted in the context that only focus on the professional environment and career is a distinguishing feature—and thus we are back to understanding the loyalty of employees of the ICT sector as addressed only to one's colleagues with high professional competences, which ensures one's development (see Figure 1).

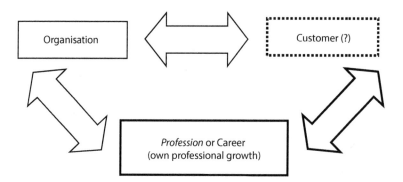

Figure 2. Directions of commitment among the audited group of IT specialists: A discussion

Source: own elaboration based on N. Kinnie, J. Swart, *Committed...*, p. 24; J. Rosiński, *Postawy zawodowe...*, p. 184.

Such an understanding would also be reinforced by reading the customer (Figure 2) not as an outsider, but rather as a person from the same organisation: the so-called "Product Owner"—a person representing the customer in the management of IT projects according to the Scrum methodology. In this methodology, which is universal for project management in the ICT sector, the task force does not meet with the end customer, but with a team member representing the customer's needs—the product

---

[37]   See J. Rosiński, *Postawy zawodowe...*, p. 178.

owner.[38] By interpreting the above situation in Scrum teams, it can be concluded that the relationship of employees of the ICT sector with the customer (Figure 2) can often mean a relationship within their own project team with an expert in the same field. That would mean the return to the characteristic relationship described in Figure 1. In other words, the customer would be another professional within the industry with whom we compare and against whom we compete, as well as try to acquire specialist competences (Figure 3).

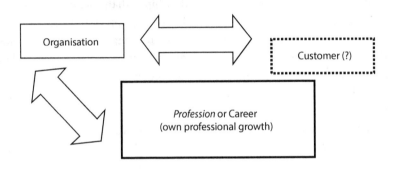

Figure 3. Directions of commitment among the audited group of IT specialists: Proposed conclusion

Source: own elaboration based on N. Kinnie, J. Swart, *Committed...*, p. 24; J. Rosiński, *Postawy zawodowe...*, p. 184.

In such a situation (the customer being an expert from the team according to Scrum), what we are dealing with is personal and professional development, as well as career overlapping and "obscuring" the customer in the professional functioning of the employee (Figure 3). The situation which takes place (described in psychology by, e.g. the theory of Transactional Analysis), when one of the elements of the system begins to be more important than the other and thus takes over the function of controlling the whole, is described as contamination.

    The situation of contamination (Figure 3) is also possible with the exclusion of the Scrum methodology. The functioning described in Figure 3 is possible when customers are treated in an instrumental manner, with their recommendations needed for career development and own professional growth. Thus, the main direction remains the career and calculative motivation.

    Regardless of adopting the final conclusion about contamination and increasing the importance of one of the components, it is worth noting a trend which appears in the behaviour of ICT workers:

---

[38]   W. Andrijew, *Zespół w metodyce zwinnego zarządzania projektami Scrum*, unpublished MA thesis, IEFiZ UJ, Kraków 2019, pp. 16–17.

- Own professional growth is linked to the loyalty to the professional group (particularly to persons with high specialist competences) while the interests of the employing organisation are marginalised.
- Calculative nature of loyalty (see: conclusions below Figure 1).

Figure 3 represents the relationship between the organisation and the customer, as organisations from their own perspective "see" the customer and the relationship with him, but from the employee's point of view, the situation is different.

Marginalising the importance of the relationship with the organisation by employees of the ICT sector is associated with a specific perception of the employing organisation as unfriendly towards the employee.[39] This mechanism can be explained on an individual level in terms of tending to maintain a consistent approach and to reduce cognitive dissonance.[40] The employee may ignore or undermine the role of information indicating the friendly character of the organisation, while giving high value to the feedback from satisfied customers or competent colleagues. Such distribution of involvement may be explained by the previously mentioned reasons of treating the employing organisation in a calculating manner, or by a high importance of material motivators. Such an interpretation seems to be consistent with the interpretation of the existing specific approach of ICT employees when it comes to the perception of the employing organisation. It would also provide a further explanation why within a group of IT professionals it is preferred to cooperate only with people with highly advanced, specialised competences.

What remains a separate question is whether this trend (Figures 1–3) is a characteristic feature only for employees of the ICT sector, or if it is a broader phenomenon; or, in other words, if it is not only a characteristic but also a distinctive feature which sets the employees of the ICT sector apart from people employed outside that sector. Research results published in 2013[41] pointed to the specificity of the ICT sector—the surveyed people from outside of the sector did not show the same characteristics as the employees of the ICT sector did. At the same time, it was already suspected that the phenomena observed in the ITC sector might become characteristic for larger market segments. The presumption that this trend could have a wider reach may be confirmed by data concerning the specificity of loyalty within the generation of millennials,[42] while the dominant area related to professional development or loyalty to the professional group (present in Figure 3) can be substituted with, e.g. personal growth or to the search for self-expression (both in the professional area and outside of it).

---

[39] See J. Rosiński, *Postawy zawodowe…*
[40] E. Aronson et al., *Psychologia społeczna…*, pp. 78–111.
[41] See J. Rosiński, *Postawy zawodowe…*
[42] Ch. Espinoza, M. Ukleja, *Zarządzanie…*, pp. 78–82.

Loyalty and the challenges for building Economy 4.0

The challenges for building Economy 4.0 associated with the nature of loyalty focused on the mercantile relationship with other professionals from the industry (outlined earlier in the text) and on their own professional development can be related to two areas:

- The society, or the entire economy (frequently described in the literature on sociology or social psychology).
- The functioning of organisations (present in communication within a given company and in specialised press titles on human resources management).

Following are two perspectives for perceiving the challenges related to loyalty.

Challenges: The perspective of society in general

In the works which present general social trends,[43] we can notice challenges resulting from the described in Figure 3 (so to speak, one-directional) nature of loyalty, such as: loyalty of the professional environment, group thinking syndrome, creating stereotypes, and "shifting goals." These concepts are confirmed by rich, dedicated literature and research materials, also in the field of social psychology.[44] It seems safe to say that social psychology shows the "mechanics" of what sociologists present in a wider perspective.

One could ask here whether these risks are in fact original, in some way new, and if the context of Industry 4.0 gives them a new meaning. The above-listed phenomena are not new or original—they have been investigated for over fifty years in social sciences. Yet, the context of Economy 4.0 may prompt these phenomena to cease to apply to task force or particular professional groups. The specificity of the professional group of ICT sector employees and its role as the "creators" of the new industrial revolution means that the challenges and risks may have a new, much wider nature that goes beyond a single sector of the economy.

The first of these challenges—workplace loyalty—is understood as loyalty not to the organisation, but rather to the professional environment. The rule is expressed in a Polish saying which can be translated as: "It's an ill bird that fouls its own nest." Workplace loyalty is favoured by intense contacts within the professional environment and similarity of social position.[45]

It is also a situation of a feedback loop, considering that we are more likely to initiate interactions with people similar to us than with people whom we evaluate as less

---

[43]   P. Sztompka, *Socjologia…*
[44]   E. Aronson et al., *Psychologia społeczna…*
[45]   P. Sztompka, *Socjologia…*, p. 83.

familiar. Interactions are also easier since they are usually seamless, conflict-free and associated with mutual understanding—they are the so-called simple transactions.[46] It is easy to visualise two IT professionals who develop codes (in a similar age, graduates of the same university, working in the same company earlier in their respective careers), complaining about a new colleague who is testing an already written piece of software, who is not formally an IT specialist ("only" a mathematician), who graduated from university rather than a technical college and is about ten years younger, which means that he has a different professional experience.

A challenge related to workplace loyalty is avoiding behaviours interpreted as directed against the interests of one's professional environment. Therefore, the following situation is possible: faulty software was written, while as an employee I know that my colleague (an expert like myself) made an error, but I will refrain from criticism and point to the sources of the error in external factors (chance, system error, error of one of the suppliers) and actively defend the colleague as an expert in the field. Such behaviour leads to a situation where the relationship within a group of specialists becomes more important than the interest of the organisation or the wider common good. Of course, this is not a new phenomenon,[47] but in Industry 4.0 it has consequences that go beyond a single organisation (e.g. hospital, office, technical service), or even a sector of the economy. In the reality of the Internet of Things and self-controlled factories, the attitude of concealing own errors in the name of protecting the unity of the professional group may have consequences even for the entire economy. Similarly to globally spreading computer viruses, errors in software can quickly infect the whole system, and protection against them is more difficult, considering that they can freely destroy the system until the software is modified, because they are not recognised as harmful.

Workplace loyalty is also associated with the syndrome of group thinking,[48] which relates to excessive identification, lack of criticism and loyalty to the group and organisation, not so much to correcting errors as to making (original) decisions. Groups susceptible to the syndrome of group thinking make risky decisions with the conviction that they are on a great mission and that their course of action is right. At the same time, they cut the group leader off from information which may affect the modification of the original decision.

In this case, it is easy to visualise as a challenge for building Industry 4.0. gigantic investments launched without a sufficiently long testing period, only so as to be the first, the largest, the technology leader, etc. To provide an analogy in the already

---

[46] E. Berne, *W co grają ludzie. Psychologia stosunków międzyludzkich*, transl. P. Izdebski, Wydawnictwo Naukowe PWN, Warszawa 2007.

[47] C. Sikorski, *Wolność w organizacji. Humanistyczna utopia czy prakseologiczna norma*, Oficyna Wydawnicza Drukarnia Antykwa, Kraków 2000.

[48] E. Aronson et al., *Psychologia społeczna…*

known phenomena, there is forcing producers of computers to install a new version of the operating system to maintain the position of the leader in terms of the number of individual licenses. Unfortunately, the haste means that the new system is significantly worse than the old one, and only after approximately one year a broad update allows for its smooth operation. While the event mentioned earlier made life more difficult for users of computers, a similar phenomenon in the situation of a self-controlled factory can cause not only emotional or financial consequences, but also those that have to do with the natural environment, and when it comes to the Internet of Things, it can actually paralyse everyday life (e.g. it is already a reality that an ATM or a car controlled by a newer, insufficiently tested version of the system software may not recognise our face and initiate the procedure of attempted theft).

Workplace loyalty and group thinking is favoured by creating stereotypes. Metaphorically speaking, it can be concluded that both of the previously mentioned processes "feed on stereotypes." In other words, a simplified perception of reality in contrast terms (e.g. good/bad) facilitates the presence of loyalty, trust and avoidance of criticism against "ours," with mistrust and critical distance toward the "others."

Creating stereotypes favours closing oneself within the group, cutting oneself off from any information which may undermine the stereotype.[49] In this case we frequently have to do with models which take the form of mitigation, justification, rationalisation, all the while ignoring reality.[50]

Certainly, the phenomenon of organisations shutting themselves off from reality and creating models removed from reality is something we can already witness. Such a form of functioning can be found in public sector organisations, performing the same activity year after year regardless of changes in the organisational environment.[51]

In Industry 4.0, stereotyped ways of perceiving reality may lead to the separation of the production of technologically great products from customers' needs. For example, we will create a customer service system which will perfectly respond to customer questions and use artificial intelligence to learn continuously, but we will ignore the fact that customers of intangible services (e.g. financial services) wish to speak to a "live human being" rather than only obtain a quick solution to a problem. The stereotypical perception will be strengthened by, e.g. the conviction that contact with a live consultant introduces elements of the unexpected into the system, and that such contact should be eliminated by constantly improving the voice interface for contact with AI and the database.

The phenomenon of "shifting goals" involves ascribing to the procedures themselves an autotelic (rather than solely instrumental) value rank, measured by the

[49]   A. Falkowski, T. Zaleśkiewicz, *Psychologia poznawcza w praktyce. Ekonomia, biznes, polityka*, Wydawnictwo Naukowe PWN, Warszawa 2011.

[50]   P. Sztompka, *Socjologia…*, p. 134.

[51]   F. Laloux, *Pracować inaczej*, transl. M. Konieczniak, Wydawnictwo Studio Emka, Warszawa 2015.

effectiveness in achieving essential goals.[52] Again it can be said that the situation is not new—considering following a procedure as the purpose of the organisation's existence is a phenomenon found in public organisations.[53]

In Industry 4.0, the consequences of this may completely paralyse life. If a public institution could, in accordance with a given procedure, refuse to grant a certain benefit, the situation is unfortunate but limited to a one-time occurrence and limited in scope. In the reality of the already existing databases and the IoT, it is easy to imagine a situation in which we agree to install an app on the phone to receive a lower interest rate for a loan or a cheaper car insurance. We are contractually bound for a year and then we realise that certain songs which we listened to while driving are now unavailable—because in the database of the insurance company, they are identified as associated with a greater accident risk. This is a minor inconvenience. However, if we are to continue this story, it may turn out that we will not be able to purchase sweets or pizza with extra cheese along the motorway, as in the name of reducing the likelihood of an accident these goods become unavailable for drivers at our age. Of course you can turn off the phone and pay in cash but the growing popularity of phone payment systems and already employed payment systems using face recognition (e.g. you can already use this technology to pay in a popular fast food restaurant and get cash from ATMs) shows that the presented vision of the risk of procedures being misinterpreted is not so distant.

Challenges: A perspective on the functioning of organisations

At the level of organisations, we have to do with a different type of description. It involves single identifiable behaviours, similar to behavioural competence indicators. The factors in question are related to social relationships in the organisation associated with mutual trust, respect, cooperation and open communication. The role of employment stability, adequate remuneration and working conditions, as well as the possibility of employee development offered by organisations is paramount in this respect.[54] Deprivation of these expectations is reflected in such "behavioural indicators" as employee turnover, complaints, absenteeism, low productivity at work, problems in interpersonal communication.[55]

While the range of issues is in itself not surprising, what poses a challenge is the fact that the loyalty programmes offered by organisations will not replace the loyalty of employers in relation to the employees, manifested by: taking care of employees, keeping promises, appreciating the involvement of persons employed, or transparent

[52] Ibidem.
[53] J. Rosiński, *Postawy zawodowe...*
[54] E. Robak, *Lojalność pracowników...*, p. 92.
[55] Ch. Espinoza, M. Ukleja, *Zarządzanie...*, p. 70.

and just principles of staff management.[56] Paradoxically, this means that Industry 4.0 can boost the demand for superiors who are not only efficient technical experts (it is with such people that employees of the ICT sector wish to work with), but also a kind of mentors understanding the specificities of their employees' functioning and using existing differences as a base for building relationships between workers in the team. This type of model is not at all distant from reality. It is used irrespective of the industry in staff management for the millennial generation.[57]

Using the differences between the supervisor and the employee (even if it is a superior only for the duration of a given project) and the ability to work with the expectations of the employee is close to the reality of how organisations function. For example, most employees[58] declare their will to change the current employer, 27.2% of respondents want to continue work for the current employer, and 11.1% have no opinion about it.[59] But if one analyses the data, it turns out that we are dealing with a lack of distinction between the needs (interests) and the way to meet them (position), typical for conflicts.[60] For example, the stance of changing the employer may conceal, e.g. the need to be promoted to project manager, and this is already an area for discussion—conflating position and need, frequently occurring among employees declaring their lack of loyalty to the employer.[61]

Such a combination of organisational challenges and the proposed way of solving the problem (relationship with the supervisor) constitutes a separate challenge for organisations in the ICT sector because it requires the development of social competences. This is a paradox of Industry 4.0: technology development has increased the need not only for advanced professional competence of programmers, but also for higher social competences of managers. What also turns out to be important is the development of social competences of ICT sector employees, e.g. as mentioned above, in terms of a better understanding of their interests, a more informed identification of their needs, distinguishing between the position and the needs, and flexible searching for different options.

Summary

In the context of Industry 4.0, loyalty specific to employees of the ICT sector creates challenges not only at the level of organisations, but also for the society as a whole. Both types of challenges (organisational and societal) require new intervention tools,

---

[56]   Ibidem.
[57]   Ibidem.
[58]   In research by E. Robak it is 61.7%.
[59]   E. Robak, *Lojalność pracowników...*, pp. 89–90.
[60]   R. Fisher et al., *Getting to Yes: Negotiating Agreement without Giving in*. Houghton Mifflin Company, New York 1992.
[61]   E. Robak, *Lojalność pracowników...*, p. 92.

seemingly focused on larger social skills on the part of the supervisors. The existing practices in which low loyalty of the employee and the fact of staying with the organisation for 2 to 3 years were simply assumed, or the existing traditional measures (e.g. loyalty programmes) used by HRM departments may not be sufficient to neutralise the risks resulting from the combined specific employee loyalty and a wider range of consequences of the development of Industry 4.0.

It seems that the presented trends, currently characteristic for the ICT sector (particularly loyalty to the professional group as opposed to the employer) might, together with the saturation of the job market by the millennial generation, be characteristic for a wider range of organisations.

Bibliography

Ajzen I., Fishbein M., *Understanding Attitudes and Predicting Social Behavior*, Prentice-Hall, Englewood Cliffs 1980.

Andrijew W., *Zespół w metodyce zwinnego zarządzania projektami Scrum* [Team in the Scrum agile project management methodology], unpublished MA thesis, IEFiZ UJ, Kraków 2019.

Aronson E., Wilson T. D., Akert R., *Psychologia społeczna – serce i umysł*, transl. A. Bezwińska, Wydawnictwo Zysk i S-ka, Warszawa 1997.

Berne E., *W co grają ludzie. Psychologia stosunków międzyludzkich*, transl. P. Izdebski, Wydawnictwo Naukowe PWN, Warszawa 2007.

Bryła M., *Lojalność konsumenta w aspekcie nowoczesnej psychologii*, "Marketing i Rynek" 2008, 5.

Bugdol M., *Wartości organizacyjne. Szkice z teorii organizacji i zarządzania*, Wydawnictwo Uniwersytetu Jagiellońskiego, Kraków 2006.

Bukowska B., Gajda K., *Pigułka z lojalności. Praktyczne aspekty budowania lojalności pracowników*, "Personel i Zarządzanie" 2009, 2.

Bukowska U., *Lojalność pracowników – ujęcie atrybutowe i procesowe* [in:] *Nauka i gospodarka w dobie destabilizacji*, ed. by J. Teczke, J. Czekaj, B. Mikuła, R. Oczkowska, Biuro Projektu Nauka i Gospodarka, Kraków 2011.

Cialdini R., *Wywieranie wpływu na ludzi. Teoria i praktyka*, Gdańskie Wydawnictwo Psychologiczne, Gdańsk 2013.

Czernek K., Wójcik D., Marszałek P., *Zaufanie w gospodarce współdzielenia*, "Gospodarka Narodowa" 2018, 3 (295).

Dembińska-Cyran I., Hołub-Iwan J., Perenc J., *Zarządzanie relacjami z klientem*, Difin, Warszawa 2004.

Dolata Z., *Jak budować lojalność zespołu?*, http://www.blog.refa.pl, 2012 (access: 4 September 2016).

Espinoza Ch., Ukleja M., *Zarządzanie milenialsami*, Wydawnictwo Naukowe PWN, Warszawa 2018.

Etzioni A., *Władza, uczestnictwo i uległość w organizacjach* [in:] *Wybrane zagadnienia socjologii organizacji. Skrypty uczelniane*, ed. by A. Marcinkowski, J. B. Sobczak, Uniwersytet Jagielloński, Kraków 1985.

Falkowski A., Zaleśkiewicz T., *Psychologia poznawcza w praktyce. Ekonomia, biznes, polityka*, Wydawnictwo Naukowe PWN, Warszawa 2011.

Fisher R., Ury W. L., Patton B. M., *Getting to Yes: Negotiating Agreement without Giving in*, Houghton Mifflin Company, New York 1992.

Jerzyk E., Disterheft A., *Proces zakupu online w świetle badań okulograficznych – rola opakowania, opisu i ceny produktu*, "Studia Ekonomiczne" 2017, 342.

Kagermann H., Wahlster W., Helbig J., *Securing the Future of German Manufacturing Industry. Recommendations for Implementing the Strategic Initiative INDUSTRIE 4.0*, Industrie 4.0 Working Group, https://www.din.de/blob/76902/e8cac883f42bf28536e7e8165993f1fd/recommendations--for-implementing-industry-4-0-data.pdf (access: 23 April 2019).

Kinnie N., Swart J., *Committed to Whom? Professional Knowledge Worker Commitment in Cross--boundary Organizations*, "Human Resource Management Journal" 2012, 22 (1).

Kleinig J., *Loyalty* [in:] *Stanford Encyclopedia of Philosophy*, http://plato.stanford.edu/entries/loyalty/ (access: 20 December 2013).

Kolasińska-Morawska K., *E-konsument nowej generacji wyzwaniem przedsiębiorstw w XXI w.*, "Studia Ekonomiczne" 2016, 255.

Konieczko A., *Zmiany w organizacji a lojalność pracowników*, "Edukacja Ekonomistów i Menedżerów: Problemy. Innowacje. Projekty" 2012, 1 (23).

Laloux F., *Pracować inaczej*, transl. M. Konieczniak, Wydawnictwo Studio Emka, Warszawa 2015.

Lipka A., *Inwestycje w kapitał ludzki organizacji w okresie koniunktury i dekoniunktury*, Wolters Kluwer, Warszawa 2010.

Lipka A., *Propozycja modelu długookresowych relacji lojalnościowych firmy z pracownikami*, "Edukacja Ekonomistów i Menedżerów: Problemy. Innowacje. Projekty" 2012, 1.

Lipka A., Winnicka-Wejs A., Acedański J., *Lojalność pracownicza. Od diagnozy typów pracowników do Zarządzania Relacjami z Pracownikami (Employee Relationship Management)*, Difin, Warszawa 2012.

Lisiecka K., *Mobilność pracowników w organizacji a ich kreatywność* [in:] *Zmieniające się przedsiębiorstwo w zmieniającej się politycznie Europie*, ed. by T. Wawak, Wydawnictwo Informacji Ekonomicznej Uniwersytetu Jagiellońskiego, Kraków 2002.

Lewicka-Strzałecka A., *Lojalność pracownika: trwała wartość czy anachroniczna cnota?*, ed. by W. Banach, Adam Mickiewicz University Press, Poznań 2014.

Maison D., *Utajone postawy konsumenckie. Analiza możliwości wykorzystania metody IAT*, Gdańskie Wydawnictwo Psychologiczne, Gdańsk 2004.

Małysa-Kaleta A., *Zaufanie w relacjach rynkowych na współczesnym rynku*, Wydawnictwo Uniwersytetu Ekonomicznego w Katowicach, Katowice 2015.

Marik V., Buncek M., Czesana V., Holoubek J., Kopicova M., Krechl J., Valasek M., *National Initiative Industry 4.0*, Praha 2015, http://www.spcr.cz/images/priloha001-2.pdf (access: 22 March 2016).

Myjak T., *Wpływ formy zatrudnienia na zachowania organizacyjne*, Wydawnictwo Adam Marszałek, Toruń 2011.

Piórkowska-Wojciechowska K., *Wybrane problemy kształtowania i badania lojalności pracowniczej*, "Prace Naukowe Akademii Ekonomicznej im. Oskara Langego we Wrocławiu" 2014, 1032.

Przewoźna-Krzemińska A., *Poszukiwanie zatrudnienia przez absolwentów uczelni wyższych a zapotrzebowanie na nich sygnalizowane przez współczesny rynek pracy* [in:] *Udział pracowników w zarządzaniu nowoczesnymi organizacjami gospodarczymi*, ed. by A. Bazan-Bulanda, A. Kwiatek, E. Robak, Wydawnictwo Wydziału Zarządzania Politechniki Częstochowskiej, Częstochowa 2015.

Robak E., *Nowe pokolenie na rynku pracy jako wyzwanie dla zarządzających nowoczesnymi organizacjami* [in:] *Udział pracowników w zarządzaniu nowoczesnymi organizacjami gospodarczymi*, ed. by A. Bazan-Bulanda, A. Kwiatek, E. Robak, Wydawnictwo Wydziału Zarządzania Politechniki Częstochowskiej, Częstochowa 2015.

Robak E., *Lojalność pracowników a zarządzanie potencjałem społecznym współczesnych organizacji*, "Zeszyty Naukowe Politechniki Częstochowskiej. Zarządzanie" 2016, 24 (2).

Rosiński J., *Postawy zawodowe informatyków. Jednostka, zespół, organizacja*, Wydawnictwo Uniwersytetu Jagiellońskiego, Kraków 2013.

Rosiński J., *Specyficzne rozumienie pojęcia kompetencji w sektorze publicznym* [in:] *Zarządzanie kompetencjami w sektorze publicznym*, ed. by I. Stańczyk, Wydawnictwo Uniwersytetu Jagiellońskiego, Kraków 2017.

Rosiński J., Marcinkowski A., *From Employee to Participant in an Organization Research Focused on IT Sector Specialists* [in:] *Organisation Management. Competitiveness, Social Responsibility, Human Capital*, ed. by D. Lewicka, AGH—University of Science and Technology Press, Kraków 2010.

Rozkwitalska M., Slavik J., *Around Learning and Industry 4.0 in Management Theory*, "International Journal of Contemporary Management" 2017, 16 (4).

Sikorski C., *Wolność w organizacji. Humanistyczna utopia czy prakseologiczna norma*, Oficyna Wydawnicza Drukarnia Antykwa, Kraków 2000.

Skalska A., *Jak na dłużej zatrzymać pracownika generacji Y w firmie*, "Personel i Zarządzanie" 2014 (1).

Smarżewska D., *Uwarunkowania lojalności pracowników wobec organizacji – aspekty teoretyczne*, "Przedsiębiorczość i Zarządzanie" 2018, 19 (8), part 1: *Wyzwania w zarządzaniu zasobami ludzkimi we współczesnych organizacjach. Od teorii do praktyki*.

Studzińska E., *Lojalność klienta – pojęcie, podział, rodzaje i stopnie*, Wydawnictwo Uniwersytetu Ekonomicznego we Wrocławiu, Wrocław 2015.

Szaban J. M., *Rynek pracy w Polsce i Unii Europejskiej*, Difin, Warszawa 2013.

Sztompka P., *Socjologia. Analiza społeczeństwa*, Społeczny Instytut Wydawniczy Znak, Kraków 2012.

Sztompka P., *Kapitał społeczny. Teoria przestrzeni międzyludzkiej*, Społeczny Instytut Wydawniczy Znak, Kraków 2016.

Śliwerski B., *Kryzys oświatowej demokracji w świetle makropolitycznych badań pedagogicznych*, "Przegląd Pedagogiczny" 2016, 2.

Świątek-Barylska I., *Lojalność pracowników współczesnych organizacji. Istota i elementy składowe*, Wydawnictwo Uniwersytetu Łódzkiego, Łódź 2013.

Urban W., Siemieniako D., *Lojalność klientów. Modele, motywacja, pomiar*, Wydawnictwo Naukowe PWN, Warszawa 2008.

The Importance of Flexibility of Human, Tangible and Intangible Resources in Selected Production Entrepreneurships: Results of Empirical Research

Michał Teczke, Ph.D.   https://orcid.org/0000-0001-9617-1936
Cracow University of Economics

Maciej Teczke, Ph.D.   https://orcid.org/0000-0002-1989-6965
Jagiellonian University

Abstract

The article presents the theoretical basis of resource flexibility. Focuses on human, tangible and intangible resources. An analysis of the literature was carried out and the results of empirical research conducted in selected Polish small and medium enterprises were presented. The study was conducted using a questionnaire and analysis of collected data. In addition to data analysis, recommendations were presented for the surveyed enterprises aimed at making the examined resources more flexible. All companies currently operate in a turbulent environment, the most important factors include the emergence of a society of risk and society of fear, social inequalities, the chaotic nature of the global market, inability to create long-term analyses due to the acceleration of changes or the emergence of global terrorism and global pandemics. Research has shown that the flexibility of individual resources depends on the sector in which a given company operates, therefore tools increasing the flexibility of individual resources must be properly selected for an enterprise.

Keywords: resources flexibility, tangible resources, intangible resources, strategy effectiveness, human resources, flexible organizations

Introduction

The flexibility of management is a subject which has for some time been broadly analysed in the management literature, and also put into practice by managers regardless of the size of their organisation. The capacity to rapidly adapt to sudden changes occurring in the market environment may, today, determine a company's success or failure.

The issue of flexibility is linked to many concepts: flexible forms of employment, flexibility of management and flexible forms of operation of organisations. These and other forms of flexible activity improve the competitive capacity of companies. The term flexibility may be popularly regarded as the ability to adapt to changing environmental conditions. Companies which have acquired such an ability are far better adapted to operating in an unforeseeable, rapidly changing environment.

Literature on the subject contains information which confirm the observation that the capacity for quick, flexible changes depends on two main factors, i.e. the size and the profile of an organisation. The flexibility of operation of large-sized companies is much lower than that of small-sized ones. The reason for this is large "inertia" of such companies. Making changes in each area of operation requires substantial time. This arises out of a large number of management levels and the organisational range. The flow of information is hindered, and as a consequence, the accomplishment of tasks delayed. As indicated, the companies from the manufacturing sector are also characterised by lower flexibility of operation compared to companies from the service sector. This, in turn, is caused by higher initial costs and a longer period of return on investment in technologies which are borne by this type of companies. It can be observed that a minor part of the world's largest organisations can minimise the significance of flexibility of operation by truly affecting how the market is formed. Such companies assume that if we were to affect the entire market directly (e.g. by unique innovativeness), then it would be the competition that would need to flexibly accommodate itself to our operations. It must, however, be accentuated once more that very few companies have such a capability.

On the other hand, small-sized companies can react to the changes market conditions particularly quickly. A small number of management levels gives them an advantage arising out of the rate of information flow. As a result, such companies can instantly change their mode of operation in order to make the most efficient use of their resources.

The concept of flexibility is inextricably linked to the concept of dynamic capabilities. These are defined as the capability of a company to integrate, build and reconfigure internal and external competence to respond to a suddenly changing environment.[1] Dynamic capabilities greatly affect the outcomes produced by companies. This is

---

[1]   D. J. Teece et al., *Dynamic Capabilities and Strategic Management*, "Strategic Management Journal" 1997, p. 516.

affected by such factors as the optimal use of knowledge in a company, an increase in the competitive advantage in a disordered environment, a decrease in the competitiveness of companies under the conditions of a changeable environment in the case of a traditional non-dynamic approach, increased impact on the operating activities which translate into the overall performance of a company.[2]

Faulkner and Bowman[3] drew attention to the factors affecting the operation of companies in a turbulent environment. These are such aspects as: intensifying globalisation processes, the growing impact of ecology on the operation of companies, social changes, and also a highly dynamic development of technology over the last decade. For companies to be capable of operating in this reality effectively, they need to adapt the elements enhancing their flexibility to their strategies. Brilman[4] indicated the features which a flexible organisation should have: the ability to keep up with environmental changes, an efficient customer feedback system, short decision-making processes and staff accustomed to changes. The synthesis of these elements promote an immediate reaction which should produce the anticipated results. In this perspective, a flexibility-oriented organisational culture occupies a very important role. It requires the employees to be prepared for changes and innovativeness.[5] In the context of management oriented to the obtainment of company flexibility, attention should also be paid to the flexibility of structures. There are differentiated five types of flexibility of organisational structures:[6] flexibility arising out of the modular structure of an organisation, flexibility arising out of the personal characteristics of the managing director, the incremental model of forming the flexibility of organisational structures, the intentionally formed organic relation inside and flexibility arising out of the specificity of a sector.

Analysing the changes which companies needed to make in order to meet the requirements of a turbulent environment,[7] such as: transition from functional areas to processes, outsourcing, structure simplification, provision of continuous innovativeness, transition from implementation employees to knowledge employees, results in increasing significance of intangible resources in an organisation. However, tangible resources still continue to be the resources of crucial significance in many companies, including mainly in manufacturing companies. An answer to how to

---

[2]   R. Wilden et al., *Dynamic Capabilities and Performance: Strategy, Structure and Environment*, "Long Range Planning" 2013, 46, pp. 72–96.

[3]   D. Faulkner, C. Bowman, *Strategie konkurencji*, transl. M. Albigowski, Gebethner i S-ka, Warszawa 1996, pp. 120–125.

[4]   J. Brilman, *Nowoczesne koncepcje i metody zarządzania*, transl. K. Bolesta-Kukułka, PWE, Warszawa 2002, p. 391.

[5]   C. Sikorski, *Zachowania ludzi w organizacji*, Wydawnictwo Naukowe PWN, Warszawa 1999, p. 260.

[6]   R. Krupski, *Zarządzanie przedsiębiorstwem w turbulentnym otoczeniu. Ku superelastycznej organizacji*, PWE, Warszawa 2005, p. 76.

[7]   M. Morawski, *Zarządzanie wiedzą w perspektywie personalnej* [in:] *Zarządzanie wiedzą w przedsiębiorstwie*, ed. by K. Perechuda, Wydawnictwo Naukowe PWN, Warszawa 2005.

provide sufficient flexibility to these resources is, for example adopting Flexible Manufacturing Systems (FMS). Undoubtedly, having adopted FMSs, a company may count on considerable gains from this, however, the adoption of an FMS involves considerable costs.[8] Due to the number and type of machines as well as their intended use and arrangement, flexible manufacturing systems can be classified into several types: flexible manufacturing model, flexible work centre, flexible production line, flexible manufacturing network.[9]

The manufacturing system allowing the flexibility of a manufacturing process to be enhanced, and consequently the flexibility of an organisation to be improved is lean management. The term refers to considerably "leaner" manufacturing systems compared to traditional mass production systems.[10] The classical concept of lean production by Womack and Jones means that a company uses half the resources, compared to mass production. This requires having two times less stock and gives the opportunity of developing a new product twice as fast.[11] All of these elements affect enhancing the flexibility of a company.

Human resources

In the case of manufacturing companies, the highest results among the characteristics of human resources were obtained by the skills and experience of employees (see Table 1). Companies in this sector are looking for employees with specialised skills, for example in the operation of machines and equipment. Employees' experience and qualifications allow these companies to work efficiently, safely and smoothly. In the production industry, any mistake can affect the functioning of the entire enterprise which directly affects its performance. Many used machines and devices with incorrect use by qualified employees may lead to accidents at work. This is connected with the production stoppage and the possibility of controlling the enterprise by relevant services such as the National Labour Inspectorate. This is why companies in this industry attach so much attention to the experience of employees.

---

[8]   A. Muhlemann et al., *Zarządzanie – produkcja i usługi*, transl. K. Wojtczak, J. Sołtys, PWN, Warszawa 1995, p. 264.

[9]   M. Uchroński, *Przegląd algorytmów szeregowania zadań w elastycznych systemach wytwarzania*, PTZP, Opole 2008, p. 2.

[10] C. Wiśniewski, *Wpływ wdrożenia zasad lean manufacturing na efektywność i jakość produkcji*, "Problemy Eksploatacji" 2010, 2, p. 37.

[11] J. P. Womack et al., *Lean thinking – szczupłe myślenie*, ProdPress.com, Wrocław 2008, p. 76.

Table 1. The importance of human resources in manufacturing enterprises according to respondents

Human resources	Influence
Employee skills	18.4
Staff experience	18.0
Level of employee motivation	14.1
Level of employee satisfaction from work	9.0
Employees' education and knowledge	7.6
Level of staff turnover	8.2
Opportunities for professional development of employees within the enterprise	11.4
Applying flexible forms of employment	6.8

Source: elaborated by the authors.

Skills are related to the experience of employees. Often, the acquisition of relevant qualifications is associated with the right amount of experience. The modern production process, which is more and more automated, requires employees to have more and more specialised skills that will allow to use the full potential of the owned machinery park.

The surveyed respondents indicated that the use of flexible forms of employment does not interest them. It is associated with a strong emphasis on the experience and skills of employees. In order to hire staff with these characteristics, enterprises have much less room for maneuver related to the use of flexible forms of employment. The specificity of this industry also affects the fact that flexible forms of employment form a small part of contracts.

Employees' education and knowledge is also at the bottom of the list of the most important characteristics of human resources. Respondents paid much more attention to the skills and experience of employees, which is why they are focused on purely practical skills.

Recommendations

In the surveyed production enterprises, emphasis on the practical features of the employees is clearly visible (see Figure 1). With the increasing degree of sophistication of the machines and equipment used, it may be necessary to pay more attention to the education and knowledge of employees. Well-educated employees can have greater adaptability to new devices, a solid theoretical foundation that will allow them to quickly master the service of new devices. In enterprises, it is also possible to pay attention to increasing the motivation of employees by improving job satisfaction; both of these characteristics indicate that the surveyed companies are moderately involved in this matter.

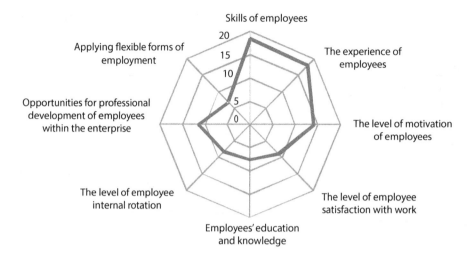

Figure 1. Key aspects of human resources in production companies

Source: own calculation.

Tangible resources

In production entrepreneurships, material resources play a key role (see Table 2). This is clearly seen in the study. As many as five characteristics are particularly important in this sector. These are: the universality of machines and devices, the ability to store goods, specialist equipment, the availability of transport, and the possibility of expanding the organisation's headquarters. These are the features necessary for the effective management of a production company. The highest result of the universality of machines and devices is seen in the high awareness of respondents regarding the importance of enterprise flexibility. Machines and devices of this type allow better adjustment of the offer to the clients' requirements. They allow tailoring the production to current needs and adjusting the size and diversity of deliveries to expectations. A trend is noticeable, which indicates that smaller—more diversified and, what follows, better adapted to the needs of customers—supply parts are becoming more and more important. Such deliveries are much more difficult to introduce and require better equipment, better developed logistics systems, but are necessary to meet the current needs of customers.

The possibilities of storing goods are an inseparable element of the functioning of production enterprises. The operating costs of an enterprise depend on the effective management of storage space. Hence, the possibility of storing goods was very high among the characteristics of material resources. Specialised equipment is necessary in the production process. No company in this sector can function without the equipment necessary for production. Equipment will vary depending on the products being manufactured; the more advanced the manufactured products, the more specialised the equipment which the company requires. The availability of transport is associated with appropriate logistic processes in the business. The greater their availability, the cheaper they can transport the produced good and the more reliable is the supply of necessary intermediates needed to produce final products. Finally, it is possible to expand the headquarters of the organisation. The fact that surveyed enterprises take it into considerations proves the good condition of the firms and that they are optimistic about the future.

Table 2. Significance of tangible resources in production enterprises by respondents

Tangible resources	Influence
Location adequacy	16.4
Modern computer equipment	15.2
Specialised equipment	20.0
Possibilities of expanding the organisation's headquarters	17.6
Up-to-date software	9.9
Functionality of office space	11.1
Possibility of storing goods	21.0
Availability of transport	18.5
Versatility of machines and devices	22.0
Availability of premises for rent	2.4

Source: elaborated by the authors.

Respondents of the surveyed companies focused on the characteristics of material resources related to production processes. Manufacturing enterprises are based mainly on material resources, hence such great emphasis is put on them in this sector.

Recommendations

Flexible production systems already play a very important role in production companies and it can be assumed that this trend will increase (see Figure 2). Therefore, the management of manufacturing enterprises should be prepared to adapt these solutions in their businesses.

The survey shows that this process already takes place because the universality of machines and devices is in the first place among the characteristics of material resources. Also, specialist equipment was quite high, which emphasises the necessity of investing in modern production systems, ensuring the ability to attract customers with high requirements.

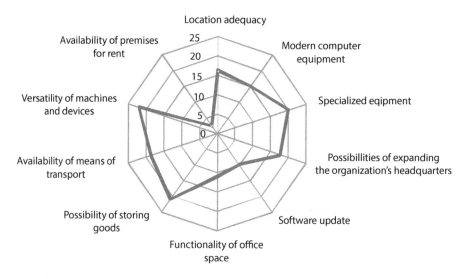

Figure 2. Key aspects of tangible resources in production companies

Source: elaborated by the authors.

Financial resources

Production companies require the greatest access to capital. This is confirmed in the study (see Table 3). The first two places are held by access to own sources of financing and access to external sources of financing.

Table 3. Significance of financial resources in production enterprises by respondents

Financial resources	Influence
Access to own sources of financing	23.5
Receivables	16.0
Balance between funds allocated for investments and retained funds (as a financial surplus)	12.3
Value of cash at hand	15.2
Level of obligations from suppliers	13.6
Access to external sources of financing	19.5
Liquidation capability of fixed assets	12.5
Ability to liquidate intangible assets (e.g. patents)	3.4

Source: elaborated by the authors.

The investments that must be made in manufacturing enterprises are definitely higher than in commercial and service businesses. The return on investment takes longer and the risk incurred is higher. For these reasons, manufacturing companies must seek access to foreign sources of financing. Finding the right investment financing partners is thus becoming an element of competitive advantage that allows to reduce the cost of investment financing.

Membership in the European Union allows the use of funds for investment in fixed assets on preferential terms, but it is necessary to have own funds for co-funding the investment. Enterprises may also benefit from the support of governmental programmes through various agencies such as the PARP or MARR. They give the opportunity to credit investments on more favourable terms than financial institutions, but to obtain them it is required to participate in competitions, which is in itself time-consuming and does not guarantee the acquisition of financing.

The least important characteristics are the ability to liquidate intangible assets and the balance between funds allocated for investments and retained funds. The first of these can have a double meaning. It may indicate a lack of intangible assets, such as patents that could be liquefied, which may indicate a low level of innovativeness of the surveyed enterprises. The second reason may be the reluctance to liquidate intangible assets so as not to lose their competitive advantage.

Recommendations

The survey showed that the most important aspect of managing financial resources is gaining access to financing (see Figure 3). Respondents indicated both access to foreign sources of financing and access to their own sources of financing.

The surveyed enterprises should benefit from the possibility of obtaining financing on preferential terms from the government and EU funds. This allows to make the necessary investments while maintaining a low cost of credit. Because access to external financing is important, enterprises must pay special attention to their balance sheet so that they can receive a loan on favourable terms.

Intangible resources

As regards the company's intangible resources one can observe symmetry among the following characteristics: availability of suppliers, efficiency of management information processes, enabling identification of threats and opportunities flowing from the environment, existing relations with other organisations and invariability of the mission and vision of the organisation (see Table 4).

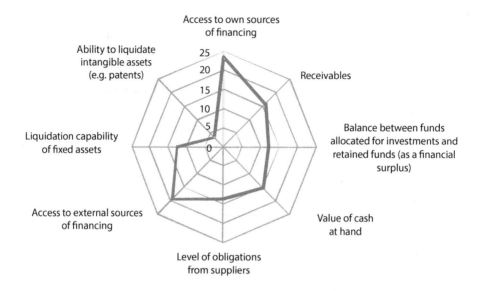

Figure 3. Key asspects of financial resources in production companies

Source: elaborated by the authors.

Table 4. Significance of intangible resources in production enterprises by respondents

Intangible assets	Influence
Reputation of company on the market	13.2
Availability of suppliers	24.0
Positive image of employer	13.8
Efficiency of management information processes, enabling identification of threats and opportunities coming from the environment	21.0
Unchanging mission and vision of the organisation	15.2
Organisational structure that gives employees freedom of action	7.8
Existing relations with other organisations	16.0
Strong organisational culture	8.0
Status of the organisation's learning processes	8.4
Possibilities of commercialisation of intangible assets owned by the company (copyrights, patents, etc.)	1.8

Source: elaborated by the authors.

The first of the characteristics is directly related to the production process. The availability of suppliers for a production company is a strategic element. In a situation where there are few suppliers offering the necessary intermediate products required for production, the business has very limited possibilities of price negotiations and in case of a sharp increase it may even be forced to stop production if it proves unprofitable at that price. Therefore, access to a wide range of suppliers is necessary for the company to be able to negotiate favourable terms with suppliers and replace the existing suppliers with others, when they fail to perform their tasks or when they raise the price. As in the case of other types of enterprises, also in manufacturing firms, attention was paid to the importance of management information processes that enable identifying threats and opportunities coming from the environment. Because production companies need more time to adapt to changing conditions, and this is associated with high costs, it is more important that the management is able to take decisions in advance that allow the company to adapt. Anticipation in this case is crucial to gain a competitive advantage. Production companies are associated with the entire network of cooperating companies, which is why maintaining relationships with them is so substantial. Good relationships allow one to receive favourable offers and the participation of a network of companies can have a beneficial effect on the business. Lastly, the respondents indicated the immutability of the mission and vision of the organisation. The mission and vision should be unchangeable; they should be a signpost demonstrating the reason behind the company's functioning and the manner in which it operates. This approach allows one to maintain continuity in business management, even with changes in the management. It also enables the preservation of the company's identity.

Recommendations

Respondents pointed to very prominent aspects related to other characteristics of resources. The highest position of accessibility of suppliers in this case is the most justified. Furthermore, the efficiency of management information processes, enabling the identification of threats and opportunities arising from the environment is an aspect that can help to gain an advantage over competitors (see Figure 4).

The company's reputation on the market has obtained quite a low result. This element appears to be one to which respondents should pay more attention. What is more, the state of the organisation's learning processes could be at a higher level. This would allow companies to react faster and to often avoid unnecessary costs.

Conclusions

According to the last PARP report, small- and medium-sized enterprises together with micro-enterprises have contributed to the generation of 50.1% of Poland's GDP in 2013. At the same time, at the end of 2014, enterprises of this size class employed 69% of professionally active people in Poland. Data presented in the report, such as

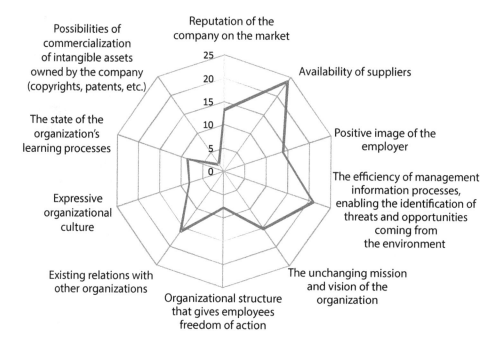

Figure 4. Key aspects of intangible resources in production companies

Source: elaborated by the authors.

the number of employees, indicate the validity of this sector for sustainable economic development in Poland.

All enterprises (including small and medium) operate in the age of destabilisation,[12] which is associated with a high level of risk of their decisions. The most important factors illustrating the variability of the environment include, among others, a high rate of technological changes as well as quick and easy access to information, including those of economic nature. Modern small- and medium-sized enterprises must also face other challenges that result from destabilisation. The most important are: emergence of a society of risk and society of fear, social inequalities, chaotic nature of the global market, inability to create long-term analyses due to the acceleration of changes or the emergence of global terrorism.[13]

It is not reasonable to compare small and medium enterprises with large business-es, taking into account only the amount of resources. Relatively minor resources of small- and medium-sized enterprises are, on the one hand, a factor increasing the

---

[12]   J. Teczke, *Flexibility of International Business under Destabilization Conditions. Management Science in Transition Period in Moldova and Poland. Responsible Use of Resources*, Moldova 2014, p. 66.
[13]   Ibidem, p. 67.

risk of their functioning in a turbulent environment, and, on the other hand, an advantage from the perspective of adaptation abilities. Large enterprises and the largest corporations have the resources to minimise the risks associated with, for example, the introduction of a new product to the market, and at the same time the possible lack of success of a single product is not able to disturb the company. Enterprises with small resources, which concerns small- and medium-sized enterprises, are much more sensitive to changes in the demand for products and services, and innovations introduced by them carry a much higher risk of failure. A tendency indicating that small and medium enterprises are quicker to notice customer needs and are able to adapt to them faster can be observed. A characteristic example may be the highly centralised brewing industry, where large groups of producers dominate the beer market. The largest corporations were forced to largely modify both the product portfolio as well as the marketing communication method in response to craft breweries, with many times lower capital, production, marketing and distribution resources. It can be considered that adaptive abilities represent a significant advantage of small and medium enterprises over their larger competitors. When determining the overall flexibility of an enterprise, it should be considered that it depends on its least flexible resources. This means that flexibility in the area of one type of resource is not enough to define the company as flexible. Only the possibility of influencing the flexibility of resources in the area of the entire enterprise's functioning would allow to satisfy the changing environment conditions.

Undoubtedly, the flexibility of an enterprise depends on the sector in which it operates, and hence—the type of resources that dominate in its operations. And so, companies operating in the service sector, often building their position on the employees' knowledge and high level of the organisation, are able to easily adapt to the changing needs of clients. Knowledge, as a kind of strategic resource, allows consulting or outsourcing companies, engaged in a wide range of activities, to adapt their offer to the client's needs.

Enterprises from the production sector, relying mainly on material resources, increase the flexibility of production to reduce the complexity of the environment.

Bibliography

Brilman J., *Nowoczesne koncepcje i metody zarządzania*, transl. K. Bolesta-Kukułka, PWE, Warszawa 2002.

Drnevich P. L., Kriauciunas A. P., *Clarifying the Conditions and Limits of the Contribtions of Ordinary and Dynamic Capabilities to Relative Firm Performance*, "Strategic Management Journal" 2011, 32.

Elastyczność jako kryterium efektywności organizacyjnej, ed. by W. Błaszczyk, I. Bednarska-Wnuk, P. Kuźbik, B. Ziębicki, Acta Universitatis Lodziensis, Folia Oeconomica, Wydawnictwo Uniwersytetu Łódzkiego, Łódź 2010.

Faulkner D., Bowman C., *Strategie konkurencji*, transl. M. Albigowski, Gebethner i S-ka, Warszawa 1996.

Krupski R., *Zarządzanie przedsiębiorstwem w turbulentnym otoczeniu. Ku superelastycznej organizacji*, PWE, Warszawa 2005.

Morawski M., *Zarządzanie wiedzą w perspektywie personalnej* [in:] *Zarządzanie wiedzą w przedsiębiorstwie*, ed. by K. Perechuda, Wydawnictwo Naukowe PWN, Warszawa 2005.

Muhlemann A., Oakland J., Lockyer K., *Zarządzanie – produkcja i usługi*, transl. K. Wojtczak, J. Sołtys, PWN, Warszawa 1995.

Protogerou A., Caloghirou Y., Lioukas S., *Dynamic Capabilities and Their Indirect Impact on Firm Performance*, "Industrial and Corporate Change" 2012, 21.

Sikorski C., *Zachowania ludzi w organizacji*, Wydawnictwo Naukowe PWN, Warszawa 1999.

Teece D. J., Pisano G., Shuen A., *Dynamic Capabilities and Strategic Management*, "Strategic Management Journal" 1997.

Uchroński M., *Przegląd algorytmów szeregowania zadań w elastycznych systemach wytwarzania*, PTZP, Opole 2008.

Teczke J., *Flexibility of International Business under Destabilization Conditions. Management Science in Transition Period in Moldova and Poland, Responsible Use of Resources*, Moldova 2014.

Verona G., Ravasi D., *Unbundling Dynamic Capabilities: An Exploratory Study of Continuous Product Innovation*, "Industrial and Corporate Change" 2003, 2.

Wilden R., Gudergan S., Nielsen B. B., Lings I., *Dynamic Capabilities and Performance: Strategy, Structure and Environment*, "Long Range Planning" 2013, 46.

Wiśniewski C., *Wpływ wdrożenia zasad lean manufacturing na efektywność i jakość produkcji*, "Problemy Eksploatacji" 2010, 2.

Womack J. P., Jones D. T., Roos D., *Lean thinking – szczupłe myślenie*, ProdPress.com, Wrocław 2008.

Wu L.-Y., *Applicability of the Resource-Based and Dynamic Capability Views under Environmental Volatility*, "Journal of Business Research" 2010, 63.

Zhou K. Z., Li C. B., *How Strategic Orientations Influence the Building of Dynamic Capability in Emerging Economies*, "Journal of Business Research" 2010, 63.

Challenges Posed for Universities by the Industry 4.0 Environment

Prof. Marcin Geryk, Ph.D.   https://orcid.org/0000-0002-5164-0716
Jagiellonian University

> We must . . . deal quickly with the fusion of the online world and the
> world of industrial production. In Germany, we call it Industrie 4.0.[1]
>
> *Angela Merkel, German Chancellor*

> We stand on the brink of a technological revolution that will fun-
> damentally alter the way we live, work, and relate to one another . . .
> unlike anything humankind has experienced before.
>
> *Klaus Schwab, Founder and Executive Chairman*
> *of the World Economic Forum*

Abstract

Industry 4.0, a term that describes the Fourth Industrial Revolution, will reshape our lives by the common use of robots. Machines will communicate with each other (Internet of Things). Those changes will alter the socio-economic environment we live in nowadays. Many jobs will disappear. The main issue that stands before universities is to predict which skills should be taught to fulfil the future job market requirements.

Keywords: Industry 4.0, education, skills in industry 4.0, educational industry, future labor market requirements

---

[1]   https://ec.europa.eu/growth/toolsdatabases/dem/monitor/sites/default/files/DTM_Industrie%204.0.pdf (access: 21 October 2019).

Introduction

The term "Industry 4.0" (or the original German: "Industrie 4.0") is currently a top priority for everybody, from business representatives, through researchers, to university leaders. There is no widely accepted definition of the term.[2] That is why the scientific debate must be continued on a global scale, as the revolution changes peoples' lives everywhere in ever so many dimensions.

Revolutions of the world industry

The term "Industry 4.0" was firstl publicly introduced in 2011 as "Industrie 4.0" (in German) by a group of representatives from different fields, such as business people, politicians and representatives of higher education institutions. The term was an initiative to enhance the competitiveness of the German industry.[3] The idea appeared to be so important that it became the leading theme of the High-Tech Strategy 2020 introduced by the German federal government.[4]

The earlier stages of the "revolutions" in industrial development dated back to the 18th century, or more precisely, to the years 1760–1840 when the introduction and wide use of machines in the industry occurred. For the first time in human history, powered by steam, machines were responsible for the shift from manual production.

The Second Industrial Revolution, between 1870 and 1914, was connected with the introduction of such systems as the telegraph and railroads. Manufacture was then scaled-up to "mass production" due to electrification and innovations in science, mostly in chemistry.

The Third Industrial Revolution, also referred to as the Digital Revolution, was described as such since the industry leaned on digital technologies in production. It began between 1950 and 1970 and brought the shift from analogue and mechanical systems to digital ones. Another term for this period is the Information Age, a result of the development of computers and information and communication technology.

So, the Fourth Industrial Revolution takes the automation of manufacturing processes to a new level by customizing and making mass production technologies more flexible. It simply means that machines will operate independently or that they will cooperate with humans. Machines will be able to collect data, analyze it, and

---

[2] M. Hermann et al., *Design Principles for Industrie 4.0 Scenarios: A Literature Review*, Working Paper No. 1, Dortmund 2015.

[3] H. Kagermann, W. Lukas, W. Wahlster, *Industrie 4.0: Mit dem Internet der Dinge auf dem Weg zur 4. industriellen Revolution*, "VDI nachrichten" 2011, p. 13.

[4] *Recommendations for Implementing the Strategic Initiative G. Industrie 4.0: Final Report of the Industrie 4.0 Working Group*, ed. by H. Kagermann et al., Acatech, Frankfurt am Main 2013, p. 77.

advise upon it. It is connected with the creation of a virtual reality where machines communicate with each other (Internet of Things), or with people (Internet of People).

A wide description of the vision of Industrie 4.0 was published by Kagermann et.al in 2013:

> In the future, businesses will establish global networks that incorporate their machinery, warehousing systems and production facilities in the shape of Cyber-Physical Systems (CPS). In the manufacturing environment, these Cyber-Physical Systems comprise smart machines, storage systems and production facilities capable of autonomously exchanging information, triggering actions and controlling each other independently. This facilitates fundamental improvements to the industrial processes involved in manufacturing, engineering, material usage and supply chain and life cycle management. The Smart Factories that are already beginning to appear employ a completely new approach to production. Smart products are uniquely identifiable, may be located at all times and know their own history, current status and alternative routes to achieving their target state. The embedded manufacturing systems are vertically networked with business processes within factories and enterprises and horizontally connected to dispersed value networks that can be managed in real time—from the moment an order is placed right through to outbound logistics. In addition, they both enable and require end-to-end engineering across the entire value chain.[5]

Challenges of the future

As in every revolution, the one under discussion here may change the societal environment we are used to living in nowadays. One such huge change might demolish the current job market. In truth, not only the market. A number of jobs are expected to disappear, especially those based mostly on manual work. There are two widely discussed scenarios relating to in this matter:[6]

- a very optimistic one—that Industry 4.0 will bring unlimited prosperity for mankind;
- a pessimistic one—modern society model will collapse along with the economic system.

It is worth mentioning that according to PwC report results, Polish entrepreneurs are those who expect positive changes involved with the implementation of the concept of Industry 4.0.[7] A research project on two thousand entrepreneurs from 26 countries led to the conclusion that many of them are successfully implementing elements of "Industry 4.0"

---

[5]   Ibidem, p. 5.
[6]   R. Krzanowski, K. Trombik, *Czwarta rewolucja przemysłowa – dobrodziejstwem czy przekleństwem? Wokół myśli Martina Forda*, "Studia Metodologiczne" 2018, 38, p. 2.
[7]   *Przemysł 4.0 czyli wyzwania współczesnej produkcji. Raport PwC*, 2017, https://www.pwc.pl/pl/pdf/ przemysl-4-0-raport.pdf (access: 21 October 2019).

as key factors to achieve efficiency and cost effectiveness. What is most important, those who took part in the project stated that the main beneficiary of the changes will be the final customer. However, entrepreneurs will also benefit from the revolution, as it may mean:

- higher revenues—the respondents expect a 1/3 increase in revenues and adequately in cost effectiveness;
- deeper customs relations—it will provide new data for market analysis;
- changes in organizational culture;
- data analysis will be provided on an unexpected scale and will lead to a higher market performance.

Besides, the Fourth Industrial Revolution creates a huge chance of development for the European Union as a whole, and for every member state itself.[8]

Should universities react to the changes?

The labor market of the future will look completely different when compared to that of today. Bill Clinton's Secretary of Education Richard Riley said: "We are currently preparing students for jobs that don't yet exist, using technologies that haven't been invented, in order to solve problems, we don't even know are problems yet."

Economists Erik Brynjolfsson and Andrew McAfee predict that we could expect greater inequality caused by the revolution, which can also lead to a disruption of labor markets. With the progress of automation in the world economy, the net displacement of workers by machines might increase the gap between returns on capital and returns on labor. This promising prediction might result in a net increase of safe and rewarding jobs, due to the displacement of workforce by technology.[9]

A further increase of the inequality gap is expected between the largest beneficiaries of innovation—those who represent the intellectual capital—the innovators, shareholders, and investors, and those who depend on labor. The demand for highly skilled workers will increase, but the demand for less-skilled workers will decrease. Among those "skills for the future" are: oral communication, persuasion, critical thinking, emotional intelligence, judgement, service orientation, negotiation and cognitive flexibility. It is all interconnected with the four main effects of the revolution on business—customer expectations, product enhancement, collaborative innovation and organizational forms.[10]

---

[8] M. Grabowska, *Innowacyjność w porządku prawnym Unii Europejskiej* [in:] *Innowacyjność polskiej gospodarki: wybrane aspekty*, ed. by K. Opolski, J. Górski, Wydział Nauk Ekonomicznych Uniwersytetu Warszawskiego, Warszawa 2018, pp. 15–25.

[9] *The Fourth Industrial Revolution: What It Means, How to Respond*, 2016, https://www.weforum.org/agenda/2016/01/the-fourth-industrial-revolution-what-it-means-and-how-to-respond (access: 27 October 2019).

[10] K. Schwab, *The Fourth Industrial Revolution. What It Means and How to Respond*, "Foreign Affairs" 12 December 2015.

The revolution will strongly rebuild the shape of the labor market so universities should take it into consideration. Focusing on the transfer of the basic skills will no longer be possible. The update of the curricula is a must and should be repeated every five years to respond to market challenges. In order to increase employability skills like the ones listed below, the following should be acquired by students:[11]

- social skills (such as negotiations, emotional intelligence);
- cognitive skills (such as creativity, analytics);
- personal/mental abilities (such as dealing with pressure and persistence);
- process skills (such as critical thinking);
- system skills (such as decision making, entrepreneurial skills);
- technical skills (such as information and telecommunication technologies literacy, active learning);
- intercultural skills;
- resource management skills (such as time management).

Examples from different countries have brought about these observations. For example in universities in Ghana, where students graduated with few technological, problem-solving and team-work skills. To inspire the students, the Ghana Robotics Academy Foundation introduced the use of robots in the teaching process to help develop problem-solving and critical thinking skills.[12]

In another study—from Portugal—serious games and gamification were adopted in order to encourage students to learn and discover in ways based on experimentation. The main merit of this innovative method was that it put education in the context of a greater involvement of students and it developed their skills in a real context. The results of the project led to the conclusion that students prefer a more hands-on approach—theoretical concepts should be empirically proven and tested by students. This will help students build technology-based skills and participate in more diverse lessons.[13]

In Poland, at the Silesian University of Technology (Politechnika Śląska) an e-learning platform is used as a good practice of the new teaching method that is a response to Industry 4.0 challenges. E-learning brings not only mobility and flexibility but, what is more important, interactivity. Everyone can take part in a chosen training or course, and their programs can be flexibly modified, for example, to suit the new requirements of the labor market. It is also a very good reaction to the need of life-long

---

[11]   B. Eberhard et al., *Smart Work: The Transformation of the Labour Market Due to the Fourth Industrial Revolution (I4.0)*, "International Journal of Business and Economic Sciences Applied Research" 2017, 10, pp. 47–66.

[12]   M. Wilson, Y. Okraku-Yirenkyi, *Impact of the Robotics Inspired Science Education (RiSE) Program on Education in Ghana*, "Journal of Engineering and Economic Development" 2019, 5 (2), pp. 11–22.

[13]   F. Almeida, *The Role of Serious Games, Gamification and Industry 4.0 Tools in the Education 4.0 Paradigm*, "Contemporary Education Technology" 2019, 10 (2), pp. 120–136.

learning and the persistent search for new skills and new qualifications required by the fast-changing business environment.[14]

Education of the future should be focused on educational development and the skills taught should be more customized and intelligent. Not all activity can be supplanted by smart robots, that is why higher education institutions should focus on pertinent information and abilities. There is a platform for creative educators where they can develop educational innovation and upgrade future learning—Education 4.0.[15]

The educational industry should adopt two main roles in Industry 4.0—educating the followers and the change-makers. The followers should be equipped with skills to respond to the changes, adapting their performance, while the change-makers should be the people who can make informed decisions related to usability, sustainability, safety or ethics in the world.[16]

The Universities of the Future research project, a Knowledge Alliance Project supported by the European Commission, has brought many highly interesting prospect implications for the higher education industry. The project lasts since 2018 till 2021 and is run by a consortium of universities, business partners and public bodies. Its goal is to identify the skills required for succeeding in Industry 4.0, the effects on education, future skills of the workforce, and, in general, the challenges of the higher education institutions.

Table 1. Relationship of skills and challenges

Challenges of Industry 4.0	Skills needed to overcome the challenges
Homogenous cultures and resistance to change	Risk-taking, flexibility, adaptability
Lack of vision of technological development	Technological literacy
Investing in the right technology	Technological literacy, business thinking
Lack of new business models	Technological literacy, business thinking
Lack of knowledge of the strategic use of information	Competencies of information management
Cybersecurity and quality control	Knowledge, competencies of cybersecurity and quality control
Sustainability challenges	Competencies, knowledge of sustainability

Source: M. Clavert, *Universities of the Future. Industry 4.0 Implications for Higher Education Institutions*, www.universitiesofthefuture.eu (access: 27 October 2019).

---

[14] S. Grabowska, *E-learning jako pożądana forma kształcenia w dobie Industry 4.0*, "Zeszyty Naukowe Politechniki Śląskiej" 2018, 118, pp. 171–180.
[15] A. A. Shahroom, N. Hussin, *Industrial Revolution 4.0 and Education*, "International Journal of Academic Research and Social Sciences" 2018, 8 (9), pp. 314–319.
[16] M. Clavert, *Foreword: Universities of the Future. Industry 4.0 Implications for Higher Education Institutions*, www.universitiesofthefuture.eu (access: 21 October 2019).

As the project results have clearly shown, technological literacy, understood as a fluency in technology usage and data management are needed for value creation. An understanding of cybersecurity is essential to quality control. The range of changes expected globally is so wide that it requires focusing on long-term decision-making processes, with proper regard for the ethical and legal issues.

One of many concluding words of the report draws a slightly blurred and unclear view of the near future of the world, where:

> A broader understanding of the society, combined with business thinking and technology literacy, enables the creation of novel business models. For creating successful technological solutions having empathy for the user is a key element. In order to engage people, align strategic objectives and obtain new resources for technological investments, leadership, communication and interpersonal skills are needed. However, these efforts should involve evaluation of the ethical implications concerning the development and use of new technologies.[17]

Conclusion

Higher education institutions are obliged not only to follow social and economic changes. They have to predict the shape of the labor market as well as the jobs that will exist in the future. This is highly bound to the way in which universities will teach their students. This responsibility forces university staff to persistently improve their curricula and to pursue further research to predict the changes that might influence our lives in the future.

Those changes are inspired by the tremendous changes in technology called Industry 4.0. The common use of robots, the Internet of Things, communication between machines without human agency—those are the main challenges that stand before us and which will reshape our future completely, but also the future of higher education institutions—even to a higher degree.

Universities should actively put research efforts on change and improvement of teaching methods. They should follow the massive popularity of mobile phones, social media, visual communication, movies and other modern technologies. They should actively respond to the challenges of the modern world.

---

[17]   Ibidem.

Bibliography

Almeida F., *The Role of Serious Games, Gamification and Industry 4.0 Tools in the Education 4.0 Paradigm*, "Contemporary Education Technology" 2019, 10 (2).

Clavert M., *Foreword: Universities of the Future. Industry 4.0 Implications for Higher Education Institutions*, www.universitiesofthefuture.eu (access: 21 October 2019).

Eberhard B., Podio M., Pérez Alonso A., Radovica E., Avotina L., Peiseniece L., Caamaño Sandon M., Gonzalez Lozano A., Solé-Pla J., *Smart Work: The Transformation of the Labour Market Due to the Fourth Industrial Revolution (I4.0)*, "International Journal of Business and Economic Sciences Applied Research" 2017, 10.

Grabowska S., *E-learning jako pożądana forma kształcenia w dobie industry 4.0*, "Zeszyty Naukowe Politechniki Śląskiej" 2018, 118.

Grabowska S., *Innowacyjność w porządku prawnym Unii Europejskiej* [in:] *Innowacyjność polskiej gospodarki: wybrane aspekty*, ed. by K. Opolski, J. Górski, Wydział Nauk Ekonomicznych Uniwersytetu Warszawskiego, Warszawa 2018.

Hermann M., Pentek T., Otto B., *Design Principles for Industrie 4.0 Scenarios: A Literature Review*, Working Paper No. 1, Dortmund 2015.

Kagermann G., Lukas W., Wahlster W., *Industrie 4.0: Mit dem Internet der Dinge auf dem Weg zur 4. industriellen Revolution*, "VDI nachrichten" 2011.

Krzanowski R., Trombik K., *Czwarta rewolucja przemysłowa – dobrodziejstwem czy przekleństwem? Wokół myśli Martina Forda*, "Studia Metodologiczne" 2018, 38.

Przemysł 4.0 czyli wyzwania współczesnej produkcji. Raport PwC, 2017, https://www.pwc.pl/pl/pdf/przemysl-4-0-raport.pdf (access: 21 October 2019).

Recommendations for Implementing the Strategic Initiative G. Industrie 4.0: Final Report of the Industrie 4.0 Working Group, ed. by G. Kagermann, W. Wahlster, J. Helbig, Acatech, Frankfurt am Main 2013.

Schwab K., *The Fourth Industrial Revolution. What It Means and How to Respond*, "Foreign Affairs" 12 December 2015.

Shahroom A., Hussin N., *Industrial Revolution 4.0 and Education*, "International Journal of Academic Research and Social Sciences" 2018, 8 (9).

The Fourth Industrial Revolution: What It Means, How to Respond, 2016, https://www.weforum.org/agenda/2016/01/the-fourth-industrial-revolution-what-it-means-and-how-to-respond (access: 27 October 2019).

Wilson M., Okraku-Yirenkyi Y., *Impact of the Robotics Inspired Science Education (RiSE) Program on Education in Ghana*, "Journal of Engineering and Economic Development" 2019, 5 (2).

Big Data in Managing Marketing Communication*

Agnieszka Smalec, Ph.D.   https://orcid.org/0000-0003-3524-6716
University of Szczecin
Researcher ID: L-3863-2018

Abstract

The huge amount of generated information is now a global phenomenon affecting all market participants, and the need to constantly collect and process significant amounts of data is becoming a daily reality for decision making. The article aims to introduce the concept of Big Data and to indicate the possibility of using large data sets by modern entities primarily in the field of communication management. Very large data sets are created not only thanks to devices enabling data transmission but also through mutual interactions of people, e.g. in social networks. The acquisition and correct interpretation of this data play an important role in market entities, especially in the field of management, including communication management, since greater availability of data means more accurate decisions, although it also raises some problems. The article was prepared based on a literature review, research reports and analysis of secondary sources. The presented considerations will be the basis for further conclusions in the direction of empirical research.

Keywords: Big Data, marketing communication, data processing and collection, communication management, data interpretation

Literature review

Modern technologies affect not only our everyday lives but above all human methods. Telephones, tablets, television, radio, smartphones and game consoles are available everywhere. The needs and expectations of today's consumers regarding communication vary and will change; they are focused on here and now. Digital transformation

---

* The project is financed within the framework of the programme of the Minister of Science and Higher Education under the name "Regional Excellence Initiative" in the years 2019–2022; project number 001/RID/2018/19; the amount of financing PLN 10,684,000.00.

includes more and more entities that change their way of thinking, acting, management, including by exploiting the potential of social media, mobile technology and other digital solutions. Cyberspace is a reflection of the idea of subject fragmentation and consumer orientation. On the one hand, it is about the multiplicity of buyers' identities, while on the other, it concerns the immediate availability of information on the Internet (which, according to D.I. Hoffman is the most important invention since the discovery of printing), allowing to immediately meet the expectations of the recipient. "The ephemeral nature of hyperreality forces enormous flexibility" of the created strategies, including communication strategies.[1] The effectiveness of many campaigns is often a derivative of the analysed data and the used technology.

Data processing and collection is becoming more convenient and cheaper. The development of modern technologies and devices that enable data transfer, results in faster information growth. Both a challenge and a problem is the proper processing and extracting from this information of what is valuable, which will allow the making of right decisions. Worldwide, 98% of data is stored digitally, which is why the appearance of Big Data is quite natural.[2] Big Data enables the improvement and optimisation of internal and external communication. Conventional data processing and storage techniques are no longer sufficient, which necessitates the search for new methods to manage huge data resources. Currently, many services, marketing systems or CRM save and collect information on the behaviour of current and future customers. There is more data, but there are also increasingly enhanced analytical tools and skills to better match the communication activities of entities. It is also possible to create future scenarios with the appropriate analyses. Data analysis flowing from many different devices, applications and search engines enables predicting phenomena. For example, already in 2009 Google engineers were able to predict the place of origin and the spread of the flu, monitoring it on an ongoing basis, mainly due to the analysis of a huge number of search queries. They correlated all queries with medical data regarding the spread of influenza in 2003–2008.[3] Data analysis in the digital world, without threatening the privacy of the individual, can be successfully used in marketing communications.

IBM was one of the first to use Big Data for data that was not stored in relational databases.[4] This concept appeared in a 1997 document prepared by NASA scientists who pointed to a problem related to data visualisation, the collection of which was so large that it occupied the entire capacity of the computer's main memory, local disk

---

[1]   L. Sułkowski, *Epistemologia i metodologia zarządzania*, PWE, Warszawa 2012, p. 243.

[2]   S. Cortés, E. Pedrol, *Big Data as a Tool for Corporate Communications Strategies*, 2016, https://www.holmesreport.com/agency-playbook/sponsored/article/big-data-as-a-tool-for-corporate-communica-tions-strategies (access: 5 July 2019).

[3]   V. Mayer-Schönberger, K. Cukier, *Big data. Rewolucja, która zmieni nasze myślenie, pracę i życie*, transl. M. Głatki, MT Biznes, Warszawa 2014, p. 14.

[4]   A. Pamuła, *Potencjał analiz Big Data w procesach obsługi odbiorców energii*, "Roczniki Kolegium Analiz Ekonomicznych" 2016, 40, p. 285.

and even an external disk. American scientists popularised this term at the beginning of the 21st century by predicting that Big Data would shape the activities of enterprises, scientists, researchers, doctors and defence and intelligence services.[5] Science, genetics and astronomers were the first to experience a rapid flow of information, which forced the invention of new ways for processing it.[6] Currently, although Big Data is used in many areas and has already partly come out of the buzzword phase, and advanced analytics have spread for good in companies, the term is still not clearly defined. To put it simply, it means large data sets (usually demographic and behavioural) that are difficult to process and to manage using existing methods and tools due to their huge size and complexity.[7] In other words, it is the ability to analyse and draw conclusions from large databases of various data, thanks to which managers can obtain information about what the consumer likes, what affects him or how he reacts in given situations. This permits the personalisation of the marketing message. Big Data is primarily a new way of explaining the phenomena that surround us. Table 1 shows how this concept evolved over time.

Table 1. Terminology regarding the use and analysis of data

Term	Time frame	Specificity of the concept
Decision support	1970–1985	Using data analysis to support decision-making processes
Board support	1980–1990	Focus on data analysis to support management decisions
OLAP (Online Analytical Processing)	1990–2000	Decision support software for analysing multidimensional databases (views and hierarchies)
Business intelligence	1989–2005	Tools to support data-based decisions with an emphasis on reporting
Business analytics	2005–2010	Focus on statistical and mathematical data analysis to support decisions
Big Data	since 2010	Focus on very large, unstructured, rapidly changing data

Source: Th. H. Davenport, *Big Data at Work: Dispelling the Myths, Uncovering the Opportunities*, Harvard Business School Publishing Corporation, Boston 2014, p. 10.

The essence of Big Data does not have to lie in a particularly large size of data, therefore, one should speak not so much of "large data sets" as of "new type of data."[8] Some authors compare Big Data to the ability to search and find a needle in a haystack. It is also worth pointing to relatively new research approaches developed on the basis

[5]   G. Press, *12 Big Data Definitions: What's Yours?*, 2014, https://www.forbes.com/sites/gilpress/2014/09/03/12-big-data-definitions-whats-yours/#40a9e8b513ae (access: 5 July 2019).
[6]   G. Błażewicz, *Rewolucja z marketing automation*, Wydawnictwo Naukowe PWN, Warszawa 2016, p. 20.
[7]   Th. H. Davenport, *Big Data at Work: Dispelling the Myths, Uncovering the Opportunities*, Harvard Business School Publishing Corporation, Boston 2014, p. 8.
[8]   V. Bosch, *Big Data in Market Research: Why More Data Does not Automatically Mean Better Information*, "GfK Marketing Intelligence Review" 2016, 8 (2), p. 59.

of digital anthropology, which include social listening, netnography and empathic research.[9] The essence of social listening is monitoring, often using Big Data, opinions expressed by consumers on the Internet about the company and its products. The concept of Big Data can, therefore, be understood as a large amount of data, enabling the receipt of specific value as a result of the process of obtaining and analysing these data, using new technologies and creating a specific architecture.[10] This architecture is understood as a skeleton for the entire process related to the use of data, starting from the designation of data sources that are of interest from a business point of view, through collection, preliminary processing, separation, analysis, data modelling, and ending with inference.[11] This involves the rapid processing of huge amounts of data, often collected in different sources and with the help of numerous tools, saved on various media and in different formats.

Some authors approach the concept of Big Data to define the characteristics of large data sets, by referring to their size, diversity in structure and format, and sensitivity to the speed of inflow and the possibility of using them in business processes.[12] Big Data includes what can be realised on a large scale, and cannot be done on a small scale, in order to acquire new knowledge or create new value in a way that will change markets, organisations, relations between entities of the environment, etc.[13]

Big Data can also be described using the 3V model[14]—important conditions that define this concept:

- Volume—extensive data sets to be processed; all correlations can be recognised only when we have access to huge data sets.
- Velocity—data is time-sensitive, it quickly becomes outdated, and therefore one should draw conclusions from these quick changes and react to them quickly, preferably in real time; fast processing, analysing and implementing changes based on the collected data; data cannot be static.
- Variety, because the data are varied: demographic data, e.g. gender, age, place of residence, as well as behavioural data, e.g. what is the response to individual or transactional campaigns (what the customer bought before), which allows finding interesting relationships between them.

---

[9]   Ph. Kotler, H. Kartajaya, I. Setiawan, *Marketing 4.0: Moving from Traditional to Digital*, John Wiley & Sons, Hoboken, New Jersey 2017, pp. 110–113.

[10] A. Katal et al., *Big Data: Issues, Challenges, Tools and Good Practices*, Sixth International Conference on Contemporary Computing (IC3), IEEE, Noida 2013, p. 404.

[11] M. Tabakow et al., *Big data – definicje, wyzwania i technologie informatyczne*, "Informatyka Ekonomiczna" 2014, 1 (31), p. 145.

[12] A. Pamuła, *Potencjał analiz Big Data w procesach obsługi odbiorców energii*, "Roczniki Kolegium Analiz Ekonomicznych" 2016, 40, pp. 285–297.

[13] V. Mayer-Schönberger, K. Cukier, *Big data...*, p. 20.

[14] D. Laney, *3D Data Management: Controlling Data Volume, Velocity, and Variety*, 2001, http://blogs.gartner.com/doug-laney/files/2012/01/ad949-3D-Data-Management-Controlling-Data-Volume-Velocity-and-Variety.pdf (access: 5 July 2019).

IBM characterises Big Data by means of four attributes, adding a fourth feature-reli-ability (veracity), i.e. the verification of possessed data; checking whether the infor-mation was obtained in accordance with the Personal Data Protection Act (GDPR), if it was not generated by robots (spam-type traffic) and is relevant to the business. The company should collect necessary and sufficient data to test the adopted hy-potheses and to build and verify models, enabling analysis and inference about the studied population. This dimension is related to subsequent Big Data properties, i.e. validity, which can be understood in the context of data quality and management based on mass, diverse, distributed, heterogeneous, often unrefined data, and with business value and the potential of large data.[15] Of importance is the value of data for the user, i.e. the ability to use the collected information to draw useful conclusions. Value is an extremely important feature that distinguishes Big Data in the context of the cost of technology acquisition and the benefits that organisations can obtain from its use. SAS, however, draws attention to two additional attributes: variability and complexity.[16]

It should be emphasised that nowadays Big Data is a fact increasingly embedded in the minds of managers, although companies are still learning to use it. It has rev-olutionised the way of thinking about how consumers purchase, work and commu-nicate. Big Data allows to discover consumer motivations, their shopping habits and elements of the offer convincing to make a conversion. The acquired data is analysed in order to find correlations, patterns and trends, helpful, among others in forecast-ing phenomena and trends as well as human behaviour, preferences and habits.[17] An example of an institution that possesses huge data is banks. Banks, based on, among others, movements on user accounts and payments, obtain a lot of information about their users. They can then offer the customer a revolving account credit so that he can afford the additional expenses. Companies release their own applications downloaded by users to smartphones, automatically consenting to access their own data during installation. Big Data is used to predict the future on the basis of the ongoing analysis of constantly growing very large data sets, collected and processed in real time, which allows, among others for a better understanding of market.[18] Big Data analyses are meant to help in predicting the future, discovering new values based on the ongoing analysis of constantly increasing very large data sets, collected and processed in real time,[19] based primarily on current, not historical data.

---

[15]   K. Borne, *Top 10 Big Data Challenges: A Serious Look at 10 Big Data V's*, https://mapr.com/blog/top-10-big-data-challenges-serious-look-10-big-data-vs/ (access: 11 April 2014).

[16]   M. Tabakow et al., *Big data…*, p. 141.

[17]   A. Stępnik, *Big Data w perspektywie memetycznej*, "Teksty z Ulicy. Zeszyt memetyczny" 2015, 16, p. 150.

[18]   M. Graczyk-Kucharska, *Big Data koniecznością współczesnego marketingu*, "Problemy Zarządzania, Finansów i Marketingu" 2015, 41 (2), pp. 267-268.

[19]   K. Ayankoya et al., *Intrinsic Relations between Data Science, Big Data, Business Analytics and Da-tafication*, Proceedings of the Southern African Institute for Computer Scientist and Information

Three main groups of companies using Big Data can be distinguished, characterised by data, skills and ideas.[20] The first group consists of companies that have data or at least access to them. It does not have to be their business goal. They may not have the skills to extract values from their data. Such examples are often social media, e.g. Facebook or Twitter. The second group comprises such companies that have this skill. These include consulting and analytical firms selling new technologies and having the specialised experience, but often without access to data or the inability to use them in an innovative way. You need a group of companies with a big data focus. The reason for their success is not data or know-how, but unique ideas and an innovative approach to the use of these data, bringing out new forms of value.

Big Data is helpful in managing communications. It should be emphasised that the most important thing in it is not just the collection of data but above all the processing of information and the practical use of the conclusions derived from it. A consumer profile is created that can be used to reach them effectively. Regardless of the company's profile, resources or location, it is important that, for example, an advertising campaign is directed to the right recipient or appears in the right time and place. An interesting source of data are also all relations, among others those formed through social media. Some of them are difficult to analyse in terms of numbers, but it is possible to examine the presence and content of keywords, the frequency of user entries or response time to emerging posts. For example, based on the analysis of entries on the Facebook profiles of a person who is a fan of extreme sports, an insurance company may offer him an additional package of benefits.

Big Data: Examples of practical applications

There are many examples of using Big Data in business management, customer relations or creating a tailored marketing message. The role of Big Data is key, among others in marketing automation, i.e. systems for automating marketing processes that allow the transmission of personalised marketing messages which respond to the needs of recipients. Marketing automation can only bring results if it is based on large amounts of real data taking into account the behaviour and preferences of buyers. Recently, as already mentioned, a significant evolution of marketing has been observed, resulting from the dynamic pace of convergence of customer service technologies, digital and marketing technologies.[21] Together, Big Data and marketing automation create an

Technologists Annual Conference 2014 on SAICSIT 2014 Empowered by Technology, ACM, New York 2014, p. 195.
[20] V. Mayer-Schönberger, K. Cukier, *Big data...*, pp. 165–166.
[21] M. Brinker et al., *Trendy technologiczne 2015. Połączenie biznesu oraz IT. Marketing wielowymiarowy*, Deloitte 2015, http://www2.deloitte.com/content/dam/Deloitte/pl/Documents/Newsletters/ (access: 5 July 2019).

effective way of collecting, sorting and obtaining insight from thousands of data points about customers, campaigns, offers, etc., and creating a comprehensive communication plan with recipients. Marketing automation will not succeed without Big Data.[22]

According to the survey "Internet Trends Report 2015," in the case of companies that have used technologies related to the processing of large data sets, the costs of maintaining IT infrastructure per year have decreased by 33%, while the costs of enterprise data storage have fallen by 38%. In turn, as results from the research carried out by Forrester, by the end of 2016, companies using data analytics in their business processes have earned over USD 400 billion. By 2020, their profit will have reached over USD 1.2 trillion. This global trend also affects the situation of Polish companies. An example is the development of the Warsaw company Cloud Technologies, which supplies data from businesses from the Internet marketing industry as well as more and more entities from other segments. It created the OnAudience platform, which is the largest Big Data warehouse in Europe.

According to the study "Forecasts of company bosses regarding development, innovation and leadership" conducted among CEOs by Frost & Sullivan among over three hundred presidents and business leaders from both Americas, the Asia-Pacific region, Europe and Africa, Big Data is one of the main determinants of business success and sustainable development of companies. Over half of the respondents (53%) indicated that the most important factor conditioning the organisation's growth and development capabilities in the next three years will be intelligent data analysis.[23]

According to a study conducted at the beginning of 2017 by New Vantage Partners LLC, almost 90% of organisations invest in Big Data, and 80% describe their investments as beneficial for the development of their business. Respondents point to many positive effects, including cost reduction, creation of a data-based organisational culture, benefits associated with innovation, new products and services. Only 1.6% of respondents said that their investments in Big Data were unsuccessful. It is worth noting that over the past five years, the surveyed companies have undertaken significant investments related to Big Data. 37.2% of the management confirmed that over the past five years their organisations have invested over USD 100 million in Big Data, and 6.5% have invested over USD 1 billion. Companies focus on innovation opportunities while reducing spending levels. At the same time, companies are trying to earn on Big Data thanks to increased revenues and finding new sources of revenue (54.8%), as well as repositioning their activities (51.6%). Of the respondents, 72.6% strive to reduce expenses by increasing the efficiency of operations by reducing operational costs, and 49.2% have achieved success by reducing costs thanks to Big Data investments.[24]

---

[22] *E-marketing. Współczesne trendy. Pakiet startowy*, ed. by J. Królewski, P. Sala, Wydawnictwo Naukowe PWN, Warszawa 2013, pp. 188–195.
[23] http://corpcom.frost.com, 2016 (access: 5 July 2019).
[24] http://newvantage.com, 2017, pp. 2–8 (access: 5 July 2019).

An example of using Big Data in management is Netfix, which combines viewers' declarations during registration and collects data about their clients regarding, among others, what they choose, how much they watch, where they watch, when they watch, what parts of films are rewinded repeatedly, what films they do not watch, what they put in the search engine window or how they browse the search results. The company, thanks to such a huge database, can personalise communication and make decisions regarding the purchase of a given series or format. Such an example is the purchase in 2011 of the right to film the British political series "House of Cards" based on the analysis of the preferences of nearly 30 million subscribers to determine how many of them really want to watch it. They then topped the best TV channels like HBO and AMC to get the rights to the American version of House of Cards, giving them two seasons with 13 episodes each season.[25]

Another example is Amazon, which uses Big Data very widely not only in the category of proposing specific products but also in solving its customers' problems. Actions taken in this field effectively build trust in the brand and lead to increased sales efficiency. It analyses the provided data, tracking what customers do to provide content that best suits their preferences and expectations. To this end, the firm uses, among others automatic system for measuring and optimisation of sent marketing messages. The home page is never the same, pointing out recommendations that aim to stimulate further purchases.

Walmart increased conversion by almost 15% when it installed a semantic search of its own production called Polaris. The system analyses texts and constantly learns to better suggest the best products. The system used directly to predict earthquakes has been modified and is currently helping police departments in Los Angeles and Santa Cruz to prevent crime. The system provides real-time crime analysis in a given area, which has enabled it to reduce thefts by 21% and assaults by 33%.[26]

Big Data analysis is also used by Wirtualna Polska in order to match the displayed content—articles, video materials, etc.—as well as advertisements as accurately as possible. In the case of the positioning of editorial materials, first editors and publishers determine what content can go to the WP homepage, and then Big Data algorithms adapt it to individual users. The machine takes actions based on previously collected information about users, as well as based on their current behaviour, deciding not only what but also where content will be displayed. Big Data mechanisms, and more specifically machine learning also allow to analyse whether users assigned to one segment also exhibit behaviours similar to those assigned to any other segments, which in the future will permit even more targeted communication that could potentially

[25] Z. Bulygo, *How Netflix Uses Analytics to Select Movies, Create Content, and Make Multimillion Dollar Decisions*, https://neilpatel.com/blog/how-netflix-uses-analytics/ (access: 5 July 2019).
[26] P. Golczyk, *Krótko o Big Data w marketingu*, http://golczyk.com/big-data-w-marketingu/ (access: 5 July 2019).

interest them. The mechanisms of Big Data analysis used by Wirtualna Polska process more and more information from year to year and support marketing activities with ever greater precision. The effectiveness of advertising based on Big Data compared to advertising that does not use the analysis of large amounts of data is always higher: from a dozen to even several hundred percent, depending on the industry, creation and broadcasting time.[27]

However, it should be emphasised that many companies are not aware of and do not know how to properly use large databases. For example, the results of a study commissioned by Cisco (Cisco Connected World Technology Report CCWTR) among 1,800 IT professionals from 18 countries, among them Poland—including identification of the strategic potential of Big Data projects and technological deficiencies hindering their implementation—show that most companies face business and technological problems related to Big Data. Over 60% of respondents said that Big Data could help in making key decisions and improve the competitiveness of their companies, but only a quarter, both in Poland and in the world, admits that they can extract strategic information from currently available data. Over two-thirds of IT managers have confirmed that Big Data will be a strategic priority for their companies, and half of the respondents believe that they need a strategic plan to take advantage of the possibilities of Big Data. It is worth adding that 73% of respondents in the world and 71% in Poland plan to include data provided from digital sensors, measuring devices, video cameras and other smart devices into their Big Data plans, however only 33% of respondents in the world (and 16% in Poland) have a specific plan for using these new data sources.[28] According to a 2017 New Vantage Partners LLC survey, 52.5% of senior executives indicated that organisational obstacles prevent full implementation of Big Data solutions, organisational and technological alignment is also a problem, and 18% report a lack of a coherent data strategy.[29]

Having access to large data sets and the ability to analyse them is considered useful in the process of building information bases for making decisions in the field of marketing communication and management.

---

[27] Ł. Kryśkiewicz, *Analityka Big Data w Polsce. Jak polskie firmy wykorzystują #BigData, aby efektywnie konkurować na rynku*, 2017, http://di.com.pl/analityka-big-data-w-polsce-jak-polskie-firmy-wykorzystu-ja-bigdata-aby-efektywnie-konkurowac-na-rynku-58022 (access: 5 July 2019).

[28] https://www.cisco.com, 2013 (access: 5 July 2019).

[29] http://newvantage.com, 2017 (access: 5 July 2019).

Summary

Big Data has great potential to create consumer behaviour and manage communication addressed to them. Based on the collected data, it is possible to create and characterise the recipient's profile to reach them more effectively. It enables the use of information in an innovative way that facilitates a better understanding of the surrounding reality. However, it is worth realising not only the benefits of using Big Data, but also certain threats associated with it. In society, it often raises dislike and fear of excessive surveillance by market players or deliberately misleading to achieve sales goals. There are both domestic and international legal regulations, which mandate some security, but the border is quite delicate. Collecting and using data is quite muddy ground, as it can violate privacy and is easy to abuse. It is therefore important to clarify the purpose of data collection and provide greater transparency of the entire process, as well as use the appropriate technological tools enabling the analysis of these large sets. Big Data is a powerful tool to help market entities get to know their own environment better, including buyers, but it is only up to informed managers whether it will be carried out in an ethical and non-damaging manner. The benefits of Big Data encourage some entities to use inappropriate techniques or to overly rely on data results. Also, it is impossible to accept data that is essentially wrong or false in exchange for the possibility of creating a much larger set of them, although some disorder may be acceptable. There is also a threat that a person will be tried not for his actual actions, but for his predispositions, which will be inferred from the collected data.

In the era of Big Data, not only the processing of mass data sources but also the ability to collect and integrate many types of data from numerous varying sources becomes a challenge. Combining "traditional" data sources (such as research results, static data) with new ones to achieve synergies and create new information is an opportunity to study the behaviour of "intelligent" communities and the phenomena which they create. Big Data enables maximum personalisation of communication and adapting the message to specific groups of recipients. In addition, Big Data can be successfully applied for internal use—data collected from communication between employees can help improve and optimise internal communication. However, this is still a poorly explored area. The implementation of Big Data analytics tools is still insufficient. This is due to, among others, the fact that companies are not aware how to analyse and select such large volumes of information. They also do not have the business know-how that would allow them to process and monetise this data. There is also a misconception on the Polish market that data analytics is a solution reserved for large entities. Meanwhile, companies from the SME sector and even micro-enterprises can also use it successfully. Big Data analytics is a flexible technology that can be adapted to the scale of business operations of any enterprise. The company itself decides what kind of data and how much detail it needs. Big Data will also not replace research, because these are complementary and not competitive aspects. Research combined with technology means a greater need for "broad" thinking, understanding, explaining and drawing appropriate conclusions to better manage communication and adapt it to the needs and expectations of recipients. Big Data must be kept up with, we must learn to manage large data sets and transform them into accessible and useful knowledge. Big Data helps streamline the management of market entities, including marketing communication management, and broadens their understanding of reality, but—which should be emphasised—it is not a magic wand and it will not solve every problem.

Bibliography

Ayankoya K., Calitz A., Greyling J., *Intrinsic Relations between Data Science, Big Data, Business Analytics and Datafication*, Proceedings of the Southern African Institute for Computer Scientist and Information Technologists Annual Conference 2014 on SAICSIT 2014 Empowered by Technology, ACM, New York 2014.

Błażewicz G., *Rewolucja z marketing automation*, Wydawnictwo Naukowe PWN, Warszawa 2016.

Borne K., *Top 10 Big Data Challenges: A Serious Look at 10 Big Data V's*, https://mapr.com/blog/top-10-big-data-challenges-serious-look-10-big-data-vs/ (access: 11 April 2014).

Bosch V., *Big Data in Market Research: Why More Data Does not Automatically Mean Better Information*, "GfK Marketing Intelligence Review" 2016, 8 (2).

Brinker M., Kunker N., Singer M., *Trendy technologiczne 2015. Połączenie biznesu oraz IT. Marketing wielowymiarowy*, Deloitte 2015, http://www2.deloitte.com/content/dam/Deloitte/pl/Documents/Newsletters/ (access: 5 July 2019).

Bulygo Z., *How Netflix Uses Analytics to Select Movies, Create Content, and Make Multimillion Dollar Decisions*, https://neilpatel.com/blog/how-netflix-uses-analytics/ (access: 5 July 2019).

Cortés S., Pedrol E., *Big Data as a Tool for Corporate Communications Strategies*, 2016, https://www.holmesreport.com/agency-playbook/sponsored/article/big-data-as-a-tool-for-corporate-communications-strategies (access: 5 July 2019).

Davenport Th. H., *Big Data at Work: Dispelling the Myths, Uncovering the Opportunities*, Harvard Business School Publishing Corporation, Boston 2014.

E-marketing. Współczesne trendy. Pakiet startowy, ed. by J. Królewski, P. Sala, Wydawnictwo Naukowe PWN, Warszawa 2013.

Golczyk P., *Krótko o Big Data w marketingu*, http://golczyk.com/big-data-w-marketingu/ (access: 5 July 2019).

Graczyk-Kucharska M., *Big Data koniecznością współczesnego marketingu*, "Problemy Zarządzania, Finansów i Marketingu" 2015, 41 (2).

Katal A., Wazid M., Goudar R. H., *Big Data: Issues, Challenges, Tools and Good Practices*, Sixth International Conference on Contemporary Computing (IC3), IEEE, Noida 2013.

Kotler Ph., Kartajaya H., Setiawan I., *Marketing 4.0: Moving from Traditional to Digital*, John Wiley & Sons, Hoboken, New Jersey 2017, https://www.nima.today/wp-content/uploads/2018/11/Marketing-4.0-Philip-Kotler-Hermawan-Kartajaya-And-Iwan-Setiawan.pdf (access: 5 July 2019).

Kryśkiewicz Ł., *Analityka Big Data w Polsce. Jak polskie firmy wykorzystują #BigData, aby efektywnie konkurować na rynku*, 2017, http://di.com.pl/analityka-big-data-w-polsce-jak-polskie-firmy-wykorzystuja-bigdata-aby-efektywnie-konkurowac-na-rynku-58022 (access: 5 July 2019).

Laney D., *3D Data Management: Controlling Data Volume, Velocity, and Variety*, 2001, http://blogs.gartner.com/doug-laney/files/2012/01/ad949-3D-Data-Management-Controlling-Data-Volume--Velocity-and-Variety.pdf (access: 5 July 2019).

Mayer-Schönberger V., Cukier K., *Big data. Rewolucja, która zmieni nasze myślenie, pracę i życie*, transl. M. Głatki, MT Biznes, Warszawa 2014.

Pamuła A., *Potencjał analiz Big Data w procesach obsługi odbiorców energii*, "Roczniki Kolegium Analiz Ekonomicznych" 2016, 40.

Press G., *12 Big Data Definitions: What's Yours?*, 2014, https://www.forbes.com/sites/gilpress/2014/09/03/12-big-data-definitions-whats-yours/#40a9e8b513ae (access: 5 July 2019).

Stępnik A., *Big Data w perspektywie memetycznej*, "Teksty z Ulicy. Zeszyt memetyczny" 2015, 16.

Sułkowski Ł., *Epistemologia i metodologia zarządzania*, PWE, Warszawa 2012.

Tabakow M., Korczak J., Franczyk B., *Big data – definicje, wyzwania i technologie informatyczne*, "Informatyka Ekonomiczna" 2014, 1 (31).

Mathematical Risk Assessment Method in the Implementation of Logistic Processes

Prof. Piotr Buła, Ph.D.   https://orcid.org/0000-0001-8741-8327
Cracow University of Economics
University of Johannesburg

Dorota Dziedzic, Ph.D.   https://orcid.org/0000-0001-8358-7780
Cracow University of Economics

Marta Uznańska, MA   https://orcid.org/0000-0001-5384-9137
Cracow University of Economics

Abstract

Organisations providing international transportation, shipping and forwarding services are exposed to risk in every stage of making business whether it is recognised and managed, addressed in a cursory manner, or altogether ignored. In order to understand the risk that exists, companies can proactively assess the probability and impact of risk in advance, or reactively discover risk after a detrimental event occurs. Operations in the logistics process are subject to the risk of disruptions that enterprises try to minimise. The purpose of this study is to explore, analyse, and derive common themes on mathematical risk assessment techniques. The article presents the application of this method in the domain of international freight wheeled transport. Assessing risk, including appraising its likelihood of occurrence, exposure, likely triggers, and likely loss, is a critical step in managing the risk inherent in this type of companies. Findings from this research indicate that organisations can assess the risk with simple and affordable techniques.

Keywords: risk management in logistics processes, logistics process, mathematical risk assessment method, risk, risk concept, logistics

Introduction

The new landscape of the 21st century, with unparalleled advancements and growth, is fraught with a variety of hazards and risks. As multinational companies operate across borderless and timeless dimensions of the international marketplace, coupled with rapid transportation systems where nothing is more certain than a change in the ecosystems, the risk is much higher than it used to be. Every organisation needs to obtain goods and services in order to carry out its objectives and goals. In the European market for land transport of cargo, the most important role is played by shippers who choose road carriers to meet the requirements of the market and customers. The choice of road transport services is not limited only by the advantages of this type of transport, but also by the very low operational and commercial attractiveness of alternative services in this field. Although the European Union's transport policy is aimed at preventing the excessive development of road transport, in order to eliminate the negative impact on the natural environment, so far in Western Europe there is no prospect of limiting the place of road transport below 65%.[1] That is why international freight wheeled transport gains great significance and why it is critical to an organisation's success to understand the risk that exists. A supplier's failure to deliver inbound purchased goods or services can have a detrimental effect throughout the supply chain.

The paper begins with a review of prior research on the concepts of risk and risk management in the logistic process within a theory context, then continues further to explain the methodology of the research method, explains the definition of weights and scale of points for individual risk criteria and shows the implementation of mathematical risk assessment method in international freight wheeled transport. This is followed by a discussion on the research findings and conclusions.

Literature review and theoretical framework

The concept of risk and risk management

Risk is a multidisciplinary category, but mainly a domain of social sciences, especially economy. Apart from every discipline's concepts, risk has one thing in common: the contingency of human actions. The natural consequence of this specific multi-subjectivity of risk is the fact that it is not an objective category in the sense of a general definition and its scientific approach to the problem. Regardless of those differences, it is indisputable that risk accompanies the activity of all entities on the market, each organisation, especially in the era of continuous and growing turbulences in business processes, the emergence of fast evolving digital technologies, increased regulatory pressure and global political landscape. In this approach, risk is an objectified uncertainty of the occurrence of an undesirable event,[2] or a threat

---

[1]   Z. Kordela, W. Paprocki, *Stan i perspektywy rozwoju międzynarodowego transportu drogowego rzeczy w Polsce*, Wydawnictwo Eurologistics, Suchy Las 2018, pp. 8–10.

[2]   See: A. H. Willet, *The Economic Theory of Risk Insurance*, The University of Pennsylvania Press, Philadelphia 1951, p. 6; F. H. Knight, *Risk Uncertainty and Profit*, MA: Hart, Schaffner & Marx, Houghton Mifflin Company, Boston 1921; A. Rowe, *An Anatomy of Risk*, John Wiley and Sons, New York 1977, p. 24;

of loss.[3] What is more, in prior research,[4] risk is perceived to exist when there is a relatively high likelihood that a detrimental event can occur and when that event has a significant associated impact or cost.[5] One can find many risk typologies, an especially interesting concept of the theoretical risk model was presented by J. Zawiła-Niedźwiecki, who combined universal typologies of risk categorisation along the dividing line into risk types: specific to industries, sectors and areas of activity; external and internal; specific and systemic, and most importantly with the assumption of openness of the concept for further detailed divisions.[6] Irrespective of any theoretical typologies, the grouping of risk takes place primarily at the level of economic practice and depends on the profile and unique determinants of the functioning of the organisation. In business, an increasingly common model of behaviour, resulting directly from entrepreneurial orientation, is taking the risk by choice, not to avoid losses, but in order to achieve anticipated or probable benefits. Hence the literature on the subject points out pure (negative or absolute) risk and speculative or neutral risk.[7] Risk is measurable. Recalling the PN-ISO 31000: 2018-08 standard regarding risk management principles and guidelines, it is understood as the "impact of uncertainty on objectives," which may cause a deviation from expectations—not only in a negative but also positive way.[8] Nowadays, the risk category is given a constructive merit in building the enterprise value, risk may concern both positive and negative effects.[9]

For the purposes of this article, the definition of risk should be reconsidered from an operational point of view. Jajuga K. accentuates that "operational risk is the risk of loss resulting from inappropriate and malfunctioning internal processes, people, systems and external events." Basel II: International Convergence of Capital Measurement

K. R. MacCrimmon, A. D. Wehrung, *Taking Risk. The Management of Uncertainty*, The Free Press, New York 1986, p. 12; W. Tarczyński, M. Mojsiewicz, *Zarządzanie ryzykiem*, PWE, Warszawa 2001, p. 11.

[3] R. Kendall, *Zarządzanie ryzykiem dla menadżerów. Praktyczne podejście do kontrolowania ryzyka*, K.E. Liber, Warszawa 2000, p. 55.

[4] See: J. Hallikas et al., *Risk Analysis and Assessment in Network Environments: A Dyadic Case Study*, "International Journal of Production Economics" 2002, 78 (1), pp. 45–55; R. Luce, H. Raiffa, *Games and Decisions*, John Wiley & Sons, New York 1957; Z. Shapira, *Risk Taking: A Managerial Perspective*, Russell Sage Foundation, New York 1995; J. Yates, E. Stone, *The Risk Construct* [in:] *Risk Taking Behavior*, ed. by J. F. Yates, John Wiley & Sons, New York 1992, pp. 1–25.

[5] G. A. Zsidisin et al., *An Analysis of Supply Risk Assessment Techniques*, "International Journal of Physical Distribution & Logistics Management" 2004, 34 (5), pp. 397–413.

[6] J. Zawiła-Niedźwiecki, *Zarządzanie ryzykiem w zapewnianiu ciągłości organizacji*, Wydawnictwo Edu--Libri, Kraków–Warszawa 2013, pp. 40–41.

[7] See: A. H. Mowbray, R. H. Blanchard, *Insurance, Its Theory and Practise in the United States*, McGraw-Hill Book Co., New York 1961, pp. 6–7; R. J. Mehr, B. A. Hedges, *Risk Management in the Business Enterprise*, Homewood, Irwin 1963, p. 3; J. Teczke, *Zarządzanie przedsięwzięciami zwiększonego ryzyka*, PAN, Kraków 1996, p. 17.

[8] PN-ISO 31000:2018-0, *Risk Management Guidelines*.

[9] D. McNamee, *Oszacowanie ryzyka w audycie wewnętrznym i zarządzaniu*, Fundacja Rozwoju Rachunkowości w Polsce, Warszawa 2004, p. 4.

and Capital Standards: a Revised Framework separates seven components of the
groups generating operational risk: internal fraud, including unauthorised activities,
theft and fraud; external fraud; HR practice and work safety (along with: employee
relations, occupational safety, divisions and discrimination); clients, products and
business practice; damage to assets; business process management (making transactions, delivery and management processes); and system defects.[10] Risk is present in
all processes in the company—its sources may be in manufacturing, technological,
commercial, IT, financial or managerial processes, it may also involve the implementation of specific functions: logistics, marketing, investment and other. Therefore, it
is everywhere within the organisation and concerns both operational processes and
strategies.[11] It is implemented through ongoing monitoring of internal processes,
evaluation of systems and people, detecting and counteracting the negative effects of
risk resulting from external events, as well as implementation of necessary corrective
actions. Strategic risk management is a long-term process with the purpose of anticipating, identifying and continuously monitoring and correcting the organisation's
strategic goals. The sum of these activities from the scope of operational and strategic
risk management consists of comprehensive risk management in an organisation.
What is of great consequence is that risk cannot be completely eliminated. There is
always an event that will change the course of processes. It is important, therefore,
to tame risk in the organisation, develop mechanisms of control and risk assessment,
monitor the course of the first level of implementation of the adopted objectives.
Likewise, every organisation must learn how to eliminate the negative effects of risk
or influence the reason for its appearance, not to mention noticing opportunities and
taking advantage of them.[12]

Risk management in the logistic process

The logistic process is an orderly series of operations related to the flow of materials,
which creates a logistic system that, in the end, results in a logistic service, proper
transportation or storage of products, in quality, quantity and time consistent with

[10] See: *Zarządzanie ryzykiem*, ed. by K. Jajuga, Wydawnictwo Naukowe PWN, Warszawa 2007, p. 16;
I. Staniec, K. M. Klimczak, *Ryzyko operacyjne* [in:] *Zarządzanie ryzykiem operacyjnym*, ed. by I. Staniec,
J. Zawiła-Niedźwiecki, C.H. Beck, Warszawa 2008, p. 39; A. M. Marinoiu, *Operational Risk in International Business: Taxonomy and Assessment Methods*, "The Journal of the Faculty of Economics" 2009,
1 (1), p. 196; J. Zawiła-Niedźwiecki, *Zarządzanie ryzykiem...*
[11] K. Janasz, *Ryzyko w zarządzaniu strategicznym organizacją* [in:] *Zarządzanie przedsiębiorstwem w warunkach współczesnych wyzwań gospodarczych*, ed. by R. Borowiecki, J. Kaczmarek, Fundacja Uniwersytetu
Ekonomicznego w Krakowie, Kraków 2014, p. 93.
[12] P. Buła, *System zarządzania ryzykiem w przedsiębiorstwie jako element nadzoru korporacyjnego*, Wydawnictwo Uniwersytetu Jagiellońskiego, Kraków 2015, p. 18.

the expectations of recipients. Logistic processes are related to the flow of materials and information from suppliers of production factors to their users, and currently also to the utilisation of waste. The logistic process can be part of logistics: procurement, production and distribution; it can include, among others, processes such as: storage, transport, communication, material flow management, packaging management and cargo units, inventory management, customer order handling.[13] Logistic processes are usually complex and the effectiveness of their implementation is conditioned by properly conducted planning, organising processes and controlling individual activities. Logistic managers are under perpetual pressure to improve the efficiency of their work results,[14] especially in terms of transformation of businesses towards digitalisation. The supply chain is expected to run much faster, everything is becoming more intelligent and connected, more autonomous devices will be operationalised and much more data will be generated.[15] Nowadays it becomes clear that an efficient initial logistics plan is indispensable, it is by no means sufficient to minimise risk in high performance systems. Therefore plans need to be complemented by the ability to make and implement sophisticated decisions in real-time in order to respond effectively to unforeseen events.[16] Significant issues to be tackled include: definition of the risk and cost of deviation from the original plan. According to the assumptions of GEMIO, there are five areas of threats in logistics, specifically: geopolitics, environment, market, infrastructure, organisation.[17] Direct impacts include outsourcing, internal procedures, customs services, the situation of carriers, while indirect impacts relate to infrastructure of logistics terminals or economic situation. The level of uncertainty of logistic processes varies depending on the type, amount of financial expenditures and the implementation method. Achieving the intended goals requires the ability to predict and control risky events and conditions that can negatively affect results. What does it mean that risk assessment is constitutive and necessary? Risk assessment requires the identification of potential sources of threats that can be recognised as having impact on logistic processes.[18] When this is done, one can find a wide range of tools for risk analysis in a logistic process.

[13]   K. Ficoń, *Logistyka ekonomiczna: procesy logistyczne*, BEL Studio, Warszawa 2008.

[14]   D. Walters, *Supply Chain Risk Management: Vulnerability and Resilience in Logistics*, Kogan Page, London 2011, p. 10.

[15]   *Eye for Transport*, Global Logistics Report 2018, https://www.eft.com/content/2018-global-logistics-report, p. 2 (access: 14 December 2018).

[16]   G. M. Giaglis et al., *Minimizing Logistics Risk through Real-Time Vehicle Routing and Mobile Technologies: Research to Date and Future Trends*, "International Journal of Physical Distribution & Logistics Management" 2004, 34 (9), pp. 749–764.

[17]   D. Książkiewicz, D. Mirkiewicz, *Bezpieczeństwo we współczesnych łańcuchach logistycznych* [in:] *Współczesne problemy rozwoju transportu zrównoważonego*, ed. by R. Rolbiecki, "Zeszyty Naukowe Uniwersytetu Gdańskiego. Ekonomika transportu i logistyka" 2012, 43, p. 45.

[18]   A. Norrman, U. Jansson, *Ericsson's Proactive Supply Chain Risk Management Approach after a Serious Sub-Supplier Accident*, "International Journal of Physical Distribution & Logistics Management" 2004, 34 (5), pp. 434–456.

Research method

The method is a deliberately used procedure (with the possibility of repeating it in all cases of a given type) aimed at achieving the intended goal, and an analysis is "a general method of operation consisting of obtaining a product through distribution of a whole into finer elements."[19] In other words, an analysis is a research method examining extracted elements of the whole and examining each of them separately. It can be considered that the risk analysis methods will include separation of ways to determine risk through the prism of the parameters characterising them.

Therefore, risk analysis methods are tools that, in an organised mode, enable identification, planning and risk management. Their goal is to eliminate interference or to reduce the risk of their occurrence to an acceptable level. Risk analysis of logistic processes includes: mathematical methods, estimation methods and mixed methods which are primarily used in internal audits.

The research method used in this case study was chosen due to the growing importance of international transport in the modern economy and to obtain insights into how and why organisations may assess risk in international freight wheeled transport. The mathematical method is based on spreadsheets, where risk is described by categories to which appropriate points or weights are assigned. Mathematical analysis includes four stages: determination of risk areas, creation of point scale and weights for individual risk criteria, risk assessment, preparation of a hierarchical list of risk areas.

Determination of risk areas

At this stage, the risk areas (categories) are separated from the areas, goals and tasks of a department or an entire enterprise. Areas (categories) that are described by those factors are the risk assessment criteria. Most often the following areas of risk are distinguished: financial risk, risk of lack of internal control, risk of lack or too complicated procedures, risk of changes in legal regulations, risk of losing a good corporate image. Table 1 presents examples of risk categories, criteria for their assessment and factors affecting the category and evaluation criteria.

---

[19]   T. Pszczołowski, *Mała encyklopedia prakseologii i teorii organizacji*, Zakład Narodowy im. Ossolińskich, Wrocław 1978, pp. 15, 117.

Table 1. Categories, criteria and risk assessment factors

Risk categories	Criteria of risk assessment	Factors affecting assessment
Financial risk	Significance/ materiality	• budget size; • expenditure on an annual basis; • amount of financial flows; • number of financial operations carried out; • the probability of financial losses and their amount; • reliability of financial statements; • risk of loss in a single operation.
The risk of insufficient internal control	Internal control	• existence of written procedures; • direct supervision; • the level of implementation of conclusions from previous audits; • clarity of control procedures; • descriptions of the evaluation criteria; • authorisation control.
The risk of too complicated procedures, processes or systems	Degree of complexity / management quality	• number and complexity of procedural steps in the examined activity; • computer programs facilitating and controlling work; • complexity of internal regulations; • complexity of legal regulations regarding an area of process; • number of related operations or subsystems in the process; • duties segregation; • information flow; • the authorities.
The risk of changes in external factors affecting the business activity	External factors	• the level of complexity and the frequency of changes in internal regulations; • political, economic and legal changes in the countries where the company operates; • strikes of employees of the enterprise; • changes in trends regarding the functioning of the company or a lifestyle; • technological progress; • external controls; • price increase, inflation, interest rates, exchange rates.

Risk categories	Criteria of risk assessment	Factors affecting assessment
The risk of an internal process	Internal factors	• quality, quantity, rotation of employees and their morale; • employee engagement; • turnover rate; • quality of subsystems' operation; • the degree of process automation; • technical and technological equipment.
Risk of system termination	Sensitivity	• data reliability; • the impact of an error on another operation, subsystem or system; • customers' sensitivity to changes in procedures and/or mistakes made; • susceptibility to corruption.
The risk of losing company's good image	Company's good image/ sensitivity	• the degree of data confidentiality as part of the ongoing process; • the impact of the process on stakeholder opinions (local community, shareholders, banks); • social pressure.

Source: authors' own elaboration.

In the mathematical method, there is no constant set of criteria for risk assessment—the selection of criteria depends on the area of research and the scope of the company's activity. Usually, 4–5 most important criteria, from the point of view of a company, are chosen. Descriptions of factors affecting the assessment of criteria are also created by the company (the person who is conducting the analysis), therefore they may be different. It is important, that they are defined in description assumptions of the analysis. After determining risk areas, it is also necessary to identify tasks or activities from the examined area of the company's activity, which will then be assessed through the prism of risk criteria.

For international freight wheeled transport, 5 risk assessment criteria have been adopted. The criteria and their factors describing these criteria are presented in Table 2.

Table 2. Factors influencing the assessment of individual risk criteria in goods transport

No.	Risk criteria assessment	Factors affecting the assessment
1	Materiality (financial losses)	number of financial operations
		the risk of loss in a single transport
		difficulties in the payment execution for the service provided
2	Sensitivity	data reliability
		the error impact on another operation or system (e.g. further transport, production or trade)
		customers' sensitivity to changes in delivery times and errors in delivery and documents
		vulnerable to corruption
3	Internal control	the level of implementation of conclusions from previous audits
		clarity of control procedures
		existence of written procedures
4	External factors	the frequency of changes in internal regulations
		petrol price increase, exchange rates
		changes in legal regulations in the countries where a company operates
		road infrastructure
		strikes in homeland and abroad hindering goods transport
5	Internal factors	quality and fluctuation of employees
		engagement and employees morale
		duties segregation
		payroll system

Source: authors' own elaboration.

Definition of weights and scale of points for individual risk criteria

The next step in the implementation of the described method is assigning weights to all specified criteria. What is significant in the mathematical method is that the sum of those weights must be equal to 1. The criteria presented in Table 2 are taken into account together. Additional criteria—always present in this method, i.e. management priority and the date of the last control (audit) must be considered separately. Tables 3 and 4 present an example weight assignment.

Table 3. Basic risk assessment criteria—weights

No.	Risk assessment criteria	Weight
1	Relevance (financial loss)	0.20
2	Sensitivity	0.25
3	Internal control	0.10
4	External factors	0.30
5	Internal factors	0.15
	Total	1.00

Source: Authors' own elaboration.

Table 4. Additional risk assessment criteria: management priority, date of last control—weight

Management priority	Date of last control	Weight
Very big	Never	0.4
Big	3 years ago	0.3
Law	2 years ago	0.2
Very low	Year before	0.1
	Total	1.0

Source: authors' own elaboration.

In the mathematical method, apart from awarding weights, basic risk assessment criteria are also awarded points to indicates the degree of risk. The most common scale used in the mathematical method is from 1 to 4 points. Detailed rules for the allocation of these points are presented in Table 5.

Table 5. Risk assessment—point scale

Relevance (financial loss)	Sensitivity	Internal control	External factors	Internal factors	Point scale
No financial implications	Low sensitivity	Frequent formal internal controls of the process	Low impact	Low impact	1
Low financial implications	Moderate sensitivity	Moderate control/or frequent informal control	Moderate impact	Moderate impact	2
Big financial implications	System is sensitive	Incidental formal and informal control	High impact	High impact	3
Key financial implications	Great sensitivity	No internal control of the process	Great impact	Great impact	4

Source: authors' own elaboration.

Risk assessment

Risk assessment consists of an evaluation of the threat to which each task/action is subjected. Tasks are assessed through the prism of the adopted basic assessment criteria (hazard assessment on a scale of 1–4, see: Table 5) and weightings given (see: Table 3). The evaluation algorithm is presented in Figure 1.

$$PEC= \sum_{i=1}^{n} \frac{wC_i \times P_i}{m \times 100\%}$$

PEC—points of assessment criteria

wC_i—weights assigned to the assessment criteria

P_i—points assigned to criterion

m—maximum value that can be assigned to the criterion

n—number of criteria

Source: S. Klauf, A. Tłuczak, *Optymalizacja decyzji logistycznych*, Difin, Warszawa 2016.

Risk assessment considering the date of the last control consists of multiplying the sum of the evaluation criteria and the weight of the last control (see: Table 4). Evaluation after taking into account the priorities of the management consists of multiplying the risk assessment after taking into account the date of the last control and the importance assigned to the priorities of the management. Subsequently the results are reduced to a common denominator by dividing each result of analysis (points of each task) by the maximum number of points that could be obtained as part of the risk analysis. An example of risk assessment using a mathematical method is presented in Table 6.

Table 6. Application of mathematical method to risk assessment

Task no.	Processes (objects) of activities subject to risk assessment	Criteria (factors) for risk assessment							Risk assessment — After taking into account			Final rating in %
		Significance 0.2	Management Quality 0.3	Internal control 0.15	External factors 0.15	Internal factors 0.2	Priority of management	Date of last control 0.1	Criteria	Priority of management	Date of last control	
1	Determining the place of loading and unloading	4	3	2	4	1	0.3	0.1	70.00	100.00	110.00	61.11
2	Car selection	4	4	2	1	4	0.4	0.1	81.25	121.25	131.25	72.92
3	Technical control of a vehicle	4	4	4	3	3	0.4	0.1	91.25	131.25	141.25	78.47
4	Driver selection	3	2	2	2	3	0.1	0.1	60.00	70.00	80.00	44.44
5	Selection of the route	4	3	3	4	3	0.4	0.1	83.75	123.75	133.75	74.31
6	Tachograph control	4	3	3	4	2	0.2	0.1	78.75	98.75	108.75	60.42
7	Compliance of goods with the order	4	4	3	4	2	0.3	0.1	86.25	116.25	126.25	70.14
8	Correctness of transport documents	4	2	4	2	4	0.3	0.1	77.50	107.50	117.50	65.28
9	Correct loading/placement of goods in the loading space of the means of transport	4	2	4	1	4	0.4	0.1	73.75	113.75	123.75	68.75
10	Securing the car against theft of goods	3	1	3	2	2	0.3	0.1	51.25	81.25	91.25	50.69
11	Refuelling	3	2	2	3	3	0.3	0.1	63.75	93.75	103.75	57.64
12	Control of drivers' working time	4	3	3	3	3	0.4	0.1	80.00	120.00	130.00	72.22
13	Tracking the route of the car using computer programs	3	3	3	4	3	0.3	0.1	78.75	108.75	118.75	65.97
14	Communication with the driver while driving	4	4	2	4	3	0.4	0.1	87.50	127.50	137.50	76.39
15	Keeping the delivery date	4	4	4	4	4	0.4	0.1	100.00	140.00	150.00	83.33

Source: authors' own elaboration.

Table 7. Hierarchical list of risk areas

Task no.	Processes (objects) of activities subject to risk assessment	Criteria (factors) for risk assessment					Priority of management	Date of last control	Risk assessment			Final rating in %
		Significance	Management quality	Internal control	External factors	Internal factors			After taking into account			
									Criteria	Priority of management	Date of the last control	
		0.2	0.3	0.15	0.15	0.2		0.1				
15	Keeping the delivery date	4	4	4	4	4	0.4	0.1	100.00	140.00	150.00	83.33
3	Technical control of a vehicle	4	4	4	3	3	0.4	0.1	91.25	131.25	141.25	78.47
14	Communication with the driver while driving	4	4	2	4	3	0.4	0.1	87.50	127.50	137.50	76.39
5	Selection of the route	4	3	3	4	3	0.4	0.1	83.75	123.75	133.75	74.31
2	Car selection	4	4	2	1	4	0.4	0.1	81.25	121.25	131.25	72.92
12	Control of drivers' working time	4	3	3	3	3	0.4	0.1	80.00	120.00	130.00	72.22
7	Compliance of the goods with the order	4	4	3	4	2	0.3	0.1	86.25	116.25	126.25	70.14
9	Correct loading / placement of goods in the loading space of the means of transport	4	2	4	1	4	0.4	0.1	73.75	113.75	123.75	68.75
13	Tracking the route of the car using computer programs	3	3	3	4	3	0.3	0.1	78.75	108.75	118.75	65.97
8	Correctness of transport documents	4	2	4	2	4	0.3	0.1	77.50	107.50	117.50	65.28
1	Determining the place of loading and unloading	4	3	2	4	1	0.3	0.1	70.00	100.00	110.00	61.11
6	Tachograph control	4	3	3	4	2	0.2	0.1	78.75	98.75	108.75	60.42
11	Refuelling	3	2	2	3	3	0.3	0.1	63.75	93.75	103.75	57.64
10	Securing the car against theft of goods	3	1	3	2	2	0.3	0.1	51.25	81.25	91.25	50.69
4	Driver selection	3	2	2	2	3	0.1	0.1	60.00	70.00	80.00	44.44

Source: authors' own elaboration.

Findings

Creating a hierarchical list of risk areas

Creating a hierarchical list of risk areas consists of setting tasks according to a decreasing final grade (see: Table 7), i.e. from the highest to the lowest level of risk. The most common risk assessment criteria are:
- high level of risk—final rating over 70%;
- average risk level—final assessment from 46% to 70%;
- low level of risk—final grade from 0% to 45%.

In the example presented above, the highest final grade was given to the following tasks: keeping the delivery deadline, technical inspection of a vehicle and communication with the driver during the ride. The higher the final rating, the more a company should pay attention to monitoring and control of task implementation.

Keeping the delivery date, as could be said intuitively, which has also been confirmed in the assessment that has been conducted in this paper, is associated with the highest risk. First of all, because it can bring financial losses to the company, dictated by the contract and penalties for failure to meet the deadline, as well as image losses and the most dangerous—the loss of a client. The technical condition of the vehicle has an immanent impact on the implementation of the transport service, and affects the timeliness, quality and safety of transported goods.

An inadequate level of communication with the driver while driving, poor performance of service may also adversely affect the performance of contracted liabilities, so it is burdened with a high level of risk. What is more, the freight forwarder often has information on the condition of roads or updates of the route dictated by other orders. Route selection is inseparably connected with the time of service provision, one of the determinants of its quality affecting the competitiveness of enterprises providing services of international freight wheeled transport. The choice of a car allows for the provision of high-quality transport services in the aspect of the safety of goods and enables comprehensive service of the order and savings. It is extremely important to manage the drivers' working time responsibly to fulfil the delivery deadline and to comply with the law in this area, that is why it has been placed in the 6th position of risk rating. The company has a different influence on the conformity of goods with the order and also on the correct loading/placing of goods in the cargo area of the means of transport, which is dictated by the provisions of the contract. Most often, the role of transport companies is limited to parking under the loading ramp and waiting for the loading to finish. Drivers should check the placement of goods on the cargo area to deliver goods without damage and to ensure the safety of transport and other road users. Other operational processes subject to risk assessment, such as correctness of transport documents, determination of the place of loading and unloading, tachograph control, refuelling, car security against theft of goods, driver's choice are burdened with a lower risk level. Both the choice of the driver and the protection of the car against the theft of goods seem to be extremely important, but nowadays this is a certain standard that is obvious and written in the contract and basic requirements, and the drivers' competences are verified by appropriate institutions issuing driving licenses.

The risk of a task performance failure is associated with significant consequences for a company. It should also be noted that both internal and external factors influence the task performance. External factors which are independent of an enterprise may significantly disrupt the task execution process (e.g. strikes blocking roads, accidents, traffic jams, sudden and severe weather events), and thus lead to material losses (e.g. penalties for delayed delivery) or intangible losses (e.g. loss of good company image).

Conclusion and discussions

The presented mathematical method of risk assessment is a relatively simple technique, helping to determine the priority of the tasks performed under the project. It helps to identify tasks whose implementation is encumbered with the highest risk, and the risk of failure would bring the greatest losses to an enterprise. The most difficult stage in this method is to develop a set of assessment criteria, their weights and a process of awarding the appropriate number of points. What is significant, the assessment of a given criterion and its significance may differ between the assessors. Nevertheless, owing to this method the company is able to assess the degree of risk of disruptions in the task implementation, and has a chance to take appropriate action to reduce its occurrence. If tasks performed by a company are receptive to external factors, the company should develop procedures to monitor them and respond quickly to emerging changes.

The research findings provide forwarders with insights into simple techniques that their companies can implement to assess international freight wheeled transport risk. It is not necessary to implement costly programmes designed to assess risk. Many organisations glean information considering transport risk from existing supplier opinions on the Internet. However, risk assessment should only be one step within an organisation's overall risk management strategy. Mathematical risk assessment techniques can help organisations go beyond simply recognising the risk of transport by providing professionals early warning indicators of potential supply problems.

Bibliography

Buła P., *System zarządzania ryzykiem w przedsiębiorstwie jako element nadzoru korporacyjnego*, Wydawnictwo Uniwersytetu Jagiellońskiego, Kraków 2015.

Eye for Transport, Global Logistics Report 2018, https://www.eft.com/content/2018-global-logistics--report (access: 14 December 2018).

Ficoń K., *Logistyka ekonomiczna: procesy logistyczne*, BEL Studio, Warszawa 2008.

Giaglis G. M., Minis I., Tatarakis A., Zeimpekis V., *Minimizing Logistics Risk through Real-Time Vehicle Routing and Mobile Technologies: Research to Date and Future Trends*, "International Journal of Physical Distribution & Logistics Management" 2004, 34 (9).

Hallikas J., Virolainen V., Tuominen M., *Risk Analysis and Assessment in Network Environments: A Dyadic Case Study*, "International Journal of Production Economics" 2002, 78 (1).

Janasz K., *Ryzyko w zarządzaniu strategicznym organizacją* [in:] *Zarządzanie przedsiębiorstwem w warunkach współczesnych wyzwań gospodarczych*, ed. by R. Borowiecki, J. Kaczmarek, Fundacja Uniwersytetu Ekonomicznego w Krakowie, Kraków 2014.

Kendall R., *Zarządzanie ryzykiem dla menadżerów. Praktyczne podejście do kontrolowania ryzyka*, K.E. Liber, Warszawa 2000.

Klauf S., Tłuczak A., *Optymalizacja decyzji logistycznych*, Difin, Warszawa 2016.

Knight F. H., *Risk Uncertainty and Profit*, MA: Hart, Schaffner & Marx, Houghton Mifflin Company, Boston 1921.

Kordela Z., Paprocki W., *Stan i perspektywy rozwoju międzynarodowego transportu drogowego rzeczy w Polsce*, Wydawnictwo Eurologistics, Suchy Las 2018.

Książkiewicz D., Mirkiewicz D., *Bezpieczeństwo we współczesnych łańcuchach logistycznych* [in:] *Współczesne problemy rozwoju transportu zrównoważonego*, ed. by R. Rolbiecki, "Zeszyty Naukowe Uniwersytetu Gdańskiego. Ekonomika transportu i logistyka" 2012, 4.

Luce R., Raiffa H., *Games and Decisions*, John Wiley & Sons, New York 1957.

MacCrimmon K. R., Wehrung A. D., *Taking Risk. The Management of Uncertainty*, The Free Press, New York 1986.

Marinoiu A. M., *Operational Risk in International Business: Taxonomy and Assessment Methods*, "The Journal of the Faculty of Economics" 2009, 1 (1).

McNamee D., *Oszacowanie ryzyka w audicie wewnętrznym i zarządzaniu*, Fundacja Rozwoju Rachunkowości w Polsce, Warszawa 2004.

Mehr R. J., Hedges B. A., *Risk Management in the Business Enterprise*, Homewood, Irwin 1963.

Mowbray A. H., Blanchard R. H., *Insurance, Its Theory and Practice in the United States*, McGraw--Hill Book Co., New York 1961.

Norrman A., Jansson U., *Ericsson's Proactive Supply Chain Risk Management Approach after a Serious Sub-Supplier Accident*, "International Journal of Physical Distribution & Logistics Management" 2004, 34 (5).

Orzeł J., *Zarządzanie ryzykiem operacyjnym za pomocą instrumentów pochodnych*, Wydawnictwo Naukowe PWN, Warszawa 2012.

Pszczołowski T., *Mała encyklopedia prakseologii i teorii organizacji*, Zakład Narodowy im. Ossolińskich, Wrocław 1978.

Rowe A., *An Anatomy of Risk*, John Wiley and Sons, New York 1977.

Shapira Z., *Risk Taking: A Managerial Perspective*, Russell Sage Foundation, New York 1995.

Staniec I., Klimczak K. M., *Ryzyko operacyjne* [in:] *Zarządzanie ryzykiem operacyjnym*, ed. by I. Staniec, J. Zawiła-Niedźwiecki, C.H. Beck, Warszawa 2008.

Tarczyński W., Mojsiewicz M., *Zarządzanie ryzykiem*, PWE, Warszawa 2001.

Teczke J., *Zarządzanie przedsięwzięciami zwiększonego ryzyka*, PAN, Kraków 1996.

Walters D., *Supply Chain Risk Management: Vulnerability and Resilience in Logistics*, Kogan Page, London 2011.

Willet A. H., *The Economic Theory of Risk Insurance*, The University of Pennsylvania Press, Philadelphia 1951.

Yates J., Stone E., *The Risk Construct* [in:] *Risk Taking Behavior*, ed. by J. F. Yates, John Wiley & Sons, New York 1992.

Zarządzanie ryzykiem, ed. by K. Jajuga, Wydawnictwo Naukowe PWN, Warszawa 2007.

Zawiła-Niedźwiecki J., *Ryzyko i bezpieczeństwo operacyjne* [in:] *Zarządzanie ryzykiem działalności organizacji*, ed. by J. Monkiewicz, L. Gąsiorkiewicz, C.H. Beck, Warszawa 2010.

Zawiła-Niedźwiecki J., *Zarządzanie ryzykiem w zapewnianiu ciągłości organizacji*, Wydawnictwo Edu-Libri, Kraków–Warszawa 2013.

Zsidisin G. A., Ellram L. M., Carter J. R., Cavinato J. L., *An Analysis of Supply Risk Assessment Techniques*, "International Journal of Physical Distribution & Logistics Management" 2004, 34 (5).

Management and Digitisation

Prof. Walter Sorg, Ph.D.

Abstract

The article is devoted to the phenomena of digitalization. It describes what changes the digitalization brings and how to deal with those changes. The text uses the framework of Integrated Management and based on it the author describes how to approach process and systemic changes. It can be achieved through horizontal and vertical integration of organization internal activities.

Keywords: digitalization, Industry 4.0, St. Gallen management concept, systemic approach, change management

Foreword

Nothing is more practical than a good theory. As important as management sciences are, they do not guarantee successful corporate development. Who has no future-oriented basic attitude and the yesterday and the today again and again questions, wrong expectations will raise. Management science developed from various traditional scientific teachings at universities and is regarded as a recognised field of research and education. It provides findings and design recommendations from a wide variety of scientific disciplines. The interplay between business administration and management theory is characterised by different schools of thought. Although there is a wealth of specialist literature on economic problems, there are no sustainable patent solutions. K. Bleicher notes a loss of consensus on goals, content and methods, among other things.

From today's point of view, there are still further development possibilities despite numerous concepts. These are often shaped by current development trends. In particular with regard to a conclusive linkage of practice and theory there is still further need for action for the enterprise management. At present, the topic of "digitisation" gives rise to a further development of management science in the economic field. Such and similar topics often reveal great uncertainty and often lead to undesirable developments. A well-positioned management is therefore an important basis for every company. For this to be the case, management science must provide the necessary tools.

This contribution is made in memoriam for Prof. Janusz Teczke, Ph.D. It is with-him that I associate some years of common work. From this time of close personal contact I have come to know his merits as a person and scientist. His personal merit lies in the further development of the "Krakow School." Of particular importance is his long-standing contact with Prof. Knut Bleicher, Ph.D. and the St. Gallen Business School. For this reason, this article expressly refers to Prof. Knut Bleicher's concept of Integrated Management in honour of Prof. Teczke.

Walter Sorg

Neuhof/Fulda in September 2018.

1. Initial considerations

1.1. Digitisation, Industry 4.0

The rapid progress of technology, in particular the quick development of information technology and information systems, is triggering equally rapid economic structural change. The use of IT, computers and the Internet is widespread even in developing countries. This development brings opportunities and risks. The networking of companies opens up new forms of cooperation not only within a company, but also in and with the upstream and downstream stages of the value chain.

The media industry, for example, is regarded as a digital growth driver. Information and communication technologies are provided that enable the transmission of data through space (communication) and through time (storage). Television, the Internet, advertising agencies, print media, the software industry, the music industry, the film industry, electronic commerce (e-commerce), the networked electronic handling of the service exchange process—everything takes place on the Internet. In particular, the automation of processes to increase work productivity is being intensively promoted. Components communicate independently with the production system and, if necessary, initiate repairs themselves or reorder materials. If man, machine and production processes are intelligently networked and the manufacturing processes run independently, then this is referred to as "Industry 4.0." This refers to the fourth industrial revolution after the invention of the steam engine, the assembly line or the computer. Industry 4.0 thus means "intelligent factories" where, for example, driverless transport vehicles take care of logistics and material flow independently. Logistics companies and technical service providers are integrated into the company network (workflow management). This means that the so-called 4th Industrial Revolution not only networks companies with each other, but also allows physical objects to be recorded and processed in electronic systems. For this purpose, they use their own Internet addresses and thus enable independent communication among themselves (Internet of Things). Data capture takes place automatically and in real time, so that the real world and its virtual image become blurred; some also speak of cyberspace.[1]

In the so-called "intelligent factory," man, machine and product are networked with each other in such a way that the entire process is largely autonomous on the basis of cyber systems. The so-called 3D printer replaces the mechanical processing of material, since pulverised materials are mixed together and fused together. This makes production more flexible, individual and efficient, which improves productivity. The production worker takes on a largely supervisory role and more qualified activities. This development requires a huge amount of digital data (Big Data) from various areas.[2]

This so-called digitalisation requires the conversion of analogue data into digital formats for further processing and storage after appropriate processing. In other words, analogue contents or processes are converted into a digital form of working method. It is obvious that there are several reasons for digitisation, in particular:

- intensive use of electronic data processing systems;
- faster machine processing, distribution, storage and reproduction;
- faster search by search criteria;
- reduced sources of error;
- availability of huge amounts of data at any time, targeted processing and analysis.

This exemplary presentation makes it clear that above all digitalisation and thus new digital products and services open up further economic potentials that place new demands on management. In order to master or exploit the digital challenge and opportunities, investments must be made in the acquisition of appropriate knowledge and skills. In addition, the necessary qualification of management and employees must be guaranteed (knowledge management). Digitisation therefore requires changes in the company. It is the task of management to bring about these changes. To this end, the St. Gallen Management Concept (SGMC) offers useful design recommendations on the basis of a continuous process of corporate development, which must be realigned and, if necessary, adapted over time.[3]

The outcome of this paper is informed by the current discussion on digitisation and industry 4.0. It is therefore first briefly described what digitisation means at its core and what this will change for enterprise management and management science (Section 1). It must therefore first be explained which understanding of management is assumed and what role management science plays. This provides answers for change management for companies. The basis for further treatment of this topic is finally the

---

[1]   R. Dillerup, R. Stoi, *Unternehmensführung. Management & Leadership Strategien, Werkzeuge, Praxis*, Verlag Vahlen, München 2016.

[2]   Cf. ibidem, pp. 796 ff.

[3]   K. Bleicher, C. Abegglen, *Das Konzept Integriertes Management: Visionen—Missionen—Programme*, Campus Verlag, Frankfurt 2017, p. 19.

aspect of integrated management (Section 2). Section 3 discusses the possible approaches to the design of integrated management.

Reference is made to Bleicher's concept, which is regarded as the key to a successful business development process. In this respect, the basis if formed by the St. Gallen Management Concept. In view of the limited scope of this work, focus is placed exclusively on strategic management. Based on this, the derivation of purpose-oriented strategies and programmemes for company management takes place. The essay concludes with essential findings and statements and an outlook for shaping thefuture.

1.2. Change: What changes will digitalisation bring?

Nothing is as constant as change. It takes place constantly in all areas and with varying intensity. Change of the current state can take place step by step, continuously in small steps and in individual areas. But it can also be a principle, a fundamental change that leads to a profound change, especially in corporate values and attitudes. Management is faced with the task of recognising this type of development as a result of digitalisation and systematically introducing and shaping it within the company in order to achieve the company's objectives. Dillerup and Stoi point out that change management should only be referred to as "incremental change," since change leadership should take effect in the event of fundamental change.[4] The question must therefore be asked: is digitalisation a continuous process of change or a radical change?

The framework conditions that determine the success or failure of a company, have changed decisively. Essentially, these are the innovations in the direction of digitisation and communication outlined above. This leads to faster business processes. Product lifecycles have shortened enormously. Daily and even faster management has a wealth of accurate, broken-down data on manufacturing processes, individual products, individual branches, etc., with the required comparative figures at its disposal. There is a shortage of time as a factor. Decisions must be made quickly (time-based management). Added to this is the increasing globalisation of the economy as a result of networking, but also as a result of more mergers and cooperations or, on the contrary, unbundling. The world is becoming smaller and virtual. As a result, different cultures with different customs and habits must be taken into account. Financial resources are also being used more heavily as raw materials become scarcer and more expensive, while costs are rising as a result of the increasing use of technology. Last but not least, there is an increasing complexity, nothing is as it was. We are at a time of particular uncertainty and undesirable developments. The management has less reaction time, but at the same time more time is needed due to the increasing complexity. The challenges facing

---

[4]   R. Dillerup, R. Stoi, *Unternehmensführung...*, p. 707.

the "management" function are more diverse than ever before, highly demanding and burdened with many imponderables.[5]

In the current scientific discussion, these changed conditions are referred to as fundamental change; Bleicher speaks of a paradigm shift in management.[6] In doing so, he explicitly establishes a relationship to the paradigm shift. If one follows these changes, it is easy to see that these are highly complex networks that take on a global dimension. Companies and management still have little to no experience of digitisation. The change also affects the company as a whole. So it can be said that a reorientation of the corporate strategy is unavoidable in order to cope with the increasing cost pressure, to increase profitability and to survive in competition, as well as to generate competitive advantages. Furthermore, focus is placed exclusively on the strategic management level. Basically, a company should not only adapt reactively, but also proactively shape the framework conditions. It is crucial that management recognises the need for **change management** as a result of digital change at an early stage and initiates the necessary change. Management science makes appropriate contributions to this. This paper is based on the St. Gallen Management Concept (SGMC) according to Bleicher, whose approach is based on a holistic integrated management concept. Here, the question is examined whether and how the SGMC fulfills these requirements for the company management on the basis of knowledge of management sciences and can offer solutions for the company management to cope with this challenge. However, there will be no recipe such as for baking or cooking.

2. Management

2.1. Classification of management sciences

In further consideration, the first question to be asked is whether management sciences are recognised as management theory. In general, it is understood as the interdisciplinary engagement with problem solving and decision making. It uses various scientific research bases, mathematical models and numerical algorithms to help companies to achieve goals with various scientific methods. To this end, models and concepts are developed, data collected and analysed in order to work with them.

This paper assumes the following understanding of the term management: "management is the process of achieving organisational objectives, within a changing environment, by balancing efficiency, effectiveness and equity, obtaining the most from limited resources, and working with and through other people."[7] Bleicher's line

---

[5]   See K. Bleicher, C. Abegglen, *Das Konzept Integriertes Management...*, p. 23.

[6]   Ibidem, pp. 91 ff.

[7]   J. Naylor, *Management*, Pearson Education, New York 2004, p. 6.

of thought is followed, which understands management in an integrative way and wants to combine economic and social scientific approaches.[8] Bleicher sees in business administration an orientation towards the management of institutions, which understands itself as interdisciplinary and develops into an interdisciplinary management science, separate from business administration, i.e. business administration as a science of management.[9]

In the meantime, management science has become a recognised field of research with explanations and recommendations for various groups and is important as a general management theory with a scientific claim. Conversely, management practice relies on well-founded scientifically management theory. This is particularly important for coping with the requirements of digitisation. However, this is associated with a high demand for management sciences, especially in scientific foundation and application relevance.[10]

Now, what does management mean? The Anglo-American term management replaces the identical German term "Führung" (leadership) and encompasses all tasks and actions for the goal-oriented design, guidance and development of a company. In general, management can be understood, on the one hand, as an institution and, on the other, as a function. As an institution, it comprises the persons with authorising powers (superiors). As a function, it means a complex of tasks for controlling a company, i.e. it is linked to functions for fulfilling tasks such as planning, organising, controlling.[11] The term "scientific management" can, however, be traced back to Taylor.[12]

In the further conceptual development, management is regarded as a cross-sectional function. In the horizontal view, the functions of management such as planning, organisation, control are seen. Vertically the objective functions' procurement, production, and sales volume are illustrated. From this it follows that management functions impact each range of the enterprise and each hierarchical level, although in different ways and extent.[13]

As a result of the varying views on the term "management," different doctrines (schools) have formed, the classical school, behaviour-oriented science or mathematical approaches, the systems theoretical approach. These have led to a professionalisation of management theory at universities (business schools).

---

[8]   *Betriebswirtschaftslehre als Management- und Führungslehre*, ed. by R. Wunderer, Schäffer-Poeschel, Stuttgart 1993, p. VI.

[9]   K. Bleicher, *Betriebswirtschaftslehre – Disziplinäre Lehre vom Wirtschaften in und zwischen Betrieben oder interdisziplinäre Wissenschaft vom Management?* [in:] *Betriebswirtschaftslehre...*, ed. by R. Wunderer, pp. 109 ff.

[10] See R. H. Jung, J. Bruck, S. Quarg, *Allgemeine Managementlehre: Lehrbuch für die angewandte Unternehmens- und Personalführung*, Erich Schmidt, Berlin 2001, Part A.

[11] Cf. H. Steinmann, G. Schreyögg, *Management. Grundlagen der Unternehmensführung Konzepte—Funktionen—Fallstudien*, Gabler Verlag, Wiesbaden 1993, pp. 5 ff.

[12] R. Dillerup, R. Stoi, *Unternehmensführung...*, pp. 9 ff, 13 ff.

[13] See H. Steinmann, G. Schreyögg, *Management...*, pp. 7, 13.

Due to the large number of different theories on management sciences, the organisation and control of companies are supported in very different ways. These are not so much scientific approaches as empirical observations. What they all have in common, however, is the view that it is a central task of management to develop the company, i.e. to set the course in a controlled manner, for an uncertain future. Bleicher sees a system-oriented, cybernetic approach to integrated corporate development as a secure way of successfully managing a company for years to come. Thus he develops a basic understanding of corporate management and at the same time the basis for the St. Gallen Management Concept (SGMC). This should not be understood as a one-off procedure, but as a permanent process par excellence. This is also a matter for the boss or a management issue.[14]

The hectic pace of day-to-day business in the operational area, often blocks the view of a long-term business model. Against this background, it is necessary for corporate management to institutionalise a permanent "Management of Change," that unites the normative, the strategic and the operational to form a permanent "Management of Improvement."[15]

2.2. Orientation of change management

One of the main tasks of management is the control of operational change processes. It is important to anchor changes in the company in a sustainable manner. Basically, the life cycle of a company inevitably leads to constant changes that require an adjustment of the strategic orientation. The awareness that **change management** means a planned and controlled initiation of change in the company is increasing. Companies have to put their strategy, business models, organisation (structure, processes) to the test again and again. The prerequisite is that management is sensitised to the growing demands of competition and thus recognises the need for proactive change management. The necessity is determined, for example, by a reorientation of the corporate strategy or increasing cost pressure. In this way, the future viability of the company can be continuously developed. This means profiling the strategic management from "yesterday and today" to "tomorrow."

Currently, the changes in technology due to digitisation are in the foreground. The task of change management is therefore to manage the company in such a way that the constant changes are not only mastered. Rather, the prerequisites must be created for the change to be actively driven forward. In this sense, change management is understood as an opportunity to further develop the company in the direction of digitisation and to lead to a reorientation of the corporate strategy. Supplementary management approaches such as IT solutions and lean management provide support for strategy implementation.

---

[14]   K. Bleicher, C. Abegglen, *Das Konzept Integriertes Management...*, pp. 82 ff.
[15]   Ibidem, p. 90.

In accordance with the principle "structure follows strategy," the organisation must be adapted to the strategy. Strengths and weaknesses of the current organisation must be analysed as follows:

- **Structure:** organisational structure, process organisation, management system, working conditions.
- **Corporate culture:** mission statement, corporate principles, regulations, culture lived.
- **Behaviour:** leadership style, information and communication, working atmosphere.

The knowledge gained can be used to determine which of the familiar change management instruments are to be used. Within the scope of this work, the focus is on strategy management (on the functioning and process—phases—of change).[16] It remains to be seen whether digitisation will induce change management, which will virtually reinvent and rebuild the company in the sense of business reengineering. For many existing things will have to be retained, especially personnel. Models must therefore be developed to support entrepreneurial decisions. In addition, it may be necessary to expand formal knowledge in mathematics, statistics, or with regard to "Big Data." Change management will concentrate, on the one hand, on the core business and, on the other hand, will redefine strategic business areas.

Change management requires constant monitoring of the change process in order to separate from old procedures and ways of conduct and to anchor them in the organisation in the long term. This means a planned procedure and interaction, as well as dialogue with the participants, guided by such things as:

- clear objectives;
- correct flow of information;
- create clarity about the future;
- provide the necessary resources;
- deal with employee behaviour, reduce fears and resistance;
- drop old working methods and routines;
- involve, inspire and convince employees immediately;
- train employees and enable them to deal with new technology;
- accompaniment of change;
- track feedback and success measurement in a way that is critical to success.

According to the current Handelsblatt ranking of the research achievements of German universities since 2014, science is intensely concerned with Internet topics, in particular digitisation, and confronts most economic disciplines, production, logistics, financing, with new challenges in the development and application of scientific methods. According to this ranking, the star among universities is St. Gallen. It remains to

---

[16]   R. Dillerup, R. Stoi, *Unternehmensführung...*, pp. 712 ff.

be said: economics should become the "driver" for change through digitisation and further develop the methods of strategic planning.

2.3. Integrated management system

In order to act in the sense of change management, it is crucial not only to analyse individual areas or aspects, but also the company as a whole in context and in its interaction with the outside world. Traditional leadership patterns are often cultivated. Profit maximisation and profit orientation are predominant. The necessity of change is recognised, but nothing changes. In order to cope with this, integrated management in the sense of Bleicher is necessary.

Integrated management as a management system is based on Ulrich's system-theoretical approach and forms the foundation for the "St. Gallen Management Concept" (SGMC) developed by Bleicher. The application of system theory to business administration has resulted in system-oriented management theory. The core of this approach combines all functions and levels of a company into a holistic system. A distinction is made between the normative, strategic and operative management levels, which are then subdivided according to structures, activities and behaviour.

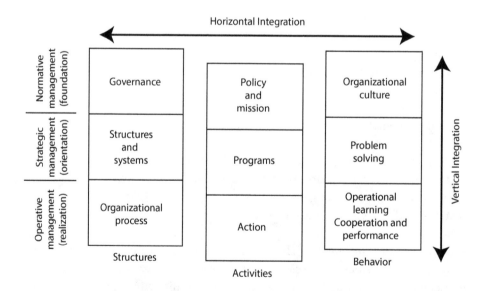

Figure 1. Integrated approach by Knut Bleicher

Source: based on K. Bleicher, C. Abegglen, *Das Konzept Integriertes Management: Visionen—Missionen—Programme*, Campus Verlag, Frankfurt 2017, p. 59.

The goal is integrated corporate development in normative, strategic and operational dimensions. Starting from the actual configuration, the focus is on the future (target configuration). Individual options for a pragmatic implementation (internal/external transition) must lead to an improvement of the company situation (performance option). This requires process competence of the management and includes topic competence. With regard to the employees of the company, mediation and implementation skills are required. In the end stands a higher performance of the enterprise.

With the integrated management system, methods and instruments are combined in a uniform structure to meet the requirements of a wide variety of management areas and serve corporate governance and compliance, e.g. quality management, security management, risk management, internal control system. The integrated management system enables synergies to be exploited and resources to be pooled, enabling lean management, for example. Unnecessary administrative and decision-making levels are avoided. Each individual system would not make this possible, or only to a limited extent. Until now, the management systems in most companies have been set up in isolation from each other. This often led to overlaps with unclear interfaces and in some cases to contrary developments. The system-theoretical approach regards companies as systems whose control is based on the control loop principle. The general definition is as follows: "A company is a complex, socio-technical system consisting of a multitude of different elements that are related to each other." Target and actual values are continuously compared in order to initiate corrective measures (operationally) in the event of deviations or to make adjustment decisions that ensure the success of the company.

The SGMC is based on these points and consists of the following dimensions:

- normative, strategic and operational management;
- structures, activities, behaviour.

The company's development is continuously included in this process. Corporate policy is translated into strategies via missions.

3. Approaches to design

3.1. Business development process

In order for the process of corporate development to be properly controlled, management needs a design framework with the help of which it can identify the appropriate approach itself. This should be developed into a core competence and become a future success potential at the top management level. This development process therefore becomes a central management task.

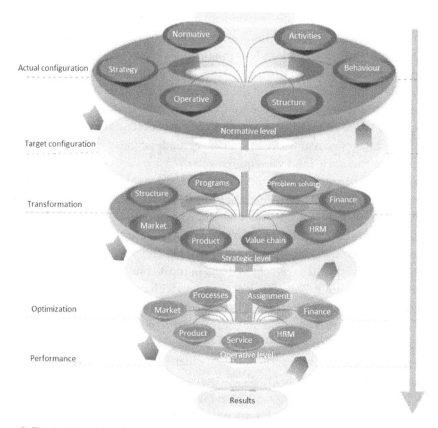

Figure 2. The business development process

Source: based on K. Bleicher, C. Abegglen, *Das Konzept Integriertes Management...*, p. 59.

The introduction of this process is leaned against the integrated approach outlined in the SGMC and takes place step by step (iteratively). This means that all measures taken must be permanently assessed, optimised and, if necessary, realigned in terms of their contribution to success. With each run it becomes possible to see through the process somewhat better in terms of learning.

It can be divided into different phases:[17]

- Initiation—a central, non-delegable topic for top management; defining role distribution, rules, communication, resources, quality measurement.
- Configuration ACTUAL/TARGET: Define actual and target status. Is the company on track or is there a lack of clarity? Derive measures.
- Transition—initiate and implement the defined measures.
- Performance—measure and optimise the new status to unfold full potential.

---

[17]   See in detail K. Bleicher, C. Abegglen, *Das Konzept Integriertes Management...*, pp. 53 ff.

The ideal typical representation of the business development process, how it can be put into practice, is briefly illustrated by the interlocking areas of reference.

The three horizontal levels are interlocked with three vertical columns. The activities result from structures and behaviour. As a rule, each level and each column is composed of three reference topic fields that influence each other in the sense of a network. These are regularly brought into line for the purpose of positioning and profiling in order to secure the long-term viability of a company. A process of corporate development can then be derived from this by realigning (actual configuration) and adapting (target configuration) all of these elements over the course of time. Each stage of development thus corresponds to a certain constellation of elements.

The precondition is an overview of the current situation in and around the company. With these iterative loops of knowledge and thought, normative management finally provides the objective and formal framework for the further development of the company (substantiating). At the strategic level, iterative and recursive alignments, themes and programmes are then concretised, which in the medium term can lead to changes in strategic success potentials (alignment). The market, product and financial situation as well as value chains and human resources are taken into account in a joint analysis of the comparison with normative management.

The operational implementation of these programmes is then thought through until they generally fit and are seen as accurate for the future. Implementation takes place at the base level. The fine-tuning (optimisation) and corrections follow in due course, so that the company can assert itself successfully under changing conditions.

As is easy to see, this concept is highly complex. However, the reference topic fields are very useful for easier handling. With their help, it is possible to move any topic at any level towards stability or change at any time.

3.2. St. Gallen Management Concept (SGMC): Brief presentation

The objectives of the SGMC are, in particular, to sustainably build up and maintain the success potential of the company, on the one hand, and the benefit potential of the various stakeholder groups (owners, stakeholders) on the other. To this end, a mental frame of reference is established. Against the background of the paradigm shift outlined by Bleicher, companies are only sustainable in the future if they pursue conscious change management. It shows how the respective levels and dimensions can be harmonised. It helps to re-align and, if necessary, adapt the continuous process of corporate development again and again. In this way, possible undesirable developments in the sense of corporate controlling can be identified at an early stage. In this respect, it is also the aim of the concept to be an advisor for the management.

For implementation, Bleicher has reduced the complexity of the concept using an example. The necessary steps are then explained by implicit reference to this example.[18]

Step 1: Defining the company foundation through normative management.
First, a picture of the company as a whole is presented:
   Actual configuration: What is good, what is bad, what are the causes?
   Target configuration: What are we today and in the future?
This is followed by considerations regarding core competencies, success and benefit potentials, intensification of value creation, own abilities. Frequent misunderstandings (e.g. the phrase "the capped flow") must be taken into account. In this way, standards for corporate culture and a corporate constitution are created. This also involves the significance of the company for the owners (shareholders) and other stakeholder groups, the increase in value, the utility contribution of the company and how this can be implemented in a vision. This results in concrete missions (programmes) for the strategic level.

Step 2: Align the company thanks to strategic management.
Normative specifications are to be taken into account in this step. The current situation with regard to markets, products, human resources, finances and the value chain must be closely examined. However, this should be customer- and need-oriented (orientation towards customer problems). Possible developments, innovative growth areas and further business opportunities, and the resulting opportunities and risks must be defined in order to maximise the number of options and alternatives. Here it is important to select various offers to use strategic concepts.

Step 3: Operational management ensures internal and external implementation.
Strategic programmes are now to be implemented and optimised in concrete terms, and priorities. Everything must be financially underpinned. This results in concrete master plans (assignments and actions) with precise directions, qualitative objectives, necessary resources, quantifiable measures (small-scale work). An integration of the individual dimensions of management requires a paradigmatically shaped guiding idea. The normative, strategic and operative elements are based on this idea, mediated by the choice of activities, structures and behaviour.[19] Bleicher calls this management philosophy, i.e. it is about fundamental questions concerning the role of management (finding meaning, ideas about the future positioning of the company in the economy and society; this then finds its way into being reflected in a vision).[20]

---

[18] See in detail K. Bleicher, C. Abegglen, *Das Konzept Integriertes Management...*, pp. 62 ff.
[19] Ibidem, p. 149.
[20] Ibidem, p. 150.

Conclusion

Normative and strategic management design, operative management steers the corporate development.[21]

It can therefore be recorded: normative and strategic management on the one hand and operational management on the other, are the two sides of the same coin. The former are aligned to the framework design (design function), in which operational execution in day-to-day business occurs. Since, according to Bleicher, the term SGMC is basically only used for normative and strategic dimensions, because operational management is all about concept-guided implementation, the concept focuses above all on normative and strategic relationships, without going into execution dimensions themselves in more detail.

In the following section, the three management levels are briefly outlined.

Normative management

This level deals with the general goals of the enterprise, with principles, norms and rules of the "game" aimed at improving the vitality and developmental capacity of the company (as a whole) and its legitimacy.

Starting from an entrepreneurial vision, corporate policy and behaviour central content become the yardstick for normative management. It takes over and is expressed in the specification of a mission for corporate development.

Strategic management—"Doing the right things"

It is aimed at the development, maintenance and exploitation of success potentials for which resources must be used.

The potential for success is expressed by the experience gained over time with markets, technologies and social structures and processes. They are able to make their mark in the implemented strategic position in the market relative to its competitors. New potentials for success should be to achieve competitive advantages over the competition in the future and to strengthen competitiveness. Long lead times often have to be calculated for this purpose with high use of resources, in particular financial resources, for which no corresponding flux of funds has yet been achieved. In addition to programmes, the focus of strategic considerations is put on fundamental design of management structures and systems, and problem-solving behaviour.

Operational management—"Doing things right"

Normative and strategic management find their implementation in the operational execution, which in the economic view is aligned with performance, financial and information management processes and efficiency.

---

[21] Cf. ibidem, pp. 150 ff.

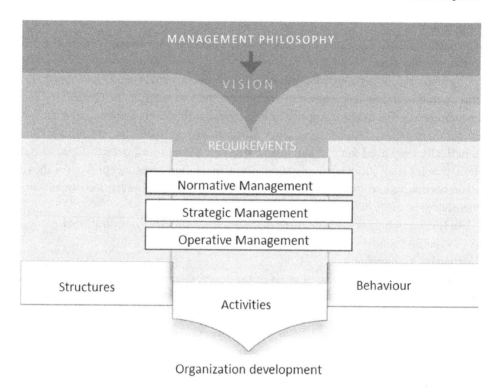

Organization development

Figure 3. Relationship between normative, strategic and operative management in a horizontal view

Source: based on K. Bleicher, C. Abegglen, *Das Konzept Integriertes Management...*, p. 35.

After all, activities, structures and behaviour have an impact on the company's development as follows in: vertical integration, norms, strategies and operations are traversed of activities, structures and behaviour. This is achieved through the concretisation of standards into programmes that are translated into specifications for activities. The structures of the management are concretised by the constitution, organisational and management systems, and disposition systems.[22]

---

[22] Ibidem, p. 157.

3.3. Strategic management: Impact through strategy

Furthermore, this contribution is limited to the treatment of the strategic management dimension. The basis for the development of strategic programmemes by strategic management is the provision of organisational structures and management systems as well as goals and measures. Future-oriented perspectives for corporate development can be derived from the standards of corporate policy. By harmonising strategic concepts with organisational structuring and system design as well as the strategic development of problem behaviour, the development of strategic success potentials becomes the content of strategic corporate management.

The corporate policy supported by the corporate culture and corporate constitution provides strategic management with long-term general goals and a basic orientation in the form of missions. These are to be concretised by means of strategic programmes. However, there are problems with the coupling of normative and strategic management. Although this can be clearly described, practical linkage is still difficult because a large number of factual, content-related and formal relationships and interactions must be taken into account. Structures and systems must support the respective corporate policy.

In order to be able to better control this complexity, Bleicher has developed reference topic fields with the help of which it is possible to move any topic at any level towards stability or change at any time.[23]

These are briefly outlined below:

Subject area 1: Organisational and management systems (structures).
The strategic intentions of a company must be supported by a corresponding design of the organisation. These are supported by the management system, which wants to steer the problem, achievement and cooperation behaviour processual in a given direction. The organisational structures thus form the framework for strategic programmes and employee behaviour. Their appropriate design largely follows model ideas of a division of labour structure. Bleicher is developing starting points for this, such as the bureaucracy model that has prevailed up to now, later steps towards reducing bureaucracy, the creation of flexible business units (to eliminate cumbersomeness), the creation of semi-autonomous units with logistical core areas, de centralisation vs centralisation ("as much decentralisation as possible, as much centralisation as necessary"), orientation towards customer-oriented problem solutions ("back to basics") due to market changes.

At present, visions of a "virtual organisation" of structural networking due to changing competitive conditions, which lead to virtual forms of corporate connections, are being discussed. This requires an IT-supported network structure (information

---

[23]   Ibidem, p. 60.

technology networking of the actors) in order to enable a temporal and spatial decoupling and distribution of division of labour processes (virtual enterprises).

Bleicher describes the consequences for structural design as an organisational paradigm shift. Against this background, the question arises as to the fundamental dimensioning of the organisation in the pursuit of the strategic programme: subject vs personnel orientation, individual regulation vs framework regulation, organisation on a permanent or temporary basis, steep vs flat configuration, individual vs external organisation or layout. This organisational structuring for the development of strategic programmes is supplemented by management systems. According to their function, all management systems are diagnosis, planning and control systems, which serve to formulate strategic concepts and control their operational execution. In order for these functions to be performed, data from the company and the environment must be processed, i.e. an information system is required (management information system to provide information for management) up to and including an early warning system. This involves the question of which information should be made available to management. A design should be chosen accordingly.

Finally, when designing the management system, a distinction must be made between a stabilising design or a change-oriented system. With regard to the management process, the focus is put on the target system and the planning and control system.

Subject area 2: Strategic programmes (activities).[24]
The search for a purposeful strategy concerns the framework within which decisions are made that determine the type and direction of the company. It therefore takes place at the level of the company as a whole and at the level of the business units (basis of strategic management). The corporate strategy concerns the implementation of a corporate policy and provides a broad framework, while the business area strategies represent a further differentiation and concretisation within this framework. The decisive factor here is the division of the company into strategic business areas in order to enable as specific a procedure as possible. For this purpose, products with similar customer groups will be grouped together (orientation towards customer problems).

A strategy generally consists of four components:
1. Analysis of the strategic starting position.
2. Determination of the future position of the company as a whole and the strategic business unit.
3. Selection of technologies and resources to achieve synergy effects.
4. Definition of criteria and standards for measuring the achievement of objectives.

So-called standard strategies are suitable for this purpose. These differ depending on the phase of the company's life cycle or strategic business unit.

---

[24]   Ibidem, pp. 367 ff.

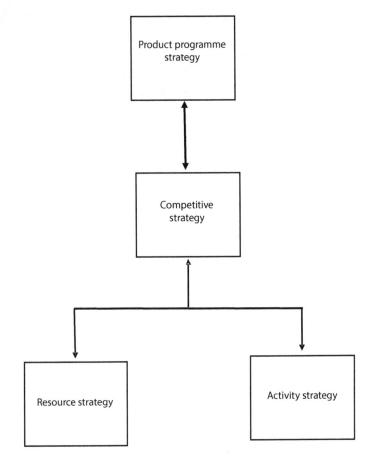

Figure 4. Sample dimensioning of strategic programmes

Source: based on K. Bleicher, C. Abegglen, *Das Konzept Integriertes Management...*, p. 385.

A distinction is made here between:
- Investment and growth strategies for existing products or services.
- Development of new products.
- Skimming or disinvestment strategies.

Further classifications differentiate between offensive and defensive strategies.

When choosing a strategy, attention must be paid to the attractiveness of markets, synergy effects, balance between risk and profit expectations as well as the development of cash flow. In addition, strategic thinking and action is always associated with concentrated use of forces to generate an "impact force," which is market-oriented and makes technological breakthroughs possible (bundling of forces).

At its core, strategic decisions are always made with regard to opportunity and risk and to gain insight into the activity of the competition.

Therefore, the relative positioning of its own activities vis-à-vis the competition, and profiling through new business systems with changed rules of competition as well as an extension of action through partnerships play a decisive role. Though, ultimately, the future is always uncertain.

Strategic programmes can be divided into four dimensions:
1. Product programme strategy.
2. Competitive strategy.
3. Resource strategy.
4. Activity strategy.

Subject area 3: Problem behaviour.[25]
A decisive point for the success of a sustainable corporate strategy is the problem behaviour of the company's employees. Strategic management is offered many concepts that also deal with the subject of learning. However the topic of behaviour should not be addresses in the context of this work.

4. Statements on the shaping of the future

4.1. Findings

The SGMC enables concrete management tasks to becaptured within the framework of the process of the development of a company in an integrated way, and to solve them in their high dynamic and complexity. The underlying order pattern with its logically delimitable division into the corporate policy, constitution and culture, as well as activities, structures and behaviour is further transformed into a normative, strategic and operational management dimension. These order-patterns mutually penetrate each other and show high interdependence. This provides a holistic, integrated frame of reference for the management. With consistent application, the management is thus able to safeguard the ability to develop and guarantee the survival of the company as a whole.

Since only one frame of reference is offered for the design of content, there is sufficient free space available for further company-specific concretisation, in particular on the strategic level. This enables the company to exploit its specific capabilities in order to build up the necessary competitive advantages over competitors. Depending on the current situation, the strategic framework programmes can then be implemented

---

25   Ibidem, pp. 405 ff.

pragmatically, i.e. securing profit, productivity, liquidity and profitability. And these are necessary to secure the existence of the company.

Attention should be also paid to consideration of the life-cycle. With regard to digitisation, it can be assumed that technological progress will proceed slowly (long start-up time). At the same time, high investments are necessary. As soon as new digital technology is introduced, progress is also possible.

Finally, in the maturity phase, improvements become smaller and smaller and productivity decreases. Therefore, in this phase new possibilities could be looked forward to. An example is the Swiss watch industry. The replacement of mechanical drives with analogue display did not take place and has not been influenced by modern digital quartz designs.

Management sciences should therefore precisely focus on the life cycle phase of the company with regard to the process of corporate development. This is because the four ideal-typical phases, which are usually distinguished, are characterised by their specific situation and therefore require corresponding strategic programmes.

What is still important for strategic management? The question is whetherit is a strategy for the companyas a whole (corporate strategy) or perhaps for a single business segment (business strategy, competitive strategy).

For strategic management, familiar instruments for the development of strategies can be offered—traditional environmental and company analysis (strengths and weaknesses), sector structure and competition analysis, opportunity and risk analysis, analysis of the value chain. Proven instruments can be used here. For that purpose Steinmann presents a traditional sequence of steps.[26]

Long-term orientation of strategic management should be based on the development of potential, from which business developments can open up with new services for new customer needs and new markets on the basis of the developing new technologies, such as digitisation. Focus should be put on the core competencies. To this end, the management must search, build, develop and secure sufficiently high success potentials. It follows from this that the control potentials turn for control parameters of strategic management. In order to achieve this, it is essential to create competitive advantages. Management must be able to use its services, and differentiate itself from its competitors in such a way that it can make a decisive contribution to customer satisfaction. This requires operative implementation on the market, which then, in the course of time, leads to an improved positioning of the company on the market.[27]

[26] H. Steinmann, G. Schreyögg, *Management...*, pp. 226 ff.
[27] Cf. K. Bleicher, C. Abegglen, *Das Konzept Integriertes Management...*, pp. 479 ff.

4.2. Linking

Strategic management carried out in this way must be integrated, profiled and harmonised. Integration takes place through a holistic approach and mutual coordination in the entire network of normative, strategic and operational management. To this end, the integrative thinking and acting of management must be strengthened and mutual relations between them shaped. This is against the background that every element of a system only gains its function and meaning as part of the whole. Thus, a holistic approach is created that enables synergies.[28] Normative, strategic and operational management have very different effects on the business development, and the influence of activity, structures and behaviour also play a role. The resulting problems may be approached situationally or with foresight. However, a definite solution is rather unlikely. Frequently, priorities are set.[29]

4.3. Outlook

As can be seen, digitisation plays a major role in corporate development and management science. There is much to be said for a fundamental change in the sense of a paradigm shift. In addition to the technical problem of digitisation, management often has little experience with this highly complex and global issue. Usually there are few suitable management strategies available.

The world's largest Internet companies set digital standards and achieve rapidly increasing annual sales and high growth rates, e.g. Alphabet (Google) or Facebook. Their primary goal is growth before profitability. As a result, they increase their profile, the number of users, and their profits. Often, this growth is also achieved through the acquisition of other companies (WhatsApp, YouTube). In the media and communications sector, companies are increasingly becoming e-commerce dealers. Volkswagen is fully committed to the trend towards digitisation and is investing large sums in networking its cars.

For many small- and medium-sized companies, the process of digitisation is more deliberate than evolutionary. A digital concept is often lacking. For this reason, individual actions are often used to test whether digitisation is actually bringing advantages. In logistics in particular, digitally controlled warehousing and driverless transport systems are being tested. In production engineering, for example, digital CAD or CAM-controlled manufacturing processes are used.

It can therefore be stated that in some industries and large companies, the technical possibilities of digitisation are used to achieve competitive advantages. This development is progressing at a rapid pace worldwide.

---

[28]   Ibidem, pp. 503 ff.
[29]   Chap. 10, pp. 571 ff.

However, many companies have not yet seized the opportunity of digitisation to establish profitable digital offerings and business models. Newspapers, for example, are experiencing declines in circulation. Digitisation at banks is faltering, Commerzbank is currently in great difficulty and has been removed from DAX. Only in online banking do banks offer secure options that enable safe and efficient payment transactions, a constant overview of all payment transactions and account movements, including due dates and evaluations of account information.

It can therefore be assumed that corporate management will develop accordingly. Therefore, management science must also offer suitable solutions. Strategic concepts and programmes do exist. Bleicher's Integrated Management concept and its specification by the SGMC with its pragmatic solution approaches, offers the appropriate framework for corporate management. What is special about SGMC is the integrated view and concentration of all company areas in the normative, strategic and operational dimension, taking into account the structure, activities and behaviour. However, the SGMC itself is very complex. It has developed a complex design framework and provides an orientation framework and food for thought for the continuous development of management. All areas and facets are included and made transparent in their complex interaction.

Especially for strategic management, practicable hints for a new strategy and strategic programme are worked out in order to bring about a necessary corporate change and to create competitive advantages. Consequently, this also applies to the process of digitisation. In this respect, the SGMC offers a holistic, integrated approach but no remedy.

In addition to coping with the far-reaching fundamental change, management can also face crises of meaning. The solution could initially be to adopt acorporate philosophy. Mastering this process can be achieved not only with changes in the organisation, processes and systems. Rather, a fundamental rethinking is necessary among all participants (paradigm shift). For it is also imperative to bring about a change in the attitudes and values of management and employees. Taking the concept of integrated management into account, the static "old" system of the company must be successively developed iteratively through a new dynamic profile with a new independent organisation. Interfaces with the outside world are of decisive importance here.

In concrete terms, this requires cooperatively managed companies instead of hierarchies, in particular teamwork to achieve synergies, the networking of employees through appropriate network constellations. Furthermore, motivation of the employees through perceived meaningfulness and participation in decision-making is decisive. Finally, corporate change should also include a stronger orientation towards so-called "customer value management" and increasingly use-oriented digital pricing. For management, this means creating the right conditions for managers and employees to share their knowledge, network and organise themselves accordingly, make decisions democratically and constantly improve performance in iterations. In this way, "digital competence" can be achieved, i.e. the ability to use one's own abilities in the digital world profitably for the company. In other words, it is necessary to develop a digitisation concept and to instruct the employees step by step on the new working technique. The SGMC offers the appropriate framework for this. Finally it can be assumed that management sciences will be further developed.

Bibliography

Betriebswirtschaftslehre als Management- und Führungslehre, ed. by R. Wunderer, Schäffer-Poeschel, Stuttgart 1993.

Bleicher K., Abegglen C., *Das Konzept Integriertes Management: Visionen—Missionen—Programme*, Campus Verlag, Frankfurt 2017.

Bleicher K., *Betriebswirtschaftslehre – Disziplinäre Lehre vom Wirtschaften in und zwischen Betrieben oder interdisziplinäre Wissenschaft vom Management?* [in:] *Betriebswirtschaftslehre als Management- und Führungslehre*, ed. by R. Wunderer, Schäffer-Poeschel, Stuttgart 1993.

Dillerup R., Stoi R., *Unternehmensführung. Management & Leadership Strategien, Werkzeuge, Praxis*, Verlag Vahlen, München 2016.

Jung R. H., Bruck J., Quarg S., *Allgemeine Managementlehre: Lehrbuch für die angewandte Unternehmens- und Personalführung*, Erich Schmidt, Berlin 2001.

Steinmann H., Schreyögg G., *Management. Grundlagen der Unternehmensführung Konzepte—Funktionen—Fallstudien*, Gabler Verlag, Wiesbaden 1993.

Naylor J., *Management*, Pearson Education, New York 2004.

Branding of Time as a New Direction in Tomorrow's Management

Prof. Kakhaber Djakeli, Ph.D.   https://orcid.org/0000-0002-4947-2362
Caucasus International University

The text is dedicated to the memory of
Prof. Janusz Teczke

Abstract

Time is the most precious good. The human civilization has improved through the management of time. Even in prehistorical societies, the understanding of time was set up by leaders guessing its importance. It was especially the human who had an idea of stopping time, which can essentially be seen in mythology and tales. The importance of the representation of a time span through painting and writing has been and still remains the need of humans. The Stonehenge and other mega structures were erected by gatherers and hunters to measure time. People are interested in how black holes are organised not because all of them share an interest in astronomy but rather due to the fact that some believe that black holes actually stop time. Time is always with people, people are concerned about time. The marketing of time forms a new era, but the branding of time which is the topic of this article is an entirely new phenomenon. Is it possible to brand time span, or to brand time in general?

Our assumption was that if time could be sold and bought, it could be branded. The research hypothesis is that companies have not made strategic brand management of their time as well as managers undertaking branding of their time have fallen into chaos. The study was conducted in two stages. We used convenience sample in telephone interview CATI, calling Georgian companies. Stage one involved a pilot study of time branding cases. Stage two consisted in inviting respondents to a marketing research laboratory at Caucasus International University for a qualitative marketing research. We used historical analyses as the approach to secondary marketing research.

The research finding is that time not only can be branded but it is obvious that Strategic Brand Management of Time can bring big advantages and additional profits for those who own this scarce resource.

Keywords: branding of time, time marketing, strategic brand management of time

Introduction

Time branding was the main idea of this marketing research study. There are few scientific papers about time branding, but evidence of this phenomenon can be seen in our culture and traditions. For example we categorise our day into: lunch time, dinner time, gym time and study time. What is this, if not an attempt to brand a time span by giving it strong and reasonable meaning? Time Management has always been a significant and unsolved issue.

Nobody knows the reason behind Paul's writing in the Second Epistle to the Corinthians, when he said: "In the time of my favor I heard you, and in the day of salvation I helped you" (Corinthians 6:2). The infamous argument for "the unreality of time" plays not an insignificant role in assessing our objective in today's science.[1]

It is interesting what the Quran says about time. The Holly Book of Muslims recalls certain events as if they concerned our lives. For example: either: "Remember Your Lord inspired the angel" (Quran 8:12) or: "And remember Jesus, the Son of Mary" (Quran, 61:6). The Quran uses more expressive forms of communication, eliminating the distance between people, Prophets and other described in this Holly Book. The Quran teaches us a new way to look at time.

Time management skills increase efficiency and satisfaction as well as reduce professional and personal stress.[2] The Time Management Matrix by Stephen Covey plays a great role here,[3] but nobody has ever spoken about strategic brand management of time.

One can say that time is an immaterial abstraction, but for marketing and especially branding, there exist unique foundations to brand time: it is the most relevant aspect of someone's or something's existence. Time can be branded in different ways either from the perspectives of culture or management, geography, psychology, economy and military, or even weather or geology.

"When in the chronicle of wasted time, I see descriptions of the fairest wights"—writes William Shakespeare in Sonnet 106, which allows us to understand how long time has been wasted by the civilisation and by ourselves. Poetry dealing with time is a good place to start the shaping of time brands too.

---

[1] W. D. Zimmerman, *The A-Theory of Time, The B-Theory of Time, and "Taking Tense Seriously,"* "Dialectica" 2005, 59 (4), pp. 401–457.
[2] E. C. Gordon, C. S. Borkan, *Recapturing Time: A Practical Approach to Time Management for Physicians,* "Postgraduate Medical Journal" 2014, 90, pp. 267–272.
[3] R. S. Covey, *The Seven Habits of Highly Effective People,* 2000, http://www.stafforini.com/docs/Covey%20-%20The%207%20habits%20of%20highly%20effective%20people.pdf (access: 5 August 2018).

Evidence of time branding in the past

Strong brands must have the ability to simplify decision making for customers, to reduce risks and set new expectations. All those can be seen in the branding of time. An important aspect here is credence. So the branding of time can be a part of goods whose quality is credence.

If strong brands can simplify decision making for consumers and manufacturers, why this rule could not be used to brand time? Let us analyse one example: children's holidays. In the summer, many tools can be used to increase the means of identification for those organisations using our concept. Means of identity, means of legal status and signal of quality—all these tools we can put into Branding of Time for companies.

However, consumers of time brands can have much more credence to responsibility, risk reduction, promise-oriented appeals to such great companies, which brand time for consumers.

"By the seventh day God finished what he had been doing and stopped working. He blessed the seventh day and set it apart as a special day" (Holly Bible)—the first brand management of time was actually described in the Holly Bible.

Time needs branding and this has actually been the subject of differentiation in various periods of history. When we describe different periods of our country's development, we accidentally begin to brand time by saying:

- In the Eolith age.
- It happened in the Bronze Age.
- Yes it was in the time of Iron Age.
- In the time of Pharaoh Ramses.

Hence, we can divide time branding into two parts: natural differentiation of time and artificial differentiation of time by man.

What is the benefit of branding time?

According to AMA, a brand is a "name, term, sign, symbol, or design, or a combination of them, intended to identify the goods and services of one seller or group of sellers and to differentiate them from those of competition."[4] This definition is more technical. In practice, a brand is more oriented towards prominence, awareness and reputation. Why do brands matter? Because consumers often simplify the purchasing process only to identify them. Brands are also important because of another thing: they exist in Branding of Time Span.

---

[4]   L. K. Keller, *Strategic Brand Management. Building, Measuring, and Managing Brands Equity*, Pearson, London 2013, p. 2.

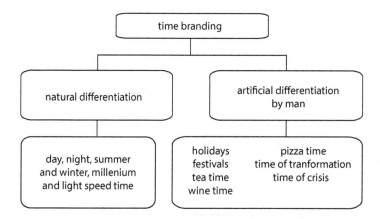

Figure 1. Parts of time

Source: author's own elaboration.

Table 1. The matrix of benefits of time span branding

Benefits of brands to consumers of products and services	Benefits of branding of time span and time brands for people	Benefits of branding of time span for corporate life
Identification of product source	Identification of one time span from another, for example honeymoon from other periods of marriage	For example, brainstorming—time span
Assignment of responsibility to product maker	Assignment of much deep meaning of time—hobby time	Assignment of much more meaning and relevance of time span for corporation—"Idea development time—once a week, 45 minutes, before lunch"
Risk reducer	Reducing the risk of unexpected events	Reducing the risk of destruction and less involvement of employees, increasing success
Promise, bond, or pact with maker of product	Promise and expectation to have meaningful time span	Promise or pact from participators
Symbolic device	Many symbolic events and special attitude for management	Symbolic events linked to time span in the company
Signal of quality	Signal to mind and body	Signal of sustainability of time process

Source: author's own elaboration.

What is the branding of time span and what happens if neither the national culture nor companies brand time?

The branding of time is a strategic and tactical activity differentiating either private or corporation time span from others to increase its meaning, relevance and value, using almost all branding tools, for better satisfaction of the final customers.

We know that national cultures have been branding their time without being aware of doing it. As our research shows, the German corporate culture differentiates their working and resting time better than any other on the continent. Branding is all about differences. If this process is managed well we should expect great brand resonance as an outcome. In countries of Eastern Europe, time is not well differentiated, which carries negative results. Time span in Eastern European companies is more generic. In Bulgaria, time as a commodity appears to be a generic product, not branded by its owner.

If time is bought and sold, why cannot it be a part of strategic brand management? This question has a reasonable answer. Time is branded by certain cultures and in these cultures, it is divided into meaningful spans. There, time is well branded and it has high consumer-based brand equity, which can be seen in the ratio of compensation.

For example, total compensation in San Jose–San Francisco–Oakland, CA, is 59 USD, whereas in Minneapolis–St. Paul–St. Cloud, MN–WI it is 37 USD—according to the employer's summary.[5]

The wages and salaries are approximately 83% of total labour costs and are obtained from the monthly wages and salaries survey.[6] This shows that time is branded differently in different companies, countries, regions and cities. Hourly labour costs ranged from €4.4 to €42.0 across the EU Member States in 2016. The lowest value can be seen in Bulgaria and Romania, whereas the highest in Denmark and Belgium.[7]

Comparing the lowest and highest hourly labour costs in countries, one cannot omit the importance of time branding. Bulgaria has the lowest labour costs per hour in €, specifically €4.4 per hour. The same goes for Georgia. This is 10 times less than the labour cost in Belgium.

What has happened with time in Georgia and Bulgaria? This questions was posed before the beginning of this article.

---

[5]   Costs per hour worked for employee compensation and costs as a percent of total compensation: private industry workers, by Census region and selected metropolitan area, March 2018. Cf. Bureau of Labor Statistics, *Employer Costs for Employee Compensation*, March 2018, https://www.bls.gov/news.release/pdf/ecec.pdf (access: 5 August 2018).

[6]   P. Hopwood, *The New Experimental Index of Labour Costs per Hour*, 2018.

[7]   Eurostat, *Labor Costs in the EU—Hourly Labour Costs Ranged from €4.4 to €42.0 across the EU Member States in 2016 Lowest in Bulgaria and Romania, Highest in Denmark and Belgium*, 2017, http://ec.europa.eu/eurostat/documents/2995521/7968159/3-06042017-AP-EN.pdf/6e303587-baf8-44ca-b4ef-7c891c3a7517 (access: 5 August 2018).

Research methodology

The research hypothesis is that national cultures and companies which do not practice strategic brand management of their time are less effective.

The study was conducted in two steps. We used a convenience sample in a telephone interview CATI conducted with Georgian companies. Stage one involved a pilot study of time branding cases in Georgian companies.

Stage two consisted in inviting every fifth interviewed person to a marketing research laboratory at Caucasus International University for qualitative marketing research. Historical analysis was our approach to secondary marketing research. The questionnaire included in the primary research was as following:

- Do you differentiate your working time from other time periods?
      Yes/No
- What features and symbols do you use for your working time?
- Do you differentiate your resting time?
      Yes/No
- How do you feel when time is not branded in corporation?
      Well / Not well
- What makes you brand time?
- What kind of services prompt you to brand time?
- What makes you loyal to your time brand?
- What components can make you happier?

Marketing study limitations

This marketing study was limited to the market of Georgia. Because we of this, our marketing research could not be extended beyond the borders of Georgia. Hence the urgency of the next stage of research development; it is necessary to conduct an extended survey of the branding of time in different countries and regions.

Research findings

The pilot stage of research shows that as many differences managers find in their working time span as effective they can be. The effectiveness of the branding of time span is evident but research needs to be continued worldwide. The effectiveness of the branding of time span is evident but research needs to be continued in different companies of the European Union, Latin and North America, Asia and Africa.

The expected findings in the case of extended research will be elaboration of special methods, methodology and tools characteristic for brand management of time span.

As a result of this research, we studied 103 companies and divided them into four different types:

a) fast growers;
b) competitive bulls;
c) lost lambs;
d) sustainable followers.

Finally, we elaborated one interesting tool named the Matrix of Time Branding.

Matrix of Time Branding

The research findings motivated me to establish this matrix of branding of time.

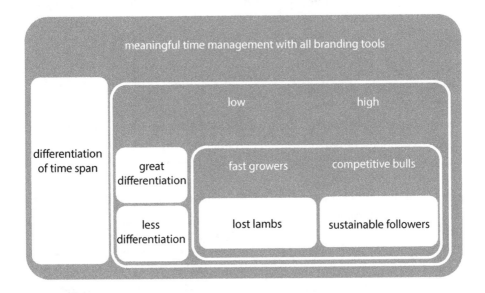

Figure 2. The matrix of branding of time span

Source: author's own elaboration.

The horizontal axis shows meaningful time management with all branding tools. The vertical axis includes the differentiation of time span. According to our matrix, we have four variants of companies categorised by how they judge branding of time:

a) Fast growers—here we can find a company differentiating its important business and non-business time periods but still does not brand it using symbols, terms, associations, names and colours. Such companies have great strategic management of their time. They organise time very well, they grow fast. As per our hypothesis, they need to turn into competitive bulls to sustain their business.

b) Competitive bulls—these companies know well how to differentiate, for example, new product development time span from other businesses. They can differentiate the time of celebration, time of sport, time of decisions, time of creative development, time of decision making. Furthermore, such a business knows how to use different symbols and names, colours, terms to increase awareness in participants, and influence their great deeds through positioning and association. In such companies people spend their time with a great sense of awareness and they are proud of their time span, which is not wasted, but well utilised by the company.

c) Lost lambs—this type of companies do not understand the benefits of branding of time. Both the employees and the employers waste their time. They are losing the market.

d) Sustainable followers—such companies like time management. Without differentiation of one time period from another, they work hard across all issues. Even if they are creative, ultimately they cannot use the results of their creativity and innovativeness, because they do not know how to make people appreciate their business.

Findings and recommendations

The importance of the branding of time is obvious on the example of different national cultures or companies. Both cultures, which influence the national type of entrepreneurship or companies can be assessed by the matrix of branding of time span.

People are concerned about time. Branding of time is a new era in business development. Branding of time span is an entirely new thing, and it is improving the market share of businesses.

Our assumption is that if time can be sold, it can also be branded, which is positively confirmed by our research. The next research hypothesis concerning companies which have failed to make strategic brand management of their time is confirmed only on the example of Georgia, but this assumption needs to be studied worldwide.

Bibliography

Covey R. S., *The Seven Habits of Highly Effective People*, 2000, http://www.stafforini.com/docs/Covey%20-%20The%207%20habits%20of%20highly%20effective%20people.pdf (access: 5 August 2018).

Bureau of Labor Statistics, *Employer Costs for Employee Compensation*, March 2018, https://www.bls.gov/news.release/pdf/ecec.pdf (access: 5 August 2018).

Hopwood P., *The New Experimental Index of Labour Costs per Hour*, 2018.

Eurostat, *Labor Costs in the EU—Hourly Labour Costs Ranged from €4.4 to €42.0 across the EU Member States in 2016 Lowest in Bulgaria and Romania, Highest in Denmark and Belgium*, 2017, http://ec.europa.eu/eurostat/documents/2995521/7968159/3-06042017-AP-EN.pdf/6e303587--baf8-44ca-b4ef-7c891c3a7517 (access: 5 August 2018).

Gordon E. C., Borkan C. S., *Recapturing Time: A Practical Approach to Time Management for Physicians*, "Postgraduate Medical Journal" 2014, 90.

Keller L. K., *Strategic Brand Management. Building, Measuring, and Managing Brands Equity*, Pearson, London 2013.

Shakespeare W., *Sonnets*, Sakartvelos Matsne Publishing House, Tbilisi 2000.

Zimmerman W. D., *The A-Theory of Time, The B-Theory of Time, and "Taking Tense Seriously,"* "Dialectica" 2005, 59 (4).

The Future of Branding

Prof. Grzegorz Urbanek, Ph.D.   https://orcid.org/0000-0002-1372-8127
University of Łódź

Abstract

In recent years, technological innovations, especially in the area of communication and information exchange have significantly accelerated. Under these conditions, brands cannot rely on a previously acquired position and their long-standing heritage, but they must actively seek new forms of reaching the minds and hearts of consumers. The main purpose of the article is to answer the question about the future of brands and their importance for the success of companies. An attempt to find answers to the above questions in the article was carried out based on the analysis of results of rankings of the most valuable global and Polish brands, as well as studies of literature on trends in brand management resulting from technological, social and cultural changes. The main conclusion from conducted research is that brands will remain one of the decisive factors in creating the value of companies. However, methods of building a brand, as well as the way of its value creation will change. Consumers will turn to brands as new institutions that will allow them to meet their more complex needs: meaning, belonging, happiness, fulfilment, self-improvement, etc. As a result, the responsibility of brands will increase, which will cause that they will have to operate in a more transparent and ethical manner.

Keywords: branding, future of brands, brand management, brand value

Introduction

The evolution of the brand from product, through trademark to carrier of unique values, has a long history. The factors that initially served as a tool for a simple exchange of utility, later turned into a carrier of benefits and an element of market protection, to finally become a billion-dollar declaration of the superiority of offered attributes. Companies that have managed to build strong brands gain a lasting competitive advantage in the market, which translates into high margins and a high return on employed capital, which in turn leads to an increase in the company value. In the case of many businesses, the brand is their most valuable asset, which may have as many as several dozen percent shares in their market value. Currently, brands account for

30% of global wealth.[1] In the context of changes that have occurred in recent years on the market, the question about the future of brands is justified. Lately, technological innovations, especially in the area of communication and information exchange, have accelerated significantly. The smartphone and tablet, the successors of the mobile phone and computer, allow people to connect from anywhere in the world, with any-one at any time. The emergence of a peer-to-peer network allows individuals to share their experience, e.g. about the brand, in real time and to spread it without filtering information and censorship. In a situation where an immediate and open exchange of information becomes a standard, brands face new challenges. The Internet, due to a two-way message exchange, increases the bargaining power of consumers in relation to brands and their owners. During the transition from mass marketing to consumer segmentation in the 1960s, brands served niches by targeting messages meeting their needs. Currently, niches are not so easy to identify. The market is populated with units that are often unpredictable, which change their tastes and are in a continuous phase of evolution. Internet users trust other consumers more than they trust companies and their brands. Under these conditions, brands cannot rely on a previously acquired position and their long-standing heritage, but must actively seek new forms of reaching minds and hearts, and consequently, consumer pockets.

The purpose of the article is to attempt to answer the question of the future of brands and their importance for the success of companies. In particular, the consid-erations carried out in the article are to help answer the following specific questions: Will the importance of brands for business success grow or decrease? Will their share in the value of companies continue to be so significant? In which industries will the importance of brands grow? Are there any prospects for niche brands? How will social media influence the position of brands and the way they are promoted? Those and many other questions are posed by researchers, analysts, marketing and advertising specialists, and finally managers of consulting companies and those that have strong brands or plan to create such. An attempt to find answers to the above questions in the article was carried out based on the analysis of results of rankings of the most valuable global and Polish brands, as well as the analysis of literature on trends occurring in brand management related to technological, social and cultural changes.

Brand bubble?

In the context of the future of brands, one of the issues that are of interest to researchers and practitioners is whether brands will maintain their importance in the economy. In relation to this topic, the key question is if there is a real value behind brands or whether

---

[1]   R. Clifton, *Brand Valuation: From Marketing Department to Boardroom*, "Market Leader" 2009, 2, pp. 51–54.

high valuation of brands and companies that own them is the effect of the so-called bubble. In the history of mankind, from time to time, there appeared price bubbles in the markets of specific assets. The bubble means inflated, above-rational numbers valuation of certain kinds of goods. The first well-described bubble was observed in the Netherlands on the market of tulip bulbs. The peak of hysteria associated with the increase in the value of tulip bulbs falls for 1636–1637, followed by a violent collapse, which led to the bankruptcy of many investors.[2] After it actually happens, the bubble, from the perspective of an external observer, seems obvious and easily identifiable. From the point of view of somebody involved in the target market, the existence of a bubble is not so clear. According to Gerzema and Lebar, there are many indications that we are currently dealing with a bubble related to too high valuations of brands of numerous companies.[3] According to these authors, in companies included in the stock index of the 500 largest companies listed on the New York Stock Exchange—the S&P 500, the bubble associated with brands amounted to USD 4 trillion, or 1/3 of the market value of those firms. The existence of a bubble is evidenced by the fact that, at a time in which the brand value being part of companies' market valuation increases, the average indicators of brands' assessment by consumers in various dimensions falls. Brands lose consumer confidence—in 1997, 52% of brands enjoyed the trust of customers, while in 2006, only 25% of brands were described by consumers as trustworthy.[4] Customers are also becoming less loyal to brands. For example, statistics from Nordic countries regarding 20 product categories show that customer loyalty has been halved within 10 years.[5] Consumer behaviour in relation to brands is well characterised by the categorisation used by users of dating portals—"involved but open to change."[6] Permanent loyalty is replaced by a temporary one—until a better offer is found. One of the effects of this phenomenon is the shortening of the average period of brand leadership in the market. According to the results of research conducted for the period of 1921–2010, for 625 brands which were market leaders, the lead time was shortened to 12–24 years in the period of 1995–2010, compared to 29–52 years in earlier periods.[7]

Is it possible, then, to talk about a bubble with regard to brand valuations? The answer to this question is not simple, because each bubble has its own specificity, genesis, and dynamics. Therefore, based on the analysis of past events, one cannot

---

[2]   E. Picardo, *Five of the Largest Asset Bubbles in History*, 2015, www.investopedia.com (access: 27 April 2019).

[3]   J. Gerzema, E. Lebar, *The Danger of a "Brand Bubble,"* "Market Leader" 2009, 4, www.marketingsociety.com (access: 26 April 2019).

[4]   Ibidem.

[5]   M. Dahlen, J. Karsberg, *Time to Forget Everything We Learned in the Past about Branding. The Future Is the Future of Branding*, "Journal of Brand Strategy" 2015, 5 (1), pp. 22–30.

[6]   Ibidem.

[7]   P. Golder et al., *Long Term Market Leadership Persistence: Baselines, Economic Conditions, and Category Types*, 2013, www.msi.org (access: 28 April 2019).

unequivocally conclude about the occurrence or value overestimation in new circumstances or the lack thereof. The past bubbles, although different in terms of the type of market, course, scale, and consequences they were concerned with, shared a common feature—lasting only a few to a dozen or so years. In the case of brands, we can talk about the increase of their meaning and value, starting from the loud acquisitions of companies with strong brands in Great Britain in the 1980s. This phenomenon has been present, without significant corrections, for over 30 years, which may indicate its durability and rationality. The fact that the increased value of brands does not have the character of a bubble is also evidenced by the relatively slow pace of the process. Figure 1 presents the total value of 100 most valuable brands according to the Interbrand ranking between 2008 and 2017.

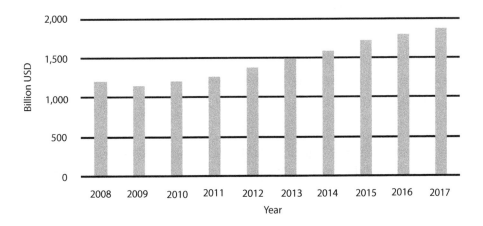

Figure 1. Total value of brands from the Interbrand brand league in 2008–2017

Source: elaborated by the author based on data from Interbrand Brand League www.interbrand.com.

In the years 2008–2017, the average annual increase in the value of brands from the Interbrand ranking amounted to 4.43%. The value of the brand, which is in principle part of off-balance-sheet assets, is part of the market value of the company's equity over its book value. From this point of view, the average annual growth of the brand's value at 4.43% can be considered moderate, because it is lower than the average cost of equity for a typical company. In other words, growth of brand value in the analysed period is slower than it results from the cost of capital. The situation is different for individual brands. For example, the average annual growth in the value of Apple in the years 2000–2011 amounted to 15.9%, while in the years 2011–2018 it increased to 30.4%. At the same time, in the period 2000–2018, once the most valuable brand in the world—Coca-Cola (currently no. 5 according to the Interbrand ranking), lost 0.5% in value annually. Amazon is currently on the fast track increasing its value between

2015–2018 by an average of 38.5% annually, and in 2018 alone by 56%. In Poland, over the period 2008–2017, the average annual increase in the value of the 100 most valuable brands according to the "Rzeczpospolita" ranking (Figure 2) was 4.54%, which was at a similar level as the Interbrand ranking.

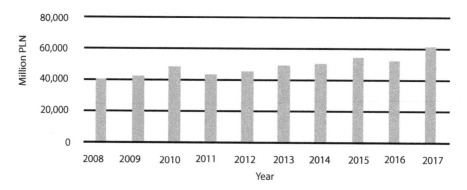

Figure 2. Value of 100 most valuable Polish brands in 2008–2017

Source: elaborated by the author based on data from "Rzeczpospolita" Brand Ranking.

Figure 3 presents the share of brand value in the market capitalisation in % of companies since 2008 to 2014, for 56 companies listed on the Warsaw Stock Exchange, for which data on the value of their brands are available.

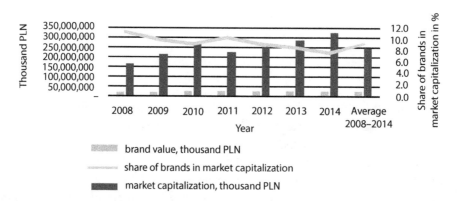

brand value, thousand PLN

share of brands in market capitalization

market capitalization, thousand PLN

Figure 3. Brand value and market capitalisation of select companies from the Warsaw Stock Exchange

Source: elaborated by the author.

In the analysed period of 2008–2014, the value of brands increased on average by 3.91%, while the market capitalisation of companies increased on average by 7.46%. This means that the value of brands follows the growth in the value of companies, but at a slower pace.

The above analyses based on data from international and national rankings of brands show that brands have a significant share in the value of firms, and their average value increases steadily in subsequent years. The results of these analyses indicate that there is no bubble effect associated with the overvaluation of brands. The average valuations of brands display a stable growth in the long-term, following the increase in the value of firms that own them.

Changes in brand significance in different areas

Observing changes in the value of brands in recent years, one can notice a clear trend consisting of a rapid increase in the value of brands of technology companies and those related to operations on the Internet, compared to traditional brands. Figure 4 shows changes in the value of brands Coca-Cola, Apple and Facebook in the period 2010–2018.

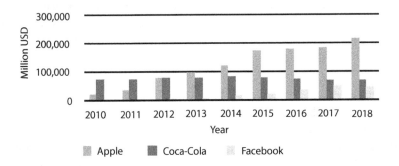

Figure 4. Value of brands Coca-Cola, Apple, Facebook in 2010–2018

Source: elaborated by the author based on data from Interbrand Brand League: www.interbrand.com.

In the case of Apple and Facebook, there is a rapid increase in their value. Coca-Cola which operates in the traditional carbonated beverages industry, and has for many years (until the beginning of the second decade of the twenty-first century) been the most valuable brand in the world, is gradually losing value. On the other hand, the value of technology and Internet brands is growing rapidly, which translates into an increase in the market value of companies that own them. In the case of 20 companies belonging to the BrandZ index of strong and innovative brands of consulting firm MillwardBrown, the return in the period 2000–2018 amounted to 226.7%, compared to 102% for the S&P 500 index.[8] The most valuable brands in this group are the so-called GAFA: Google, Apple, Facebook, Amazon. These are brands and companies that currently drive global growth and innovation, following the consumer revolution on the Internet. Each of these companies is itself a complex platform and all expand across Internet-related areas. These companies compete and cooperate in different ways, specialising in specific sectors: Google—Internet search, Apple—devices for communicating with the Internet, Facebook—social media, Amazon—online commerce. Their common feature is to offer Internet-related products or services and activities in the area of data mining. GAFA companies collect, store and use new tools for data analysis, which allows them to use data as the basis of their business model and the main source of competitive advantage. Their market value is directly related to the amount of held data and what they do with it. Data can be combined, classified and reorganised to obtain new qualitative information that carries commercial value. In this way, companies such as Google and Facebook have revolutionised and redefined the advertising market.

Companies operating on the Internet that have created platforms around their brands, consisting of a network of customers and co-operators based on their mutual interest, benefit from the self-perpetuating effect of demand-side economies of scale. It results from the fact that the value of customer service consumption is greater when the number of consumers and entities cooperating within the platform increases. A prerequisite for entering the self-supplying demand cycle is to gain a critical mass of service users earlier than competitors, which allows gaining an advantage in terms of the ability to collect and use data to improve the offer and commercialise information. Google (now Alphabet) and Facebook are classic examples of entities whose services benefit from the self-reinforcing effect of demand-side economies of scale. The Google search engine, thanks to its innovative algorithm, has gained initial advantage in the search engine market as well as a high market share. As a result, based on a database updated on a daily basis, the company is able to adapt the search results on the Internet faster and better, in line with the expectations of its users, compared to competitors who can do without having such a large and constantly expanding database. For that reason, every new user, who wants to get the best search results, should use Google. The example of Microsoft is proof of the durability of benefits from the demand-driven economies of scale. The company has been drawing benefit from this effect for many years in relation to its Windows operating system and Office software. Although Microsoft has been overtaken by GAFA companies in many fields related to the Internet, it continues to earn profits on software, which still maintains the highest share in the office software market.

Another readily visible trend is the growing importance of brands from Asian countries, primarily China, as they compete more and more effectively with traditional brands from the United States and Europe. Currently, among the 100 most valuable

---

[8]   BrandZ Top 1000, *Most Valuable Global Brands*, 2018, www.millwardbrown.com (access: 5 May 2019).

global brands according to Interbrand, as many as 14 are Chinese.[9] An important phenomenon is also the dissemination of brands and their significance for the organisation's success in areas other than those related to running a business. Brands are increasingly appreciated in such sectors as education (universities), sports, tourism, art, literature, as well as promotion of the state. Brands are also increasingly vital in non-profit organisations, such as charitable institutions, which often compete for customers' pockets with commercial brands.[10]

Brands in the age of the Internet and social media

The development and dissemination of the Internet, as well as the growing popularity of social media such as Twitter, Instagram, and Facebook, have a significant impact on the way brands are managed and, consequently, for their future. In early 2019, Facebook—a social network that allows registered users to create profiles, upload photos, and videos, send messages and keep in touch with friends, family, and colleagues—had over 2 billion users, more than the most populated country in the world. There are over 400 million blogs on the Internet.[11] The number of social media users of various types is growing rapidly, followed by content created and sent within them. The rapid development of new media for communication will have an impact on the functioning and management of brands.

For a long time, the Internet has been used by users as a place for finding information and viewing interesting content. The second stage of developing the so-called Web 2.0, primarily characterised by the transition from static websites to dynamic or user-generated content, has made a significant revaluation of the way the Internet is used. First an information provider, the Internet has become the place to create and exchange users' own content through social media, blogs, discussion forums, etc. Easier access to the Internet through mobile devices has caused the shift of interactions from sporadic to a permanent social experience.[12] Social media, also known as media created by consumers, can be defined as new online sources of information that are created, initiated, disseminated and used by consumers interested in sharing information about products, services, brands, personalities, and other issues.[13]

In the beginning, marketing was only on the periphery of social media culture. It changed very quickly—social media became a platform for marketing activities. These media have changed the way of marketing communication. Traditionally,

---

[9]   www.interbrand.com (access: 22 June 2020).
[10] W. Ollins, *Wally Olins o marce*, Instytut Marki Polskiej, Warszawa 2004.
[11] www.statista.com (access: 22 June 2020).
[12] C. Kohli et al., *Will Social Media Kill Branding?*, "Business Horizons" 2015, 58, pp. 35–44.
[13] P. Blackshaw, M. Nazzaro, *Consumer-Generated Media 101: Word-Of-Mouth in the Age of the Web-Fortified Consumer*, 2006, www.yumpu.com (access: 28 April 2019).

this communication took place from the company to the consumer, with elements of feedback. Currently, communication is two-sided, and an additional element of mass communication between consumers has emerged, the subject of which may be assessment of the company's offer. Before, this type of communication between consumers took place on the principle of "word-of-mouth" marketing, but it concerned mostly a small group of friends with whom the consumer had a direct, most frequently physical contact. Nowadays, thanks to social media, messages can be spread on a large-scale network, limited only by the number of friends connected to the consumer's website. In addition, messages can spread in the network on the basis of a chain reaction between the friends of friends, etc. From this point of view, social media seems to be an excellent platform for promoting brands, although they do not constitute a significant sales channel for products—according to some studies, it is less than 1% of all e-commerce.[14] Their role is rather to attract people to a traditional or online store, by creating positive opinions about the brand. Brands in social media should serve the same goals of the organisation as in the case of activities outside of them. They should build a sense of consumer participation in the organisation, attract the acceptance and communication of brand values, encourage the public to engage in dialogue and brand promotion, help gain and maintain a competitive advantage, convey vision and brand messages and build its differentiation, check whether the brand is properly communicated and understood by the public. As a result, the brand's use in social media should lead to building positive associations related to it, its perceived quality and increased brand awareness.[15] In connection with the accomplishment of these goals, marketers try to communicate messages, influencing the perception of brands and purchasing behaviour of media users, thanks to the "viral" spread of information. It is very difficult in practice, because media users have full control over what they read, what they pass on and what they accept. Consumers learn to use social media to their advantage in finding exactly what they want. Thus, companies have a very limited impact on this in the network. Under these conditions, the attempt to shape the tastes of recipients without addressing their actual expectations has little chance of success. Interestingly, even the brand's acceptance by the media user does not necessarily translate into desirable behaviour in the form of purchasing. Research on the so-called "likes" on Facebook indicates that liking does not translate into the tendency to buy. Likes are a meaningless gesture of friendship not translating into action.[16]

Many companies have invested a lot of resources in the implementation of the so-called brand content, creating materials for social media, aimed at building an

[14] A. Lutz, *Forrester: Facebook and Twitter Do Almost Nothing to Drive Sales*, 2012, www.smartinsights. com (access: 15 March 2019).

[15] J. Yan, *Social Media in Branding: Fulfilling a Need*, "Journal of Brand Management" 2011, 18 (9), pp. 688–696.

[16] L. John et al., *What's the Value of a Like?*, "Harvard Business Review" March–April 2017, pp. 108–115.

audience around their brands. It consisted of an attempt to bypass traditional media and create relationships directly with consumers, founded upon online platforms built around the brand. The brand on the web was to become a kind of centre for the users' community. These types of activities did not bring the expected effect, because in general consumers were not interested in joining such organised hubs. Most users treat brand links as spam. Rankings of subscribers on YouTube and Instagram show that only three channels related to brands have reached the top 500 most popular on the web. The leader among brands—Red Bull—spending $2 billion annually on branded content had 4.9 million subscribers, which gave it only the 184th place in the ranking.[17]

The failure of companies in creating platforms of brand users in social media is primarily the result of a new way of functioning of mass culture and grouping of communities around specific ideas or themes. Social media have created digital communities that have become influential innovators of culture, leading to the creation of the so-called crowd culture.[18] Nowadays, crowd culture is created around every topic: from fans of TV series, through conspiracy theorists, to joggers. Everyone can subscribe with just a few clicks on the computer. They are so effective in grouping interested parties around specific topics, as well as creating creative entertainment, that companies have no chance to compete directly with them by offering an alternative or own projects. Instead, marketers should look for ways to join the already existing independent platforms of users and "infect" them with their own messages. Such communities are used, among others as a source of information about products for their present or potential members. Therefore, it is in the interest of the company to create a positive image of its brands in such communities and to facilitate (also from the technical side) their functioning. Such communities are able to gather dispersed groups of people who share similar interests. Membership in such a group improves their information resources in relation to the seller in a situation when he wants to use the ignorance of his clients, for example to offer the same product at different prices depending on the client's profile. Access to information can be an incentive for many potential customers to join a community. As Internet communities cannot be controlled by companies, the question arises whether it is wise to sponsor them. The answer is—it is better to sponsor them than to lose them. A community that is favourable to the product can be a powerful marketing tool.[19] Within the community of users, an effective way to promote brands starts with trying to identify brand advocates and to reach through their mediation. This group usually constitutes around 2% of all consumers, but is very influential because its opinions can shape the choices of many consumers through blogs and other platforms.

---

[17]   D. Holt, *Branding in the Age of Social Media*, "Harvard Business Review" March 2016, pp. 41–50.
[18]   Ibidem.
[19]   J. Daum, *Intangible Assets and Value Creation*, Wiley, Chichester 2003.

The chance for niche brands

Consumers have a broader choice, which makes them more selective and limits their interest to the offer that best suits their tastes. From all sides, they are attacked by advertising messages and other more subtle forms of persuasion, which are to make them buy the products of specific brands. The effect is the fragmentation of market preferences. An example is a market for music albums. Currently, fifty best-selling albums of all time come from the 1970s and 1980s, and none were created after 2000, although the market is now much larger.[20] The development of social media and other communication-based forms on the Internet creates new opportunities for new and niche brands. These new brands challenge traditional ones. While it can be expected that large brands will continue to be present on the market and retain significant market shares, the trend will work for the benefit of niche brands. The Internet and social media work in their favour, because they allow them to reach narrow, scattered groups of recipients with the message, and also physically with the product itself thanks to e-commerce. Often, niche brands appear in the sales offer of the largest distributors, such as Amazon or Alibaba, which enables cost-effective and easy access to potential customers. These brands can quickly gain consumer acceptance thanks to good user ratings and the use of trust on platforms where they are present. This is called the long tail phenomenon, which is supported by the ability to communicate with the recipients. In the past, the possibility of implementing a niche strategy was limited by the risk associated with the customers' lack of certainty as to the quality of such an offer. It was unprofitable for companies to pay for quality promotion in niche markets. At present, the quality guarantee for niche products is contained in the positive opinions of other users (word of mouth), who can exchange online opinions in social media, thus sparing companies in their task. The second element of support for niche brands is online distribution. Thanks to this, the limitation of the space of store shelves has been eliminated, which increases the diversity of the market offer. In addition, low transaction costs, combined with a common return policy make it easier for online purchases.

The challenge for smaller and aspiring brands is to increase the widespread use of algorithms by consumers to choose the offer. Algorithms have become the current intermediaries in sales channels and allow consumers to get a higher value by indicating better-priced brands, or such that offer faster delivery, and are characterised by specific parameters. Algorithms pose a threat primarily to brands whose purchase does not require a lot of commitment. These are brands whose purchases are customary and, therefore, one can entrust their choice to the algorithm. More sophisticated algorithms,

---

[20]   C. Anderson, *The Long Tail. Why the Future of Business Is Selling Less of More*, Hyperion, New York 2018.

by conducting conversations with the client in real-time, can also influence the purchase of high involvement products. To maintain control over the market, the brand has two options. First, it should be visible for the algorithm. Second—it should find access to the client over and beside the algorithm. Because influencing the algorithm is particularly beyond the reach of small brands, they may remain in its orbit by "cheating" the algorithm, or by expensive operations related to positioning of the brand on the website or, at worst, by the application of the low pricing strategy. A more effective way to maintain the interest of consumers is to release the brand from the power of algorithms, by finding a way to reach customers outside of them, while maintaining the possibility of finding a brand by an algorithm. To this end, it should be ensured that potential customers can also contact brands outside the network, in the real world, also through traditional promotional activities. In this context, there is a new trend consisting of the simultaneous development of online distribution and maintaining direct contact with the client in physical stores.

Creating customer relations in an Internet era

Technological changes, Internet development and easy access to information have changed the traditional approach to marketing and brand management. Products are becoming more and more similar in terms of physical parameters, and it is difficult to achieve a long-lasting differentiation in this field, which is the quintessence of brands' existence. The offered level of quality and functionality ceases to be the result of unique competencies in this field. It rather becomes just a matter of choice. Material goods are consumed not only because of their functional characteristics but also as symbolic signs of taste, lifestyle, personal identity, as well as belonging and social status. In the process of creating themselves, consumers buy and use products of specific brands in order to confirm their desired image and articulate aspirations.[21] It means that gaining a competitive advantage is conditioned by differentiation of the offer in symbolic and emotional dimensions. However, one should not neglect to promote the functions and parameters of the product, because even if the primary motive for buying a brand is emotions, the consumer often needs a reasonable excuse to justify his emotional choice.[22]

In the era of the Internet and digital information, brands have new communication tools with potential clients at their disposal. Due to the universality of their use, it has never been as difficult as before today, to break with its message to consumers. The limitation does not lie in the real possibility of reaching the client with information,

---

[21]   M. Batey, *Creating Meaningful Brands: How Brands Evolve from Labels on Products to Icons of Meaning* [in:] *The Definite Book of Branding*, ed. by K. Kartikeya, Sage Publications, Thousand Oaks 2014, pp. 22–41.
[22]   D. Ogilvy, *Ogilvy on Advertising*, Crown, New York 1983.

but with his readiness to accept it in the surrounding information noise. The key in these circumstances is to gain the consumer's attention, not through a simple marketing message, but a consistent story about the brand that reaches the needs and desires rooted in the mind of the consumer. Having a choice of services and products on the screen that offer similar functionality, customers choose those that are better known to them. Creating unique messages and stories allows the brand to gain differentiation in the consumer's perception and to penetrate his awareness. Such a story can be built based on real characters of clients and people associated with the company, such as its founder, like in the case of the Jack Daniels brand.[23]

A vast majority of consumers in developed countries have basic needs met while suffering from a deficit of time. Consumers become impatient—they want to experience as much as possible, expecting immediate gratification for their purchases. In this way, time becomes a deficit good, which is a new type of currency that consumers use in "negotiations" with brands. The total cost of buying a brand is then the sum of the paid money, as well as the time spent to buy and "learn" the product. Therefore, the simplicity of the purchase process and the ease of "learning" related to the product become an essential component of the brand's offer. Products whose handling is more comfortable and more intuitive, create more value for the customer. Companies use artificial intelligence to improve items and personify the offer. It requires the collection and analysis of information on the profile and history of consumer activity. Consumers, though they remain sceptical about the protection of their identity, are increasingly accepting the use of their personal and purchasing data to adapt the offer to their needs. As a consequence, the importance and popularity of voice assistants based on artificial intelligence, such as Siri (Apple), Alexa (Amazon) or Cortana (Microsoft), increases. Voice assistants, among others, facilitate the use of devices and purchases, and guide through the process of learning a product or service. Thanks to machine learning, the assistant recognises user preferences and provides more tailored recommendations.

The pressure to keep promises made by brands is growing. It is primarily the result of shifting the bargaining power in the brand-buyer relationship to the consumer. Consumers, thanks to the Internet, can organise themselves into pressure groups. Also, the popularity of various types of programmes where brands are rated is growing. The extent to which they keep their promises and, what is equally important, what actions they undertake for this purpose are examined equally. As a result of their application, consumers can relatively quickly assess not only the actual value of the brand but also track the quality and origin of its components, working conditions in its producing plants or impact on the environment. A key element in creating a consumer-brand relationship is mutual interest and communication. Communication

---

[23]   M. Batey, *Creating Meaningful Brands...*

means the manner, place and time of the best communication with the client in order to develop and strengthen relationships. Companies try to create the desired brand identity, but it is customers who ultimately determine its real meaning.[24] The role of managers is to strengthen, revive and modify the meanings associated with the brand so that they work to the company's advantage. Branding, therefore, means firstly defining the desired meanings, and secondly signalling and activating these meanings. Brand management is a complicated task. Because brands operate in an ever-changing socio-cultural context and their perception by consumers is a derivative of personal experience, there is often a dissonance between the intentions of the company and consumer perceptions of the brand. Its reduction requires a shorter distance between the brand and the consumer, which means establishing closer relationships in order to build value for both parties. In this context, branding is less and less concerned with the sale of products and more related to the invitation to cooperation, which will allow creating an offer adequate to the expectations and aspirations of the consumer.

Conclusions

The change of operating conditions of companies as a result of globalisation, technological changes and the development of the Internet, has resulted in increased competition and a shift in its character. It creates new challenges for business management, including brand management. In these new conditions, brands will remain one of the decisive factors in value creation. The methods for building brands will change—the significance of symbolic and cultural elements of the brand's equity will increase at the expense of functional features and basic associations. Brand growth leaders will change as well. These will be primarily brands related to information technology and those whose business model is based on the Internet. Large, traditional megabrands will remain on the market, but they will have to redefine their strategies, even demolishing traditional barriers between product categories and modifying value propositions. Disintermediation—limiting the use of intermediaries between producers and consumers, thanks to the development of the Internet and the growing popularity of e-commerce, will increase the importance of niche brands serving small segments of the market. It means that the market is not definitively and permanently divided between large players. The scale of operations in terms of marketing effectiveness is not as important as it used to be. New brands, if they offer propositions of innovative value for customers, can successfully break into the market, reaching customers in a cost-effective manner.

---

[24] Ibidem.

The role of the brand will also change—they will become critical culture-creating factors. In the postmodern world, primarily in developed countries, institutions that traditionally created the framework of social trust—governments, political parties, moral authorities, religion—are often challenged and criticised. Under these conditions, with the fulfilment of the basic needs of food and shelter, consumers will turn to brands as new institutions that will allow them to meet their more complex needs: meaning, belonging, happiness and self-improvement. This will result in an increased responsibility of brands, which will have to operate more transparently and ethically, both in terms of business and public perception.

Bibliography

Anderson C., *The Long Tail. Why the Future of Business Is Selling Less of More*, Hyperion, New York 2018.

Batey M., *Creating Meaningful Brands: How Brands Evolve from Labels on Products to Icons of Meaning* [in:] *The Definite Book of Branding*, ed. by K. Kartikeya, Sage Publications, Thousand Oaks 2014.

Blackshaw P., Nazzaro M., *Consumer-Generated Media 101: Word-Of-Mouth in the Age of the Web-Fortified Consumer*, 2006, www.yumpu.com (access: 28 April 2019).

BrandZ Top 1000, *Most Valuable Global Brands*, 2018, www.millwardbrown.com (access: 22 June 2020).

Clifton R., *Brand Valuation: From Marketing Department to Boardroom*, "Market Leader" 2009, 2.

Dahlen M., Karsberg J., *Time to Forget Everything We Learned in the Past about Branding. The Future Is the Future of Branding*, "Journal of Brand Strategy" 2015, 5 (1).

Daum J., *Intangible Assets and Value Creation*, Wiley, Chichester 2003.

Gerzema J., Lebar E., *The Danger of a "Brand Bubble,"* "Market Leader" 2009, 4, www.marketing-society.com (access: 26 April 2019).

Golder P., Irwin J., Mitra D., *Long Term Market Leadership Persistence: Baselines, Economic Conditions, and Category Types*, 2013, www.msi.org (access: 28 April 2019).

Holt D., *Branding in the Age of Social Media*, "Harvard Business Review" March 2016.

John L., Mochon D., Emrich O., Schwartz J., *What's the Value of a Like?*, "Harvard Business Review", March–April 2017.

Kohli C., Suri R., Kapoor A., *Will Social Media Kill Branding?*, "Business Horizons" 2015, 58.

Lutz A., *Forrester: Facebook and Twitter Do Almost Nothing to Drive Sales*, 2012, www.smartinsights.com (access: 15 March 2019).

Ogilvy D., *Ogilvy on Advertising*, Crown, New York 1983.

Ollins W., *Wally Olins o marce*, Instytut Marki Polskiej, Warszawa 2004.

Picardo E., *Five of the Largest Asset Bubbles in History*, 2015, www.investopedia.com (access: 27 April 2019).

Yan J., *Social Media in Branding: Fulfilling a Need*, "Journal of Brand Management" 2011, 18 (9).

Managing editor
Zofia Sajdek

Technical editor
Renata Włodek

Proofreading
Katarzyna Zajdel, Nativic
Rafał Pawluk

Typesetting
Marta Jaszczuk

Jagiellonian University Press
Editorial Offices: ul. Michałowskiego 9/2, 31-126 Krakow
Phone: +48 12 663 23 80, +48 12 663 23 82, Fax: +48 12 663 23 83

CPSIA information can be obtained
at www.ICGtesting.com
Printed in the USA
JSHW061758160323
39040JS00003B/21

9 788323 348597